Inviting Transformation

Third Edition

Inviting Transformation

Presentational Speaking for a Changing World

Third Edition

Sonja K. Foss
University of Colorado Denver

Karen A. Foss
University of New Mexico

WAVELAND
PRESS, INC.
Long Grove, Illinois

For information about this book, contact:
Waveland Press, Inc.
4180 IL Route 83, Suite 101
Long Grove, IL 60047-9580
(847) 634-0081
info@waveland.com
www.waveland.com

Contents

Acknowledgments

We never intended to write a public speaking book. In fact, for years, we steadfastly refused even to consider the possibility because we did not believe the world needed another public speaking textbook. There came a time, however, when we felt we had something to say about public speaking that had not been said before and that maybe needed to be. We decided that we wanted to write a book on the subject so that we no longer would have the experience of lecturing on a concept in a public speaking class, turning to write it on the board, and finding ourselves thinking, "I don't believe this anymore; this doesn't fit my experience." The result is *Inviting Transformation*. Our primary intent with this book is to expand the options for public speaking—or what we prefer to call *presentational speaking*—so that all of us are better prepared for the changing world in which we live.

Once we decided we wanted to write a book on presentational speaking, the writing was helped along by many others. Our publishers, Carol Rowe and Neil Rowe, have been extremely patient and supportive through all three editions of this book. Thank you for trusting us and our vision for this book. Special thanks to Sally Miller Gearhart and Sonia Johnson for sharing with us their notions of transformation that are at the heart of this book. Ongoing conversations with several others about these ideas also were invaluable: Karen Carlton, Deborah Fort, Cindy L. Griffin, Josina M. Makau, Steve Moore, and Ann Skinner-Jones. Sonja's advisees at Ohio State University supplied valuable insights about translating theory into practice: Kimberly Barnett Gibson, Gail J. Chryslee, Debra Greene, D. Lynn O'Brien Hallstein, Cristina Lopez, Helene Shugart, and Catherine Egley Waggoner.

Our thanks also go to those who read the book in manuscript form and offered honest feedback and valuable ideas: Robert Trapp, Gail J. Chryslee, Judith A. Hendry, Ann Skinner-Jones, Stephen W. Littlejohn, Melissa McCalla Manassee, and Barbara J. Walkosz.

We tried out versions of this book on students at Ohio State University, Humboldt State University, the University of Colorado Denver, and the University of New Mexico. Our students provided important feedback and allowed us to use their speaking plans and presentations as models. Teaching assistants and instructors in presentational speaking at the University of New Mexico and the University of Colorado Denver—Carmen Lowry, Kristy Frie, Mary E. Domenico, and Elizabeth A. Brunner—provided syllabi, exercises, exams, sample presentations, and insights. Instructors using the book at the International College at Beijing of the University of Colorado Denver—Victoria DeFrancisco, Jennifer Gruenewald, Laura K. Hahn, Cheris Kramarae, and Sharon M. Varallo—were helpful in addressing multicultural dimensions. We are especially grateful for the confirmation all of you offered that we were on the right track.

Others helped behind the scenes in various ways. Kelly O'Connor Mendoza served as a research assistant, and Marcel Allbritton and Joseph Milan helped with the instructor's manual. Leah Charney, Christina Villa, Adrianne Devereux, and Anthony J. Radich allowed us to tape a discussion at the Western States Arts Federation (WESTAF) to use as a sample presentation, and Kendis Paris transcribed two of the presentations at the end of the book. Eric Berson provided companion passes on United Airlines to make the process of getting together to write this book easier.

Finally, as always, our thanks to Anthony J. Radich and Stephen W. Littlejohn for enduring yet another book with patience, good humor, and love.

1

Inviting Transformation

Not that long ago, most people in the United States were raised in homogeneous communities. They grew up, went to school, attended church, and worked with people who were pretty much like they were and who agreed with them on basic issues and values. They rarely met people who were very different from them. But recent changes in the world make such communities a rarity. People are now able to connect easily with people around the world and thus come into contact almost daily with people who are different from them in significant ways.

~ THE CHANGING WORLD: ENCOUNTERING DIFFERENCE

What is responsible for the changes that have connected diverse people? You might be surprised to hear that the fall of the Berlin Wall in 1989 was one of the primary causes of such changes. The Wall, which separated West Germany from East Germany, represented "a struggle between two economic systems—capitalism and communism." The fall of the Wall encouraged a view of the world as a single community because "there was only one system left and everyone had to orient . . . to it one way or another."[1]

Developments in transportation that allow for ease of travel also have caused increased exposure to difference. Because of these developments, you are able to leave your home community and venture out into the world. The beginning of regular transatlantic jet service in 1958 was a major catalyst for such travel. "In one fell swoop," boasted Juan Trippe of Pan American World Airways, "we have shrunken the earth."[2] The increased mobility that characterizes the world also means you not only can leave your community to travel but also to relocate to new places for school or work or to live in areas you enjoy or to be with people you love.

Another change is new technologies such as cell phones, e-mail, social networking, and search engines such as Google. All of these allow

1

you to communicate almost instantaneously with people all over the world. As a result, you can contact and develop relationships with people who live in other countries whose lives are substantially different from yours. You have access to information and resources you would not have had the opportunity to encounter even a few years ago.

As a result of such changes, the world, in the words of author, reporter, and columnist Thomas L. Friedman, has "flattened."[3] What he means by this is that "all the knowledge centers on the planet" are now connected "into a single global network."[4] As a result, "it is now possible for more people than ever to collaborate and compete in real time with more other people on more different kinds of work from more different corners of the planet and on a more equal footing than at any previous time in the history of the world."[5]

Friedman contrasts current changes with those that came before and concludes that the recent changes in the world have gone "to a whole new level."[6] What he calls *Globalization 1.0* began when Columbus sailed from Spain in 1492 and lasted until about 1800. This period of globalization, which opened trade between the Old World and the New World, focused on "how much brawn—how much muscle, how much horsepower, wind power, or, later, steam power—your country had and how creatively you could deploy it."[7] In Globalization 1.0, the primary question asked was: "How can I go global and collaborate with others through my *country*?"[8] Globalization 1.0, Friedman explains, "shrank the world from a size large to a size medium."[9]

The second period of globalization, Globalization 2.0, lasted from 1800 to 2000 and was marked by the creation of a global economy and a global market. Multinational companies looked globally for markets and labor, and, particularly with the dawn of the Industrial Revolution, began producing goods to sell on multiple continents. The major forces behind this era of globalization were "breakthroughs in hardware—from steamships and railroads in the beginning of the period to telephones and mainframe computers toward the end."[10] The big question that characterized this period was: "How can I go global and collaborate with others through my *company*?"[11] This era, Friedman asserts, "shrank the world from a size medium to a size small."[12]

Globalization 3.0 began in about 2000 and was characterized by the power of "*individuals* to collaborate and compete globally."[13] New developments in software and the creation of a global fiber-optic network have enabled individuals and groups to go global easily and seamlessly. Individuals in this era ask: "Where do *I* fit into the global competition and opportunities of the day, and how can *I*, on my own, collaborate with others globally?"[14] Globalization 3.0 is "shrinking the world," Friedman says, "from a size small to a size tiny."[15]

In the era of Globalization 3.0, virtually everyone is exposed to difference. As Friedman notes, "Globalization 3.0 is going to be more and more driven not only by individuals but also by a much more diverse—non-Western, non-white—group of individuals. Individuals from every corner of the flat world are being empowered."[16] As opportunities for connection increase in this period of globalization, you undoubtedly are discovering the ways the people you encounter are different from you in their political perspectives, ethnicity and race, religious and spiritual traditions, occupations, economic class, learning styles, dress, educational levels, and values, to name a few. You probably are discovering that "reality is multiple and not singular" and that the universe is not homogeneous. In fact, it might more appropriately be called a *multiverse* instead of a *universe*.[17]

⌁ RESPONDING TO DIFFERENCE

The question of how to live with difference has never been more important than it is now. Encountering worldviews, value systems, beliefs, and practices that are different from your own, as frequently happens in the era of Globalization 3.0, can be challenging and even scary. Several options are available to you for responding to such difference: (1) isolating yourself; (2) criticizing others; (3) attempting to change others; and (4) welcoming difference.

Isolating Yourself

One way in which you might choose to respond to diversity is by isolating yourself and trying to protect your beliefs and values from challenge. Chat rooms and blogs that present one perspective—Little Green Footballs, Townhall, or Talking Points Memo, for example—are fun and affirming because they align with your worldview, but they are also examples of isolationism. You also protect your views when you tune into television channels where the perspective on the news matches yours. If you only watch the Fox News channel or only watch or listen to *Democracy Now!*, for example, you are exposing yourself to one viewpoint. You do the same thing when you attend college and don't reach out to new people you encounter on campus, hanging out instead with your high-school friends. In all of these instances, the response to encountering difference is to isolate and protect your worldview from perspectives that differ from yours.

Criticizing Others

A second response you may choose when you encounter diverse worldviews is to criticize different perspectives. When you choose this response, you expose yourself to differences, but you scrutinize them and then evaluate or judge those differences to be stupid, silly, incorrect, immoral, or bad. Criticizing others who are different from you can range from criticizing your sister because of her choice of clothing to blaming a racial group for rising crime in your neighborhood to accusing all individuals from the Middle East of terrorism. Stereotyping is often part of this process—attributing characteristics to an entire group of people. You might decide, for example, that all members of one ethnic group or all people from one country or all adherents to a particular religion are somehow inferior and wrong.

Attempting to Change Others

Probably the most common response to difference is to try to change those who are different from you. When you select this stance toward difference, you seek uniformity among those you encounter and try to get them to become more like you—to believe and act as you do. If you can get others to change to be like you, your own beliefs are affirmed. You also are likely to feel a sense of power or increased self-worth because your efforts to change someone were successful.

When you try to change others, you do so using four primary modes of rhetoric or four approaches to communication: (1) conquest rhetoric; (2) conversion rhetoric; (3) benevolent rhetoric; and (4) advisory rhetoric.[18] The way we are using the term *rhetoric* here may be unfamiliar to you. *Rhetoric* is an ancient term for what is now called *communication*. The term comes from the classical Greeks, who were the first in the Western tradition to study rhetoric in a systematic and formal way. Both terms—*rhetoric* and *communication*—mean the same thing: the study of how humans use symbols to communicate.

Conquest Rhetoric

The goal of conquest rhetoric is winning. In this kind of rhetoric, you are successful if you win the argument, your view prevails, or you get your way. The purpose of this mode of interaction is to establish your idea, claim, or argument as the best among competing positions. Conquest interactions follow one basic rule: "*Every disagreement has to end with a winner and a loser.*"[19]

Conquest rhetoric is a very common form of rhetoric in US culture. It is an inherent part of many of the most cherished American political, legislative, and judicial systems of public communication and decision making. These systems are designed to uphold the rights of individuals, to discover the truth about a situation, and to arrive at judgments concerning controversial issues. In other words, they provide mechanisms that allow individuals to live together, despite differences, in civil ways.

In political, legislative, and judicial systems, conquest rhetoric is directed at determining the correct position and rejecting opposing ideas or positions. Conquest rhetoric is used in the political context, for example, when presidential candidates debate. Determining a winner and a loser is an important part of the process. The election itself constitutes conquest rhetoric in that one candidate wins, and one loses. In Congress, passage of a bill means that supporters of the bill have won, and opponents have lost. A decision by a jury that finds a defendant guilty or not guilty is another example of conquest rhetoric. One side—either the defense or the prosecution—is victorious, and the other is the loser. Although individuals or groups submit to the other in conquest rhetoric, they usually do not change their minds. They go along simply because they do not have a choice. Their perspective has lost, so they acquiesce on the surface—taking whatever steps are required so that they can be the winners in the next contest.

Conversion Rhetoric

Conversion rhetoric is communication designed to change others' perspectives on an issue or to change how they behave in some way. It is designed not to defeat an opponent or a position but to convince others of the rightness or superiority of a perspective. The primary method involved in conversion rhetoric is persuasion. Advertising, marketing, and sales are examples of conversion rhetoric. Religious groups engage in conversion rhetoric when they try to persuade others to believe as they do. Activists in groups such as the Sierra Club or the Silent No More Awareness Campaign engage in conversion rhetoric when they direct their efforts toward persuading the public to adopt their views on the environment or abortion. When you and a friend are planning to see a movie, your friend uses conversion rhetoric when she tries to persuade you to see a romantic comedy rather than the action film you want to see.

Benevolent Rhetoric

Benevolent rhetoric is designed to provide assistance to individuals out of a genuine desire to make their lives better. In this type of communication, the speaker seeks to change audience members out of a concern for their well-being. Benevolent rhetoric usually assumes the form of providing information to others that they can use in their lives in some way. Those who decide they want to learn more about a subject and possibly make a change in their lives have the opportunity to secure more information about the potential change. The primary goal in this mode is to benefit others—in contrast to conquest and conversion rhetoric, in which the primary goal is to benefit the speaker in some way.

Health campaigns are examples of benevolent communication. A campaign that encourages workers in outdoor settings to use sunscreen is designed to alert individuals to the dangers of skin cancer and to suggest health practices that will reduce the likelihood of developing it. In an interpersonal context, when you see someone doing a task in a way that seems inefficient and suggest another way to accomplish it, you are using benevolent rhetoric. The individual may or may not choose to adopt your suggestion, but the communication is created from your genuine desire to make life easier or better.

Advisory Rhetoric

Advisory rhetoric is communication designed to provide requested assistance. It is developed in response to an implicit or explicit request from others for advice or information. Individuals who are the recipients of advisory rhetoric are interested in learning, growing, and changing. They deliberately seek out interactions with or information from individuals who can help them accomplish these goals. In advisory rhetoric, communicators provide guidance by offering new ideas that encourage others to broaden their understanding in some way.

Counseling and education are the paradigm cases of advisory communication. Individuals who choose to see a counselor to work through difficulties in the hope of leading happier lives or who choose to develop themselves through education deliberately expose themselves to new perspectives they believe will be useful to them. You benefit from advisory rhetoric when you ask a friend who is highly knowledgeable about cars for her advice on what kind of car to buy. Advisory rhetoric is even taking place when you ask a clerk in a Motor Vehicles Department how to go about getting a driver's license, and you willingly accept the advice or assistance offered. Advisory rhetoric is marked by someone's request for assistance—unlike conquest, conversion, and benevolent rhetorics in which the information given is unsolicited.

Welcoming Difference

When you encounter difference, you have options other than isolating yourself, criticizing, or trying to change those who are different from you. You can stay open to diversity—embracing challenges to your thinking as opportunities for growth and change. In this option, you deliberately look for difference; you seek variety, newness, surprise, and even what might be uncomfortable. You approach difference, in other words, in an open and inquiring way, delighting in the exploration of new ways of thinking and being.

People do not simply observe the world and absorb what it offers. Instead, individuals rely on the "lens of self" to help them make choices from everything that is available.[20] You "construct the world through lenses" of your "own making and use these to filter and select" the things to which you want to pay attention.[21] As you interact with the data around you, you develop your own interpretation of those data. Your interpretation will be different from everyone else's because people are different—there will be as many different interpretations of what is going on as there are people observing. If only one person is observing something, only one interpretation of the situation is possible. We believe that being open to diversity is the best way to respond to difference because you will experience multiple interpretations of an issue.

Because every perspective is necessarily partial, alternative viewpoints enhance your understanding and make you wiser. When you observe or experience a situation, you get part of it, someone else gets another part, and these parts contribute to understanding the whole. Thus, you depend on others for the fullest understanding of an issue. When more and more people are included in the process of observing what is going on and contributing their unique interpretations, understanding grows. "The more participants we engage in this participative universe, the more we can access its potentials and the wiser we can become."[22]

The story of the blind men trying to understand an elephant by feeling different parts of the animal is an example of the wider resources available when you actively seek diverse perspectives. One man decides an elephant is long, slim, and flexible because he feels the trunk. Another thinks an elephant is flat and wide because he feels an ear. Another concludes that an elephant is a round and stout creature because he feels a leg. An openness to diverse perspectives allows you to connect your pieces of reality with others who see things differently: "Instead of labeling 'us' as right and 'them' as crazy, blind to the obvious, or refusing to see, we find out that they know something we don't. When we collaborate, we can see the whole elephant."[23]

The assumption that diverse perspectives represent resources for understanding requires that you approach difference with genuine appreciation and not simply tolerance. The connotations of the term *tolerance* convey a judgmental attitude toward difference. Tolerance implicitly suggests that you are willing to put up with individuals who hold views different from yours, but you still disapprove of them and wish their perspectives aligned with yours. In contrast, openness to diversity means that you embrace allowing another person to be different from you—celebrating and appreciating those differences because of the richness they bring to your world. You are delighted with those who hold different perspectives because those differences provide you with new ways of looking at and understanding the world.

When you encounter someone with a different vision and understanding of the world, you have an opportunity to gain a more comprehensive perspective. You may think or act differently as you see, know, and understand things you didn't before. As your exposure to difference transforms you, so, too, is the world changed. A change in your perspective can have an impact on your external material conditions in a number of ways.

One way in which your own transformation creates changes in the external world is that you may come to see something you saw as a problem as less of a problem than you did before. When you reinterpret or gain a new perspective on it, you might find that it isn't as big of a deal as you once thought, and you no longer feel the need to focus your time and energy on it. Consider the following example. An elderly man with severe pain in his feet enrolled in a program of meditation. "That first day he told the class that the pain was so bad he just wanted to cut off his feet."

At the end of the program, he said "the pain hadn't changed much but that his attitude toward his pain had changed a lot. . . . His feet were less of a problem."[24] The Dalai Lama provides an explanation for why a change in interpretation can diminish the perceived severity of a problem:

> It seems that often when problems arise, your outlook becomes narrow. All of your attention may be focused on worrying about the problem, and you may have a sense that you're the only one that is going through such difficulties. This can lead to a kind of self-absorption that can make the problem seem very intense. . . . But if you can make comparisons, view your situation from a different perspective, somehow something happens.[25]

Your transformation may alter conditions in the outside world through opportunities for discovering resources and for innovating that were not available to you before. When you transform yourself by adopting a new vantage point, you see the resources out in the world as more abundant than you did previously. You might discover people in your environment who direct you to resources you didn't know about before, or you might come up with a solution to a problem on your own that you could not see before. Your perception of the availability of a greater number of resources provides more options for you to use to alter your conditions: "When your mind changes, new possibilities tend to arise. . . . Your thinking expands in scope."[26]

Asset-Based Community Development (ABCD) is an example of the process of discovering and employing resources that were not initially conceptualized as resources. ABCD is a worldwide movement designed to reframe into assets conditions formerly seen as problems—abandoned storefronts and blighted neighborhoods, for example. It uses the skills of a community's citizens—young people, disabled people, artists, and thriving professionals—as well as the resources of its formal institutions—businesses, schools, libraries, parks, and social service agencies—to construct community assets in imaginative ways.[27] A change in interpretation prompted by ABCD, then, allows for the observation and use of resources that people in a community did not previously perceive.

There's another explanation for how changes in the outer world can result from small individual acts. It's the phenomenon known as the *butterfly effect*—the idea that a "small effect can have significant consequences."[28] Meteorologist Edward Lorenz, who identified the butterfly effect, discovered in his modeling of the weather that "a nearly imperceptible change in a constant will produce a qualitative change in the system's behavior" and that "small initial differences will amplify until they are no longer small."[29] Thus, "the flap of a butterfly's wings in Brazil today may make the difference between calm weather and a tornado in Texas next month."[30] Theoretical physicist and cosmologist Stephen Hawking provides another example of the butterfly effect:

> If the density of the universe one second after the big bang had been greater by one part in a thousand billion, the universe would have recollapsed after ten years. On the other hand, if the density of the universe at that time had been less by the same amount, the universe would have been essentially empty since it was about ten years old.[31]

A very small change in a cause, then, can drastically alter an effect, suggesting that, as you change, the world itself may change.

Former *Washington Post* reporter and staff writer for *The New Yorker* Malcolm Gladwell offers yet another explanation for how individual change creates larger societal changes, an explanation derived from his analysis of dramatic changes in American society. He discovered that a "small number of people" in a "small number of situations" start "behaving very differently, and that behavior" spreads to people "in similar situations." Each transformation, no matter how small, gains strength because it is connected to other changes. Gladwell gives the label *the Tipping Point* to "that one dramatic moment . . . when everything can change all at once."[32]

Welcoming the input that others' divergent perspectives provide and allowing those perspectives to transform you is an option for responding to difference that provides opportunities for a better and more expanded understanding of the world. We call this option *invitational rhetoric*. Invitational rhetoric involves a deliberate exposure to and consideration of diverse voices as beneficial rather than detrimental to your thinking. The differences of others constitute an invitation for you to reconsider and expand your perspectives in the face of something different.

⟶ DEFINITION OF INVITATIONAL RHETORIC

An invitation is a request for the presence or participation of someone.[33] "Invitational rhetoric constitutes an invitation to the audience to enter the rhetor's world and to see it as the rhetor does."[34] When you issue an invitation, you ask someone to come somewhere or to engage in some activity with you. You invite your audience members to see the world as you do and to consider your perspective seriously. The object of invitational rhetoric is understanding—reached as communicators engage in a "sharing of worlds through words."[35] The goal is not to win or to prove superiority but to clarify ideas—to achieve understanding for all participants involved in the interaction. In invitational rhetoric, the speaker and audience jointly consider and contribute to thinking about an issue so that everyone involved gains a greater understanding of the subtlety, richness, and complexity of that issue.

Ultimately, the result of invitational rhetoric is often more than an understanding of an issue. Because of the nonjudgmental and nonadversarial framework in which the interaction takes place, the participants themselves understand one another better. For example, using invitational rhetoric, you might explain to a friend why you want to work during spring break. You then would listen carefully to your friend's explanation of why he believes the two of you should take a trip during spring break. Both of you would come to a greater understanding of the issue, but you also would understand one another better because you would have a clearer idea of the motivation and rationale for your respective perspectives.

Invitational rhetoric brings benefits to both the speaker and the audience. You initiate communication with others because you believe you can offer opportunities for growth. By offering your perspective in the form of a presentation, you invite the audience to see and experience the world in new and more complete ways. At the same time, you are open to learning from the perspectives of others as you engage with them. You enter an interaction seeking to share your perspective with others, and you compare it with the perspectives that audience members offer you. You may choose, as a result, to engage in a process of questioning and rethinking your own viewpoint that leads to your own transformation.

← ASSUMPTIONS OF INVITATIONAL RHETORIC

Eight key assumptions characterize invitational rhetoric, all of which help you use this mode of rhetoric to approach difference as a resource: (1) understanding is the purpose of communication in invitational rhetoric; (2) participants in invitational rhetoric listen with openness; (3) in invitational rhetoric, speaker and audience are viewed as equals; (4) invitational rhetoric involves power-with instead of power-over; (5) participants change only when they choose to change in invitational rhetoric; (6) participants enter invitational rhetoric willing to be changed; (7) invitational rhetoric creates a world of appreciation for difference; and (8) invitational rhetoric is one of many options in your rhetorical toolbox.

Understanding is the purpose of communication in invitational rhetoric.

The purpose of invitational rhetoric is understanding. Both you and your audience enter an interaction seeking to understand the ideas and attitudes of the other. You adopt the frame of reference of the other concerning the issue under discussion. As psychotherapist Carl R. Rogers explains this idea, "To be with another in this way means that for the time being, you lay aside your own views and values in order to enter another's world without prejudice."[36] The goal of understanding in invitational rhetoric encourages both the speaker and the audience to

> venture outside the walls that normally protect them from hearing things that don't fit their worldview. . . . They feel a new curiosity about the words and beliefs of people who see things differently. . . .

It is more than hearing another's point of view—it is making room
for that point of view.[37]

You certainly may acknowledge, in invitational rhetoric, the different
roles people assume or the different status positions they have, but you
still attempt to create "symmetry, empathy and connection," even in
"relationships that are characterized by contrasts in power, knowledge,
and control between the participants."[38] Regardless of their formal positions, you approach your audience members with respect and openness,
seeking to discover what they know and understand.

There are multiple terms for the focus on understanding that characterizes invitational rhetoric. Philosopher Martha Nussbaum uses the term
narrative imagination to characterize the communicator's stance in this kind
of interaction. Narrative imagination involves the "ability to think what it
might be like to be in the shoes of a person different from oneself, to be an
intelligent reader of that person's story, and to understand the emotions
and wishes and desires that someone so placed might have."[39] Other terms
for this kind of understanding are *trial empathy, trial identification,* and *transient identification.*[40] In invitational rhetoric, you try on another person's
perspective to experience how it feels and to discover how it makes sense
to that person. At the end of invitational interaction—if you have genuinely
worked to understand someone else's perspective—you should be able to
express that person's perspective "so clearly, vividly, and fairly" that the
other person says, "'Thanks, I wish I'd thought of putting it that way.'"[41]

Participants in invitational rhetoric listen with openness.

When you listen to other people talk, you may find yourself listening
in various ways, but many of them involve listening to win. You may listen, for example, to formulate a good comeback to what the other person
is saying. You may listen only for what you already know or for what you
expect to hear. Maybe you have a tendency to interrupt the other person
so you don't even hear the entire explanation. You are listening, in other
words, to win or to have your perspective prevail in the situation.

In invitational rhetoric, listening is different. It is done with openness
and with the intent to understand. Listening is "an invitation—a hosting.
This hosting of other is as a guest, as a not-me."[42] One way to think
about listening with openness is to invert the two parts of the word *understand* so that listening becomes *"standing under"*—consciously standing
under "the other's perspective, letting it wash over, through, and around"
you, letting it inform and even challenge your thinking. By standing
under the perspective of another, you turn listening for mastery or control of others—for winning—into listening for receptivity and openness.[43] As psychologist Michael P. Nichols suggests, "To listen is to pay
attention, take an interest, care about, take to heart, validate, acknowledge, be moved . . . appreciate."[44]

Listening in invitational rhetoric requires a certain degree of inner emptiness and a stance of detachment. In this stance, which communication professor Lisbeth Lipari calls *listening being*, "the listener's emptiness is a form of inner silence that has suspended the noise of inner discursive thought. This form of inner emptiness facilitates a focus and attention that enables one to really absorb the other's words."[45] This stance is not unlike the philosophy of dialogue explored by philosopher Abraham Kaplan: "If I am really talking with you, I *have* nothing to say; what I say arises as you and I genuinely relate to one another. I do not know beforehand *who* I will be, because I am open to you just as you are open to me."[46] Lipari describes this stance as an essential part of the process of listening being: "In *listening being* I come to the conversation empty—not empty of my experience or history—but empty of the belief that my experience or history defines the limits of possible meaning and experience. Thereby, in *listening being* I am being empty of possession and of all intentions other than the intention of engagement with you and of the what-will-happen."[47] She elaborates: "What I do need to do is to stand . . . with you, right next to you, and to belong to you, fully present to the ongoing expression of you. Letting go of my ideas about who you are, who I am, what 'should' be. I let all that go, and stay present, attending, aware."[48]

Listening in invitational rhetoric looks different, then, from the listening you might be inclined to do. Invitational listening means you do not interrupt the other person but give her time to say what she wants. You make an effort to think from the perspective of the other, trying to make his perspective vivid in your own mind. You don't argue mentally; you finish listening before you speak; and you don't assume you know what the speaker is going to say next. You do not assume the speaker is using particular words in the same way that you are interpreting them, and you paraphrase or restate the speaker's message, asking questions to test your understanding of what you heard. As you listen, you are asking yourself questions such as: "What could I say to show I understand?" "How attentive am I to the speaker?" and "How are my experiences and values affecting what I am hearing?"[49]

In invitational rhetoric, speaker and audience are viewed as equals.

In traditional models of speaking, you as the speaker take center stage; all eyes are on you, and you generally are assumed to be the expert on your topic. Such a privileged stance typically characterizes speaking in the conquest and conversion and sometimes the benevolent and advisory modes of communicating. In these modes, the speaker is viewed as superior to the audience—seen as having more knowledge, experience, or resources than others do.

Audiences also are viewed in a particular way in traditional models of speaking. Audience members are seen as uninformed, misguided, or naive. The belief systems and behaviors they have created for living in the world are devalued and considered to be inadequate or inappropriate simply because their views differ from the speaker's. There is an approach of "let me help you, let me enlighten you, let me show you the way" toward the audience.[50] Even if an audience member is someone you love and respect, when you use traditional models of speaking, you unintentionally reduce that person to someone who is inferior and who is not able to make an informed decision without your input.

The relationship between the communicator and the audience is different in invitational rhetoric. The speaker and the audience are regarded as equal peers, and you are a facilitator rather than an all-knowing expert. You encourage others to contribute equally to the interaction with you. You may have access to knowledge or resources that those with whom you are interacting do not—knowledge or resources they may find helpful—but you do not claim that your experiences or your perspectives are superior to theirs. This view is summarized by writer Ursula K. Le Guin when she asks how can one person's "experience deny, negate, disprove, another experience? Even if I've had a lot more of it, *your* experience is your truth. How can one being prove another being wrong? Even if you're a lot younger and smarter than me, *my* being is my truth."[51]

In invitational rhetoric, audience members are seen as having experiences and holding perspectives that are valuable and legitimate. You conceptualize audience members as authorities on their own lives who hold the beliefs they do and act as they do for reasons that make good sense to them. Self-determination, then, is part of an invitational worldview. Grounded in a respect for others, self-determination allows individuals to make their own decisions about how they wish to live their lives. As former activist Sonia Johnson explains, the principle of self-determination involves a trust that others are doing the best they can at the moment and that they simply need "to be unconditionally accepted as the experts on their own lives."[52]

Invitational rhetoric involves power-with rather than power-over.

The power employed by the speaker in invitational rhetoric is not the ability to affect what happens to someone else or the ability to control others. It is not the kind of power that has been labeled *power-over*, which is defined as "my ability to get you to do something *you otherwise wouldn't do*."[53] In this traditional kind of power, the assumption is "that in order to get what I want, you will have to give something up and you won't want to do that. That means, in turn, that my side will have to exert power over yours in order to prevail."[54]

In contrast, the power you enact in invitational rhetoric is power-with, where power to create knowledge and make decisions is shared between the speaker and the audience. The resources, ideas, and creativity of all participants are accessed and valued as everyone thinks together to solve a problem or make a decision. In power-with, decisions are made not because one person suggests an option or persuades others but because the group, as a collective, comes to believe a certain plan is good.[55] Power-with is "dependent on personal responsibility, on . . . creativity and daring, and on the willingness of others to respond."[56] Power is not a quality to exercise over others but is something that can be employed by all participants in the interaction so that it energizes, facilitates, and enables everyone involved to contribute to and learn from the interaction.

Participants change only when they choose to change in invitational rhetoric.

A particular view of change characterizes invitational rhetoric. An openness to and appreciation of diverse perspectives means that you do not try to change the perspectives of others. In fact, in invitational rhetoric, you do not want to change others because when you make such an effort, you miss the opportunity to explore how their different perspectives can help you gain a fuller understanding of an issue, yourself, and the world. Changing others also is very difficult to accomplish. Thus, another assumption of invitational rhetoric is that change happens only when people choose to change themselves.

Many approaches to persuasion implicitly suggest that changing another person is possible and almost easy, even when the beliefs that are the target of the persuasion are deeply held. According to these theories, individuals gladly embrace a new way of believing or acting when they are presented with, for example, logical or emotional appeals, vibrant metaphors, or dynamic modes of delivery. Persuasion is seen as a natural outcome of the use of these kinds of appeals.

Our experience of trying to persuade others is different from what these theories describe, and we suspect yours is, too. You probably have found that changing someone else is very difficult, especially on issues about which they care deeply. When someone tells you what you should do or how you should think, what is your likely response? If you are like most people, you get defensive and even angry and suggest all sorts of reasons why what you are doing or thinking works just fine for you. You usually "dig in your heels" and maintain your position with greater commitment than before. Myles Horton, founder of the Highlander Folk School for community-based organizing, describes what often happens when people try to change others: "If people have a position on something and you try to argue them into changing it, you're going to strengthen that position."[57]

In invitational rhetoric, then, change happens only when people choose to change themselves. Change is the result of inner motivation and readiness to change. Rhetorical theorist Sally Miller Gearhart explains the process in this way:

> No one can change an egg into a chicken. If, however, there is the
> potential in the egg to be a chicken . . . the "internal basis for
> change"—then there is the likelihood that in the right environment
> (moisture, temperature, the "external conditions for change") the
> egg will hatch. A stone, on the other hand, has no internal basis for
> hatching into a chicken and an eternity of sitting in the proper condi-
> tions of moisture and temperature will not make possible its trans-
> formation into a chicken.[58]

Change happens when an environment is created in which individuals
decide to change themselves. At most, as a speaker, you are able to create
an environment in which audience members are willing to consider
changing. With your presentation, you might plant an idea in someone's
mind that she might continue to think about after your presentation. As
a result, she may or may not decide to make a change.

Participants enter invitational rhetoric
willing to be changed.

The process of transformation more readily happens in invitational
rhetoric than with many of the other modes of rhetoric because participants in invitational rhetoric enter communication situations willing to be
changed. In contrast to conquest or conversion rhetoric, the risk involved
in invitational rhetoric "is not that you may lose but rather that you may
change."[59] As Rogers notes, "if you are willing to enter [another's] private
world and see the way life appears to him . . . you run the risk of being
changed yourself."[60] Because you are open to new ways of understanding,
you are willing to yield your perspective or to change your mind about
what you believe. A willingness to change is not compromising your
beliefs or surrendering your values. Instead, it is a genuine shift in perspective that results from a consideration of another's views.

To be willing to change violates a very strong tenet of human nature:
"Human beings like to be right. It is programmed into us as a survival
mechanism. If you were to question everything, you wouldn't survive."[61]
When the things you know to be true and right are challenged, you often
find that you are very uncomfortable. In an invitational interaction, you
may be asked to call into question the things that are most important to
you, which can be a frightening process. As consultant and author
Annette Simmons points out, "There is always a risk when you engage in
the process of learning. Even though you can be assured that this mental
redesign will incorporate a higher level of understanding than you have
right now, the potential disruption is daunting. Like renovating a house,
it can be inconvenient to add that new wing."[62]

Another way to think about invitational rhetoric is that it is much
like the "I-Thou" relationship described by philosopher Martin Buber—a
turning toward the other. Invitational rhetoric involves meeting
another's position "in its uniqueness, letting it have its impact."[63] You

enter the communication situation willing to dismantle your point of view, willing to revise yourself. Gearhart offers an example of this willingness in her life. She is strongly opposed to the hunting of animals, but she deliberately leaves open the possibility that hunting is acceptable: "And that means that I've got to risk believing that hunting . . . may be in some cases a viable thing for human beings to do. And that's scary."[64]

Invitational rhetoric creates a world of appreciation for difference.

You have a choice about the kind of rhetoric in which to engage—conquest, conversion, benevolent, advisory, or invitational. Whichever one you choose creates a different world in which to live. Communication isn't just words and sounds and gestures that reflect your world. It is the means through which you create that world. By the choices you make in your use of communication, you create your reality. This relationship may sound backwards from how you think of the relationship between communication and reality. You may assume that reality is outside of you in the external world, and you use communication to name and talk about that reality. But reality or knowledge is the *result* of the process of communication. Reality is not fixed; it changes according to the symbols or the communication you use to talk about it. Linguist Deborah Tannen explains that often when we think we are using language, language is using us. The terms with which we talk about something shape the way we see it and the way we think about it. "This is how language works. It invisibly molds our way of thinking about people, actions, and the world around us."[65]

Some examples will clarify the relationship between the symbols you choose and the reality you experience. How you choose to name or label a situation determines how you respond to it. If you call a person a *friend*, for example, that is different from calling the person an *acquaintance* or a *lover*. Each label orients you in a different way to that person, and you treat him accordingly. You experience and treat a rambunctious child differently depending on whether you call her *gifted*, *spoiled*, or *obnoxious*, for example. Similarly, you experience a colleague differently if you describe him as *ambitious* and *motivated* or *pushy* and *aggressive*. You've also probably had the experience of deciding you were not going to have a good time at a party and then having exactly the lousy time you predicted through your self-talk.

Each of the types of rhetoric creates different kinds of worlds. For example, the use of conquest and conversion rhetorics creates an adversarial and contentious world. Tannen uses the term *argument culture* to describe the nature of this world and suggests that it is marked by "a pervasive warlike atmosphere that makes us approach public dialogue, and just about anything you need to accomplish, as if it were a fight."[66] This tends to be a world of negative emotions because conquest and conversion rhetorics often produce feelings of inadequacy, humiliation, guilt, or angry submission for some and feelings of superiority and domination for others.

Examples of the adversarial world that conquest and conversion rhetorics have created are readily apparent. Negative political advertisements distort candidates' records and predict catastrophic consequences if the opposing candidate is elected. Road rage consumes drivers as they try to keep others from passing them and try to get revenge through words, gestures, or worse on those who do. Children experience the harassing behavior of bullies in their schools; at the college level, the bullying becomes hazing. People rant and rave on the radio or on television—intimidating, insulting, and humiliating others who are different from them or who hold perspectives different from theirs. Her description is harsh, but linguist Suzette Haden Elgin describes the world that conquest and conversion have created in this way: "Everybody bickering and badmouthing and putting each other down; everybody nagging and griping and sneering, whining and carping and bellyaching."[67]

Another outcome of an adversarial world is that it continually creates the conditions for the next conflict. When positions are polarized and entrenched, conquest and conversion modes of communication continue, and additional conflict is the inevitable outcome. Most important, however, the adversarial world created by conquest and conversion rhetorics tends to shut down opportunities for transformation. Acts of power-over practically guarantee another cycle of disagreement and conflict because no one likes to lose. People resent the imposition of power and resist that power, using whatever means are available to them. In the adversarial world, different perspectives are not seen as opportunities for growth but as irregularities to be squashed and squelched.

In contrast, if you choose invitational rhetoric, you are creating a different kind of world through your communication—a world of appreciation for difference. This is a world characterized by respect and appreciation for others. You are grateful for the different perspectives that others have because they give you new information about the world that helps you understand something better. Tension dissipates as you let others believe and act as they choose, delighting in how different their choices are from yours. In this world, people feel safe, are valued, and have the freedom to make their own decisions about their lives. The outcome is civility in the exchange of ideas and appreciation for the diversity those ideas provide.

Invitational rhetoric is one of many options in your rhetorical toolbox.

You may be thinking that an invitational mode of communication is not practical if you wish to be successful in your personal and professional life. Because conquest and conversion rhetorics are prominent features of the contemporary world, you may believe you need to employ these kinds of communication to accomplish your goals. We want to make clear that invitational rhetoric cannot and should not be used in all situations. We are not asking you to forego the other modes of rhetoric and to use invitational rhetoric exclusively.

Conquest, conversion, benevolent, and advisory rhetorics have their place, and when situations require their use, they are the appropriate modes to use. In systems based on modes of rhetoric such as conquest and conversion, you may find that you must operate according to the conventions of those systems. In a legal context, for example, argumentative rather than invitational methods are necessary for pleading criminal and civil cases. On the job, you will encounter situations where you need to use persuasion to convince someone to adopt your proposal in order to be effective. In situations of crisis, when time is short and decisions must be made quickly, conquest rhetoric may be your only feasible choice. There also are times when you must argue against offensive or dangerous ideas, as Yugoslavian poet Charles Simic suggests: "There are moments in life when true invective is called for, when it becomes an absolute necessity, out of a deep sense of justice, to denounce, mock, vituperate, lash out, in the strongest possible language."[68] Conquest and conversion rhetorics are legitimate and valuable options that help achieve particular communication goals in many situations.

You may discover, however, that there are opportunities for invitational rhetoric in contexts that are predominately conquest or conversion in nature. Even in environments such as the legal context, opportunities for using invitational rhetoric exist as speakers engage in pretrial conferences and bargaining, for example. There are increasing opportunities to resolve disputes by mediation in cases involving personal relations and labor relations.

Even when conquest and conversion rhetorics are seemingly the norm, you may discover that you can use invitational rhetoric. You are likely to be more successful in all aspects of your life if you are able to take in new information and seriously consider its application and relevance to an issue, if you recognize that others may believe differently from you, and if you genuinely try to understand others' positions. The invitational mode also enables you to secure important information, to build community rather than competition, and to create a safe environment for the sharing of ideas. As philosopher Janice Moulton notes, "A friendly, warm, nonadversarial manner surely does not interfere with persuading customers to buy, getting employees to carry out directions conscientiously, convincing juries, teaching students, getting help and cooperation from coworkers, and promotions from the boss."[69]

To summarize, the world today exposes you to differences of all kinds. You can respond to the differences you encounter by isolating yourself from them, criticizing those who are different from you, trying to change others so they become like you, or welcoming and appreciating those differences. If you choose the latter option, you are engaging in invitational rhetoric, a mode of communicating in which your goal is to invite others to understand your perspective just as you try to understand theirs. The perspectives of others are not seen as impediments or obstacles to achieving your goals but as resources that encourage you to move beyond your own perspective to gain a more comprehensive view of an issue or a subject.

In invitational rhetoric, you listen to the other person with openness and with an intent to understand. You and the audience are equal as you each explore the other's perspective, and the kind of power you employ is power-with rather than the more traditional power-over. You also are aware that change happens only when people decide to change themselves. You issue an invitation for others to participate in your world rather than seeking to change those with whom you come into contact, and you yourself are willing to be changed by what happens in the interaction. Invitational rhetoric creates a more respectful, appreciative world in which to live, especially in situations when you encounter difference. Finally, invitational rhetoric, although it offers many positive benefits, should not be used by communicators in all interactions.

In this book, you will be learning about invitational rhetoric as a framework that you can use for enjoying, cultivating, responding to, and contributing to the diverse perspectives you encounter. We turn now to the various options that are available to you for practicing invitational rhetoric in your presentations.

2

Defining Presentational Speaking and Interactional Goals

Rather than the term *public speaking,* we prefer to use the term *presentational speaking* to encompass the kind of communication that is the focus of this book. In general, we believe that every time you speak, you are making a presentation. Each time you do, you have a goal in mind—a reason for communicating. In this chapter, we define the term *presentational speaking* and discuss the five interactional goals that are your reasons for engaging in presentational speaking

⟶ PRESENTATIONAL SPEAKING

When you think about giving a speech or making a presentation, a standard image probably comes to mind: one person standing behind a lectern, looking out at an audience of many people. In this conception of public speaking, the speaker does all the talking, and any participation by the audience is limited to asking questions at the end of the speech. You probably associate this kind of speaking event with public settings such as lecture halls, classrooms, senate chambers, courts of law, churches, and campaign rallies.

Perhaps the thought of engaging in this kind of speaking terrifies you. You imagine yourself as that speaker, and you immediately get anxious, recalling those times in the past when you had to give a speech. If you are using this book in a public speaking class that is required for graduation from college, you may be worried that you will not pass the course. Stage fright may overtake you. Your knees, hands, and voice shake; your mouth goes dry, or you feel like you are about to throw up. What you are feeling is best described as *public freaking* rather than *public speaking.*

In this book, we do not limit our discussion of communication principles and strategies only to those speaking situations in which one person speaks to an audience in a formal speaking context. Most of your communication does not take the form of formal public speeches. In fact, most people give those kinds of speeches relatively infrequently. If you develop communication skills that only enable you to speak at events that traditionally are defined as *public speaking*, you will be ill equipped to communicate in the variety of situations you encounter every day.

Presentational speaking suggests that you give many presentations during the day, but they are not all taking place in public, formal settings. As you move through your day, you engage in all kinds of communication—communication in the form of mini-presentations. When people ask your views on something and you offer your opinion, when you raise your hand in class or at a meeting to answer a question, when you converse with a friend about the movie you just saw, or when you give advice about something to your teenaged son or daughter, you are giving a presentation. Similarly, presentational speaking includes the communication used by a coach who gives a pep talk to a wrestling team, a new manager who introduces herself at her first staff meeting, a sales representative who meets with a client, a department administrator who presents ideas to her supervisor, and a homeowner who interviews a contractor in preparation for remodeling the kitchen. In all of these situations, communicators are engaged in presentational speaking.

Presentational speaking, then, includes all communication that occurs in the course of a day. Sometimes you will have considerable time to plan your presentation; other times, you will have little or no time for advance preparation. Whatever form your presentation takes, the basic process of communicating is essentially the same. The tools for constructing presentations offered in this book are designed to be useful across all of your communication encounters. They apply across the continuum of speaking contexts and formats—from casual, informal, one-to-one presentations to formal situations in which you address a large audience.

Not only do we believe that conceptualizing your communication as a series of mini-presentations is a more realistic way to think about presentational speaking, but we also believe that thinking about your communication in this way can help with the fear of speaking mentioned earlier. When you realize that you are always giving presentations, you will feel more assured. The daily practice will increase your confidence. If you can transfer the comfort you feel in contexts when you have an audience of one or two to larger audiences, you will discover that such audiences are not as problematic as you might think. (We talk more about speech anxiety in chapter 9, so check out that chapter if this is a problem for you.)

⌐ INTERACTIONAL GOALS

You communicate all the time, and you have various reasons for your presentations. Each reason is an *interactional goal*—what you hope to accomplish as a result of your decision to speak. The particular goal you select depends on the context or situation in which you are speaking.

Rhetorical theorist Lloyd Bitzer labels the context for speaking the *rhetorical situation*.[1] It is the context in which you communicate in order to respond to an exigence. An exigence, according to Bitzer, is a need, problem, or defect in a situation.[2] When you speak, your discourse comes into existence because of some situation to which you want to respond, and you enter the discussion in order to contribute to the situation in some way. Kenneth Burke, another rhetorical theorist, talks about communication in a similar way as "answers to questions posed by the situation in which they arose."[3] In other words, when you give a presentation, you do so because you see a situation to which you believe you can contribute. Your interactional goal is the strategy you choose for responding to that situation.

The idea of invitation introduced in chapter 1 is a good starting place for understanding how interactional goals function. When you host a party, you generally have a reason for doing so. Maybe you want to celebrate a birthday or have friends in to watch the Super Bowl or play Pictionary. You decide whom to invite, and when you call, text, or send an e-vite to them, you let them know the purpose for the gathering. An interactional goal functions the same way. It helps you understand, in advance of your presentation, why you are speaking, and it communicates that reason to your audience in the course of your presentation. To return to the party analogy, you communicate with your friends so that they will know that they will be attending an end-of-the semester party rather than a birthday party, a baby shower, or a housewarming party.

There are five major interactional goals or purposes for speaking: (1) to assert individuality; (2) to articulate a perspective; (3) to build community; (4) to seek adherence; and (5) to discover knowledge and belief.

To Assert Individuality

As a speaker, you continually engage in communication that reveals who you are as an individual. You reveal your identity and your uniqueness, for example, through your clothing, your friends, the kinds of music to which you listen, where you live, your major in school, and your choice of occupation. In some instances, however, the assertion of individuality is the main purpose of your communication, so this interactional goal becomes the focus of your presentation. In a presentation designed to assert individuality, you emphasize who you are as a unique individual. You reveal something about your values, beliefs, attributes, roles, and/or experiences to help your audience members come to a better understanding of you, your perspectives, your personality, and your worldview.

Presentations to assert individuality are used in a variety of situations. The workplace is one of the most common contexts for presentations focused on asserting individuality. In a job interview, for example, asserting individuality is your primary goal. You want the interviewer to recognize your abilities and fit with the organization, and you want to make such a good impression that you stand out from the other candidates being interviewed for the position. Every aspect of your presentation is geared toward achieving this end, including how you answer questions, the questions you ask, how you dress, and the attitude you convey. Once hired, the process of asserting individuality continues. When you introduce yourself to your new coworkers, you are asserting individuality. Every day on the job, you have opportunities to let others learn more about you through your interpersonal communication, formal presentations, reports, memos, and e-mail messages.

Although the workplace is a common place where asserting individuality occurs, conversations with acquaintances, friends, and family members also can be presentations of self-assertion. When you are introduced to someone you do not know, you are asserting individuality when you engage in small talk with that person. When you want to impress your future mother-in-law, convey that you are a bright student to the faculty of the department where you hope to attend graduate school, or be noticed by the cute guy on the floor above you in your residence hall, asserting individuality is your goal.

You cannot possibly communicate every facet of yourself to everyone you encounter—and probably would not want to if you could. The process of asserting individuality, then, involves a selection process, and you continuously make choices about what to reveal about yourself. You disclose different kinds of information to someone on a first date than you do in a medical school interview, for example. The choices you make about how to assert your individuality depend on your expectations for the interaction, your audience, and the setting in which the interaction takes place.

Your choices in a presentation focused on asserting individuality also depend on the larger cultural context in which it occurs. Asserting individuality is a very Western notion grounded in individualism—the privileging of the self over the collective or the group. In the United States, where autonomy and independence are highly valued, presentations to assert individuality are common. In cultures in which the collective is valued over the individual self, however, efforts to preserve the consensus and harmony of the group are seen as more important than the assertion of individuality. In Japan, for instance, communicators tend to seek unanimous agreement or consensus on an issue, and preservation of the collective harmony of the group is privileged over individual expressions of difference or individuality. In some cultures, asserting individuality is discouraged for other reasons. Among native children in Alaska, distinguishing oneself from the group by speaking up and asserting individuality is undesirable because it is considered boasting.[4]

The goal of asserting individuality also must be balanced against the interests and needs of others. Individuals who talk only about themselves or who believe that everything they have to say is so important that they must share their perspectives on every subject are examples of the excessive assertion of individuality. Similarly, the speaker who is asked to speak to an organization for half an hour but goes on and on, convinced that what she has to say is more important than what anyone else might contribute, is asserting individuality at the expense of the contributions of others. Both of these examples serve as reminders that, to be effective, the goal of asserting individuality must reflect a balance between the assertion of self and concern for and interest in others. Your desire to assert your individuality should not be valued at the expense of everyone else and their interests.

We have been discussing self-assertion as if what others learn about you is largely under your control. Important to remember, however, with the emergence of social networking sites and ever-growing amounts of information on the Internet, is that others may be able to learn all kinds of things about you very quickly. You simply are not able to control your presentation of self to the degree that you could in pre-Internet days. In fact, 77 percent of recruiters acknowledge running searches of job candidates on the web as a way to screen applications.[5] Nothing is private anymore, and nothing is ever really erased from the Internet. Monitoring your own social networking sites and those of others where information about you might be posted is important if you want to manage the communication available to others about who you are.

To summarize, the goal of asserting individuality is centered on the act of self-expression. In presentations designed to assert individuality, you attempt to reveal aspects of your identity and your uniqueness as a person. The cultural context in which you are speaking and a concern for the interests and contributions of others in the interaction affect the choices you make in constructing these kinds of presentations.

To Articulate a Perspective

A second interactional goal for presentations is articulating a perspective. When this is your goal, you share information or present your viewpoint on a subject so that all participants in the interaction have a better understanding of that subject. Articulating a perspective requires that you share information or express a perspective as fully and carefully as you can.

Articulating a perspective is different from advocating for a position. When you articulate a perspective, you may believe strongly in your perspective and may hope that your audience members find it attractive enough to consider adopting a similar point of view. But your goal is not to persuade them to adopt it. Your interest is in explaining the perspective, developing it in all of its richness and complexity, and giving it the best opportunity to be understood. Presentations focused on articulating a perspective are designed to offer—not to advocate for—a perspective.

Presentations in which your goal is to articulate a perspective range from simply sharing information—sharing perspectives developed by others—to offering your own opinion. When an airline agent provides information about flight times and fares to a potential traveler, a supervisor explains the correct way to fill out a time sheet to a new employee, or a teacher explains to her first-grade class how to write the letters of the alphabet, information is being shared. What you think about the information is not the issue. In a professional situation, you might be asked to present a report on your findings about the advantages and disadvantages of moving the organization for which you work to a new location. You advocate neither for nor against such a move but lay out the relevant information for making the decision.

At other times, you hold a particular perspective and offer it to others. In this kind of presentation, your focus shifts from the information itself to your view about that information. In a discussion with friends about the movie you just saw, for example, you might offer your opinion about how good you thought the movie was. Even when you have a particular perspective you are offering, the basic point of this goal is important to keep in mind: You are explaining why you feel as you do rather than trying to convince others to share your view.

Clearly, however, presenting information and presenting your perspective are not separate processes. When you are presenting information, you are also offering your perspective. This is because language is always a "carrier of tendency."[6] Rhetorical theorist Richard M. Weaver describes this characteristic of language by suggesting that "we have no sooner uttered words than we have given impulse to other people to look at the world, or some small part of it, in our way."[7] Your choices of what to discuss, the main points to offer, and which details to highlight construct a perspective. Because you can never communicate everything about a subject, you are making selections about content and language, which means you cannot help but communicate your way of seeing that subject matter.

If you are a travel agent booking a cruise for a client, for example, you might begin by discussing how fun a cruise can be, by noting how inexpensive cruises are for the money, or by describing a favorite cruise that you took to Mexico. Each of these introductions carries with it the suggestion that the client look at the world as you do and focuses the audience's attention in a particular direction. Each subsequent decision you make in your presentation does the same—how you organize ideas, the ways in which you elaborate ideas, or your manner of delivery. Every decision you make about the presentation contributes to the creation of a particular perspective on the information you are offering.

Articulating a perspective is used more than any other interactional goal because it is the foundation of any presentation. For example, when you give a presentation in which you assert individuality, the nature of your unique perspective is the starting point for asserting your individuality. You cannot help but articulate a perspective as you talk about those areas of your life that you see as original, interesting, or noteworthy. Virtually every presentation, then, has some element devoted to articulating a perspective. You need to make choices about how much of your presentation to devote to this goal, what information to include, and how you want to present it to an audience so that it serves as the foundation for your other interactional goal(s).

To Build Community

At times, the interactional goal you choose is to build community. A community is a group of individuals who share core values, ideas, interests, beliefs, and/or practices and feel connected to one another as a result of what they have in common. When community is a value, qualities such as connection and shared interests are privileged over individual interests. When you privilege the interactional goal of creating community, you are concerned about and committed to the stability and preservation of the knowledge, themes, beliefs, values, and practices that form the core allegiances of the community you are addressing. Presentations to build community are of three main types: (1) creating community when it does not exist; (2) reinforcing a sense of community when it already exists; and (3) restoring community when it has been disrupted.

Creating Community

When a sense of community does not exist and you want to create it, you direct your efforts toward encouraging people to get to know and trust one another. Kenneth Burke discusses the way identification works as a rhetorical strategy to bring people together. For Burke, identification with another—whether through "speech, gesture, tonality, order, image, attitude, idea,"[8]—is a way of making connections and forming relationships. In a presentation oriented toward building community, you help people see what they have in common. You might want to try to create community, for example, among new members in an organization who will be working together as a team or among neighbors in a newly formed neighborhood association.

Community can be created in another way as well—through identifying a common enemy. Individuals who ordinarily might be on different sides of an issue or belief often come together against a shared enemy. Those who support different soccer teams, for example, might join together in support of a single national team if their country makes it to the World Cup. Similarly, many in the US from different political persuasions have come together against the common enemy of terrorism. In every case, a group comes together because of a perception that differences among themselves are less important than the differences between them and another group.

Reinforcing Community

Most of the time, you do not need to create community where none exists. Often, your primary task will be to remind community members of their commonalities. In collectivist cultures, for example, community is a natural and accepted part of the culture. In this context, your primary task is to reinforce existing feelings of community. You want to reiterate and reemphasize the core commitments and values that are central to the group—to remind them of what they already share with one another.

Reminders can be communicated in a number of ways. Asking the group to engage in a shared ritual—reciting the Pledge of Allegiance, singing "We Shall Overcome," or marching together in the annual Gay Pride parade—reinforces solidarity and reinvigorates commitment to the community. Organizations often institutionalize rituals to reinforce community. One example of an annual ritual is the company picnic at which the founder speaks.

Telling stories about events and experiences important to the group is another way to remind group members of their shared sense of community. Perhaps a particularly inspirational moment was the catalyst for forming the group. Sharing the story of that moment highlights the values on which the community was built. Or maybe the group bonded during a river-rafting trip, and your references to that weekend are enough to reaffirm the group's commitments to one another. In a presentation in which your goal is building community, your focus is on strengthening the shared bonds and common worldview that created the initial in-group feeling that forms the basis of community for members.

Restoring Community

Disruption of an existing community can stem from a conflict in a group or unexpected events or tragedies. Perhaps a faction of a church has split from the main congregation, a strike has divided a community, or a conflict between two coworkers is harming the collegial atmosphere of a work environment. Other examples are when a new manager has been brought into a work group or a divorce has disrupted a group of friends. Abraham Lincoln's Gettysburg Address, in which he sought to unify the North and the South, is an example of this kind of presentation.

When a community has been disrupted, you attempt to reestablish the shared worldview that once bound the community together. This effort can involve efforts to reenergize the group around the common perspectives the group members once shared by talking about experiences and commitments important to them. Sometimes, your task will be to focus on helping the group see beyond the situation or events that led to the disruption. This might mean showing the group's members why they need not be concerned with certain issues or allegations, suggesting that certain problems that are disrupting the group can be handled rather easily, or minimizing the importance of an event or experience.

Another approach to restoring community is to find common ground among the parties to transcend the differences that are dividing them and to reach a new understanding of shared interests. To redirect the energies of two coworkers whose behavior is disrupting the workplace, you can help them see that they share a goal of working in the best interests of the company. A divorcing couple might find common ground in what is best for their children, reaching a new sense of togetherness based not on their own relationship but on their mutual desire to have their children thrive. Winning the state championship may become the common ground that unites a sports team that has been fractured by perceptions of differences among players.

To Seek Adherence

In some instances, you direct your efforts toward asking others to consider accepting your way of thinking or to consider adopting beliefs or behaviors that you advocate. You encourage others to change in a particular way. In these cases, you are seeking adherence. *Adherence* literally means to bind—to stick to or to hold fast. Seeking adherence, then, involves an effort to convince others to accept, adopt, support, or align with your point of view. You are seeking to persuade your audience to take your perspective or to agree with you about something by making a change in attitude and/or behavior.

You may choose to seek adherence as your interactional goal in a variety of situations. Sales and marketing are primary contexts for this goal. Efforts to sell or advertise products involve presentations in which you seek adherence. At other times, you want to sell proposals or ideas. In these cases, you advocate a particular option because you believe it will work best for an organization or an individual. You believe strongly in a product or plan and its benefits and would like your audience members to choose it over others so that they can realize the same benefits.

Another common situation in which your interactional goal is to seek adherence is when you are in a supervisory role. You may be responsible for producing particular results within an organization, and you want to persuade your employees to produce the kind of work necessary to create the desired results. You have a particular outcome in mind, and your presentations to your staff are designed to help them achieve that desired outcome.

Seeking adherence is also your goal when you offer advice in personal relationships. As a parent, you seek adherence when you talk with your child about options and choices you believe would help create a positive and productive future. A mother might ask her son to consider the consequences of dropping a particular class or to consider certain factors when choosing a college. In a romantic relationship, you might use the goal of seeking adherence when you encourage your partner to do any number of things you think would be good—to dress up for a holiday party, go back to school, or give up smoking, for example.

The goal of seeking adherence may seem antithetical to invitational rhetoric. After all, many of the assumptions of invitational rhetoric—for example, understanding is the purpose of communication or the speaker and the audience are equals—seem to contradict the effort to seek adherence. There are ways to engage in seeking adherence, however, that do not violate the principles of invitational rhetoric.

Seeking adherence can be invitational if you express your position with care. Offer your audience members as complete a picture as you can of your viewpoint—articulating your beliefs clearly, comprehensively, and respectfully. If audience members have the opportunity to consider a well-expressed perspective that avoids manipulation or deception, they may choose to change. Burke suggests the importance of offering a complete perspective when he asks communicators to "advocate their choice by *filling it out!* That is: let each say all he can by way of giving body to the perspective inherent in his choice. Let each show the scope, range, relevancy, accuracy, applicability of the perspective. . . . And only after each has been so filled out, can we evaluate among them."[9] Offering your perspective as carefully, thoughtfully, and completely as possible is one way in which seeking adherence can be accomplished invitationally. A presentation to seek adherence would look very much like a presentation to articulate a perspective when this particular strategy is used.

A second way in which you can create an invitational presentation designed to seek adherence is by including opportunities for you to learn about and understand the audience's perspective. One common way to do this is to ask for questions at the end of your presentation. Instead of assuming that you have the superior perspective that you want to impose on your audience, you enter the interaction interested in what your audience members believe about it. While you may start out thinking your perspective is perhaps the most workable, efficient, or best for the situation, you are willing to alter that perspective once you hear from your audience members. The perspectives audience members share may allow you to come up with an idea that is even better than your original one. Furthermore, because you are taking into account your audience members' views, they are more likely to continue sharing ideas, which leads to the generation of even more ideas.

You also seek adherence invitationally when you express unequivocally that audience members are free to decide whether they want to do what you are asking. A speaker who communicates to audience members that they have choices and have the right to exercise them creates a very different atmosphere for an audience than a speaker who argues for a point of view as if it were the only reasonable view to hold. When you speak to your audience members in a way that acknowledges and values their perspectives, they will be more willing to listen, knowing they can choose whether or not to change.

The interactional goal of seeking adherence can be enacted in ways that honor the integrity of others and their viewpoints. Such an approach to persuasion is more respectful of the range of perspectives on any given issue. Individuals are more willing to change when they do not feel coerced, and the changes that do occur typically are more thoughtful, better integrated, and longer lasting than ones produced in more manipulative ways.

To Discover Knowledge and Belief

In some interactions, the speaker and audience are unsure of their views on a situation or uncertain about how to handle something. They come together to sort out the knowledge and actions available to them. The interactional goal in this situation is to discover knowledge and belief. Together, the speaker and audience members explore a subject to discover what they know and believe about it and how best to respond on the basis of that information. When you choose this interactional goal, you assume the role of facilitator, but you do not have any more answers than other group members about how to handle the issue. You are not there to control or dictate what others say but to ensure that participants feel comfortable sharing their opinions, thoughts, and feelings about an issue.

As a facilitator, your first responsibility is to arrange for the time and place in which the group can interact. This might happen at a regular staff meeting for employees, when homework is done if you're talking with your teenaged daughter, or whenever there is ample time and an appropriate place to cover an issue thoroughly. You are responsible for framing the subject for discussion, guiding those present through an investigation and analysis of the subject, and summarizing the insights produced by the discussion. Even in informal situations—talking with your daughter or with a roommate, for instance—you assume the role of facilitator, although the steps in the process are not as obvious as in a formal meeting. The essence of your role as facilitator, regardless of the degree of formality, is like that of a midwife—coaching and assisting others to share, think through, and talk over various perspectives. The goal is to come to a better understanding of issues, to generate new ideas, and perhaps to reach a decision that serves as the basis for action.

To discover knowledge and belief is substantially different from the other four interactional goals. You do not enter the interaction with an idea or a proposal you already have developed or knowing what you believe. Instead, you genuinely do not know what you think or believe or how to handle a situation. You hold no perspective yet or, at best, have a sketchy, tentative one and allow the discussion to direct the development of your perspective. The interactional goal of discovering knowledge and belief is selected most often in two situations—when you want to generate new ideas or find solutions to a problem that will take advantage of all of the expertise in a group or when you are unsure or unclear about what you know or believe and use talk with others to figure things out.

The most common situation in which you construct presentations to discover knowledge and belief is when you want the help of the group in generating ideas in order to solve a problem or figure out how to do something. Involving the input of others usually means a more comprehensive set of options than if you tackled the problem alone. The assumption is that more options will allow you to make an informed decision or a more effective and productive one.

For example, let's assume that you are a manager at The Gap, and your boss has asked you to develop a plan for distributing holiday bonuses. You want the input of the other workers in order to devise a plan that is fair and equitable. You call a meeting and facilitate a discussion that allows multiple proposals to be voiced and discussed. After hearing all of the ideas, you either can choose to adopt one of the proposals in its entirety or to develop your own plan by incorporating various elements from the proposals. Or perhaps you are the advisor to a school newspaper and are trying to decide what kinds of changes in format would be beneficial. You realize that you do not know what students think of the newspaper, and you call a meeting at which students can express their views.

Although the goal of discovering knowledge and belief is common in workplace and educational settings, these are not the only contexts in which such presentations occur. Perhaps a friend talks to you about the difficulties he is having in an intimate relationship, and you help him figure out what to do. When your daughter comes home from junior high, discouraged by always being picked last for teams in her PE class, you help her see what her options are. Maybe your partner is trying to decide whether to change careers, and together you brainstorm other career possibilities.

When members of a group are unsure or unclear, presentations to discover knowledge and belief offer opportunities to enhance understanding. Members talk through their ideas to express what previously was unstated. A group that gathers to develop its mission statement, for example, may have a vague idea that there are some principles and commitments that unite all of the group members, but they cannot easily articulate them. As they think together about their mission, they voice these principles and select language to communicate the group's commitment. Theologian Nelle Morton has labeled this phenomenon *hearing into speech*,[10] a process whereby hearing others generates insights of which people were previously unaware and could not have articulated without the input from others.

Through the discovery process, you and the group arrive at an opinion or decision and also learn how productive different opinions and ideas can be in helping frame an issue more fully. You often have a more creative and comprehensive understanding than you would have developed by tackling an issue on your own. Furthermore, the process of discovering knowledge and belief may strengthen group solidarity and foster a greater commitment to the ideas or solution the group has generated. People support what they create, and when they are part of the process that brings new ideas into being, they are more likely to advocate for and commit to those ideas.

For the interactional goal of discovering knowledge and belief to be successful, it must take place in a context in which talk is valued as a means of coming to know and making decisions. Everyone involved must share a belief in the possibility of arriving at an acceptable solution or decision by talking things through. This kind of talk is valued in the US educational system, where many classes incorporate some kind of sharing of opinions, beginning with show and tell in kindergarten and progressing to more formal discussions and debates in high school and college.

In contrast, in many cultures within and outside of the United States, joint talk to discover or create ideas is not seen as appropriate or useful. In a situation with a highly authoritarian parent, for example, the goal of discovering knowledge and belief between parent and child is very unlikely. A father who "knows best" and does not tolerate challenges to his authority probably will not be willing to hear the opinions of his daughter about when she is old enough to date. In China and Denmark, for example, discussions often are not seen as a legitimate way to develop ideas. Instead, ideas are supposed to come from experts and authorities and not through discussions among groups of nonexperts.

Steps in the Process of Facilitation

Regardless of whether you are generating ideas or discovering what you believe about something, the goal of discovering knowledge and belief typically involves a brainstorming process that includes three possible steps: (1) definition of the problem; (2) joint search for ideas; and (3) evaluation or decision.

Definition of the Problem.   In the first step of the brainstorming process, you state the problem or issue for the group as clearly, concisely, and comprehensively as you can. You want to make sure all of the participants in the interaction have a clear understanding of the subject or issue about which they will generate ideas.

Defining terms is one way to provide an overview of the problem. For example, if you are a member of the Parent Teacher Association at your child's school and have been asked to facilitate a discussion on the best way to decrease violence in the schools, you need to be sure the group members agree on what they mean by *violence*. Otherwise, there will be ongoing confusion about what exactly is under discussion. Is the issue bullying, students carrying weapons, hate speech, or something else? If the group is not aware of the problem, you need to spend more time on this step. In such a case, you might want to prepare a visual aid that summarizes the background and basic facts involved.

Search for Ideas.   The second step in the facilitation pattern is a joint search for ideas. You and your audience members talk together to discover what you know or believe about a subject or to generate ideas that might solve a problem. As the facilitator, this step consists of asking questions of the audience to stimulate discussion. You might ask such questions as: "What can you tell us about yourself and your life that would help us understand your commitments in terms of this issue?" "What do we stand for as a group?" "What could we do to improve our effectiveness as an organization?" and "What are different ways that we might solve this problem?"

You might want to use formal brainstorming techniques at this stage of the facilitation. In brainstorming, you ask participants to generate as many solutions as they can to a problem while someone records all of the ideas so that everyone can review them. What is important in the brain-storming process is that there is no judgment or even commentary on the ideas generated. Any idea, no matter how silly or unworkable it seems, is recorded because even those ideas that appear to be unusable may stimulate further thinking.

You may discover, in your search for alternatives, that the group needs more information. Perhaps some creative solutions have been offered to a problem, but you do not know, for example, if they violate company policy or whether they can be implemented in the time available. When this is the case, you can give individuals particular assignments such as making calls to the appropriate people or looking up relevant policies to get the information you need. You set another meeting time when participants report on what they have found, and the idea-generation process will begin again, taking into account the new information.

Evaluation/Decision.   In most cases, the group will decide which of the ideas or solutions generated is the best and will be implemented. The first task in the evaluation/decision step is determining the criteria group members will use to evaluate the ideas generated in the brain-storming process. Criteria might include workability of the solution, sim-plicity of the solution, lowest cost, or whether the solution meets everyone's needs. As the facilitator, you lead the participants through the suggested ideas or solutions one by one, helping them apply the criteria they have developed.

As you apply the criteria to the suggested options, frame the evalua-tion process positively so that those whose ideas are being evaluated do not feel hurt or dismissed by the process. Instead of asking which ideas are unacceptable or bad, ask which appear to be the most promising and should be given the most serious consideration. The discussion at this stage is a process of clarification. As each idea or proposal is discussed, group members become increasingly clear about what they want, and often the best solution becomes obvious to everyone.

The chair of a university department might use a presentation to discover knowledge and belief to brainstorm with her faculty members about how the department can save money on copying costs. In the first stage, definition of the problem, she would share with the faculty how high the copying bill for the department is each month. In the second step of the process, the joint search for ideas, she would ask the faculty members to brainstorm ways in which they can reduce the number of copies they make. They might generate ideas such as using a system such as Blackboard or WebCT on which to post materials, developing individual websites on which they could post their syllabi, e-mailing handouts to their students instead of copying and distributing them, making double-sided copies, and putting course materials on reserve in the library. In this case, the consensus or evaluation step probably would not be necessary because there is no need to come to consensus on which option the faculty members will use. All ideas can be used by faculty members to reduce copying costs. The presentation would end with the chair encouraging the faculty members to use all available options and to think carefully about alternatives before heading to the department's copy machine.

If the faculty members wanted to develop a departmental policy to follow concerning copying, they would have to come to consensus on the option or options they would be required to follow. They might use criteria such as amount of money saved and amount of additional work for faculty as criteria by which to evaluate the various options.

Asking Questions to Facilitate Discussion

Throughout the process of facilitating a discussion to discover knowledge and belief, asking questions is critical. Participants must be committed to the use of questions as a way to learn and understand. By their very nature, questions invite levels of reflection on both content and process. Questions also can produce collective energy and commitment among participants in ways that are highly motivating and satisfying. When a questioning framework rather than one of assertion is used, participants can be more creative and collaborative and are likely to be more open to a greater range of possibilities.

As the facilitator of a group, you need to ask good questions to achieve the kind of interaction and input you want from the group. In advance of the interaction, generate questions that will help ensure that all perspectives are heard, that will prevent any individual from monopolizing the discussion, and that will keep the discussion on track. Listed below are suggested questions for specific situations:

- To draw out a silent member.
  "Does anyone who hasn't spoken care to comment?"
  "Roger, what is your opinion of . . . ?"

"Cecilia, from your experiences in local government, would you comment on that?"

- **To suggest the need for sharing personal experiences.**

  "Does anyone know of instances where this has worked?"

  "How has this affected each of you personally?"

  "Will each of you be thinking about your own experiences in this matter so that I can ask each of you for your reaction later?"

  "Have any of you had experiences with this in another company that you would be willing to share with us?"

  "What is at the heart of the matter for you?"

  "How did you get involved with this issue? What is your personal relationship to it? Do you have a personal history with it?"

- **To call attention to points that have not been considered.**

  "Does anyone have any information on [an unexplored point]?"

  "What has been your thinking on [an issue that has not been covered]?"

  "Before we continue, would it be profitable to explore another angle?"

  "Whose lives are affected by the issue? In what ways are they affected?"

  "Whose perspectives are not represented in our discussion?"

- **To suggest the need for additional information.**

  "Do we have enough information to decide now?"

  "Should we form a subcommittee to research and bring back the information we need on this issue?"

- **To prevent a few from monopolizing the discussion.**

  "Excuse me, Sally. Before you continue, may I ask if anyone has a comment on the point you've just made?"

  "Thank you, Anthony. May we hear from someone else who hasn't expressed an opinion?"

- **To keep the group on track and on task.**

  "That's interesting. How does this point fit in with the issue being considered?"

  "I might have missed something you said. Will you please explain the connection between your suggestion and the main issue?"

  "Does the group feel that this point bears directly on the issue at hand?"

  "Would we make more progress if we confined our discussion to the facts of the case rather than to the people involved?"

  "Since we don't seem to be able to resolve this difference now, could we move on to the next point? Perhaps further discussion will reveal additional information that will help us resolve this issue."

  "What are we up to in this conversation? What do we want to see happen here?"

  "Shall we go back and revisit our purpose to see if we're still working toward that end?"

Because the interactional goal of discovering knowledge and belief involves a group in the decision-making process, you cannot accomplish this goal in a short classroom presentation. If you want to try out this goal in a presentational speaking course, you probably will need to shorten the process in some way. Devote your presentation to just one step of the process—generating ideas, for example—rather than taking the group through the entire process from idea generation to evaluation. You also could make use of this goal for the introduction of your presentation only. Perhaps you ask your audience to generate definitions of something—the word *friend*, for example—that you then use in the body of your presentation. You may ask audience members to offer a few examples of their expectations about something, which you later incorporate into your presentation. Of course, if you have the option of speaking for 15 or 20 minutes, you can try out this goal in a presentation that incorporates the full decision-making process.

⟶ MULTIPLE INTERACTIONAL GOALS

We have been talking about interactional goals as if you will select only one for any given presentation. Although you are likely to have a primary goal, most presentations have multiple goals. If you want the approval of your manager to change the accounting process for a project, your primary goal will be to seek adherence. As part of that presentation, you need to explain why the proposed change makes sense in light of the overall project, which requires you to put together information about the nature and status of the project—to articulate a perspective. At the same time, you are seeking to present yourself in a positive light to your manager—to have her see you as a competent individual—so the goal of asserting individuality also is at work.

When you are designing a presentation that has multiple interactional goals, your primary focus should be on the goal that is most important for what you want to accomplish. For example, a classroom teacher has several options in dealing with a group of disruptive students. He could respond with the goal of asserting individuality by focusing on how he is personally insulted by the students' behavior and their lack of respect for what he is trying to do in the classroom. He could adopt the interactional goal of creating community, choosing to engage in a series of activities designed to create cohesiveness among the students. Yet another way he could approach the situation is by engaging in a discussion designed to discover why the class is choosing to behave so disruptively, structuring his interaction around the goal of discovering knowledge and belief. Although all of these goals might be at the heart of the teacher's presentation, he would want to decide which goal is most important to him and design a presentation that features that goal.

Interactional goals are the core of a presentation. The goal you select names a situation in some way and encompasses your response to it. It becomes your chosen approach for addressing the need you have defined as operating in this situation. The goal you choose for your presentation—to assert individuality, articulate a perspective, build community, seek adherence, or discover knowledge and belief—serves as your guide for the other decisions you will make about your presentation.

3

Creating Environment

Now that you have identified the interactional goal or goals of your presentation, you are ready to begin thinking about your specific speaking context. You want to consider how you can create an environment that will facilitate an invitational approach. Your aim is to encourage your audience members to consider your perspective carefully as well as to share their perspectives with you.

⟶ CREATING EXTERNAL CONDITIONS FOR TRANSFORMATION

To create an environment that allows audience members to be receptive to transformation, you want to create particular external conditions in the speaking situation. When these conditions are present in an interaction, the possibilities for transformation on the part of the speaker and the audience increase, and audience members feel free to contribute to the interaction. When both you and the audience consider new perspectives, the opportunity to understand one another is enhanced. As you prepare and deliver your presentation, the communication options you select either will facilitate or impede the development of these conditions in your particular speaking situation. The four external conditions you want to create in the speaking environment are: (1) safety; (2) openness; (3) freedom; and (4) value.[1]

Safety

Safety is the condition of feeling free from danger or risk. When you create safety in a speaking situation, audience members trust you, are not fearful of interacting with you, and feel you are working with and not against them. Safety is required for transformation because if participants in an interaction do not feel safe, they are reluctant to share ideas, making the emergence of new perspectives difficult. In a speaking situation, safety means feeling secure physically and intellectually.

The foundation of safety is the experience of well-being at a physical level, which includes the physical environment in which the interaction occurs. Physical safety may be an issue if you are communicating in a difficult physical situation—the site of a recent natural disaster such as an earthquake or hurricane, for instance. If you are using dangerous equipment or tools as part of your presentation—weapons or power tools, for example—you and your audience undoubtedly will be aware of issues of physical safety.

Issues of physical safety, however, are rare in most presentational speaking situations. Most meeting rooms, classrooms, and auditoriums are safe physical spaces. What you have to contend with more often is a general context of fear about safety in contemporary culture. Several explanations can be offered for such feelings of fearfulness. The mean-world hypothesis suggests that the media—and television in particular—have projected a distorted view of how dangerous life is. As a result, people believe the world is a violent place.[2] School shootings, such as the one at Columbine High School in Littleton, Colorado, have intensified parents' fears.[3] And, of course, the terrorist attacks of September 11, 2001, led many US citizens to feel fearful in ways they did not before—afraid to fly, afraid of anyone of Middle-Eastern descent, and afraid for the sanctity of US boundaries.

As a result of feelings of fearfulness, people with whom you are interacting might fear for the safety of themselves and their families and be afraid to take risks or to go outside of what is comfortable and familiar. What this means for a speaking context is that some individuals may be generally less adventuresome, less willing to try new things, and less willing to take risks. When individuals are affected by vague concerns about physical safety, your efforts at achieving understanding and transformation may be less effective than they might be in a different climate.

In most speaking situations in which safety is problematic, lack of intellectual safety rather than physical safety is the issue. Intellectual safety concerns the degree to which participants feel they can safely share, explore, and question ideas and whether their statements will be treated with respect and care. In some situations, intellectual safety is less a matter of personal preference and more an issue of potentially severe consequences. Certain audiences do not feel safe expressing perspectives that are different from those of their supervisors, church officials, or governments. Intellectual safety means that neither the speaker nor audience members can dismiss ideas with which they do not agree. Rather than immediately judging someone as silly, stupid, or ignorant for believing something, both the speaker and audience are willing to listen to ideas that are different from their own in order to have the fullest perspective possible on an issue.

Intellectual safety also means that both the speaker and audience members are willing to admit that they do not know something. Admitting ignorance and mistakes can be as difficult for some people as listening to differing perspectives. Being comfortable with engaging knowledge—the known, the strange, and the unknown—is all part of intellectual safety.

In a speaking situation, you can facilitate a feeling of safety in several ways. One is to pay attention to the environment and the kind of format for interaction that you establish. Some participants may feel safest engaging in high self-disclosure in a setting in which the chairs are arranged in an intimate circle. Others feel safest sitting in rows of chairs in a large lecture hall, where there is no expectation for them to reveal personal information. Similarly, safety for some might mean energetic participation in heated debate, while for others, such participation feels unsafe.

You also can generate a feeling of safety by asking a group to construct its own communication guidelines for an interaction. Typically, the guidelines that groups generate cover some topics explicitly designed to help participants feel safe. They might develop ground rules such as "speak only for yourself, not others"; "be respectful when commenting on the opinions expressed by others"; "try to understand where others are coming from when they express an opinion"; and "give everyone who wants to speak the opportunity to do so." With these kinds of guidelines in place, participants might feel safe to share their perspectives with other group members.

Keep in mind that there will be some in your audience, no matter how small it is and no matter how many guidelines the group has developed to encourage participation, who do not feel comfortable speaking up. With a bit of planning, you can ensure that the perspectives of these audience members are "heard" without violating their sense of safety. You might ask group members, for example, to write down questions or comments, which you collect and incorporate into the discussion. Another option is to ask your audience members to write down a question as they enter the room, which you then quickly organize into categories to use to structure the discussion. You also can ask for a written straw vote on an issue to see how audience members are feeling about an issue or ask audience members to send questions to the front to be answered in the question-and-answer session at the end of your presentation.

Another way in which you can help create the condition of safety for your audience members is by modeling how to respond to others in ways that facilitate a feeling of safety. If you listen to the ideas and feelings of others with respect and care and do not degrade or belittle them or their beliefs, you will show that you truly value all opinions and perspectives. If an audience member challenges you, demonstrate openness and make a real effort to understand the perspective of the challenger.

You also want to model that you feel safe yourself, perhaps by taking some risks. If self-disclosure is a feature that means safety for your audience, you might want to talk about your children or tell a story in which you demonstrate that you made a mistake. Such disclosures can communicate to audience members that they also can feel free to take risks. As consultant Annette Simmons suggests: Use yourself as "'exhibit A' to prove this is a safe place."[4] She adds, "If you feel safe, you communicate that to everyone. If you don't, you can't. A relaxed, confident, peaceful composure tells the group that you, at least, believe in this process and believe in them."[5]

Openness

The second characteristic required for a transformative environment is openness, a genuine curiosity about perspectives different from yours. Openness is the operationalization of the key idea behind invitational rhetoric—diverse perspectives are resources. Both you and your audience members acknowledge that the greater the diversity of the perspectives you encounter, the greater the understanding you will have of a subject. The availability of diverse perspectives, then, increases opportunities for transformation. If both speaker and audience approach such diversity thoughtfully and respectfully and with an attitude of appreciation and delight, openness will function as a resource.

One way to communicate openness to your audience in your presentation is to acknowledge other perspectives on an issue. Showing awareness of alternative viewpoints reveals that you have considered perspectives other than your own—and you have had to consider them carefully enough to be able at least to reference them. Demonstrating openness by showing an awareness of various viewpoints on an issue will go a long way to creating an environment in which transformation is possible.

Another way to demonstrate openness is to allow your audience members an opportunity to articulate their perspectives on an issue—in small break-out groups, by sharing their opinions on charts or a mural, by voting on ideas or formal propositions, or using some other mechanism by which they can express their views. A question-and-answer session after the presentation also allows the articulation of contrasting opinions, allowing audience members to hear the perspectives of others and further facilitating an environment of openness.

Freedom

Freedom is the power to choose or decide from among the options available. It allows each participant in the interaction to make decisions about what to believe and how to act. When freedom is present in a speaking situation, there is no pressure on audience members to make the same choices as the speaker.

You can develop freedom in a speaking situation in a number of ways. Freedom is created when you do not place restrictions on the nature of the exchange. Participants feel free to bring any topic into the interaction and are not limited to the perspectives you raise. In addition, all assumptions are open to questioning and rethinking. If audience members challenge assumptions you consider sacred or bring up topics you would rather not talk about, you do not exclude those topics from the discussion or discontinue your interaction with those who initiated the topics.[6] Probably the most important way you can create the external condition of freedom is to communicate to listeners that they do not have to adopt your perspective. If your audience members are truly free, they can choose not to accept your viewpoint without fear of reprisal, ridicule, punishment, or humiliation. You communicate to them that your relationship with them does not depend on their sharing your views.

The condition of freedom is at the heart of an invitation to transformation because whether to change or not is a choice. If your interactional goal is seeking adherence, for example, you help create the condition of freedom by conveying to your audience that changing minds or behaviors is not the most important aspect of your interaction with them. You are more interested in maintaining your connection with them, understanding them, learning from them, and enjoying the process of interaction than you are with convincing them to see things your way or to act as you do.

Sonja has a former student who is working on a PhD in communication and who has decided that she does not want to become a professor; she wants to work with nonprofit organizations instead. Some of her professors are telling her that she is good at research and has what it takes to make it in the academy, so she should continue on that path. In their interactions with her, they are not open to hearing what makes her happy; rather, they imply that if she leaves academia, they will no longer have a relationship with her. Other professors demonstrate what we mean by *freedom*—assuring her that her relationships with them will not be damaged if she leaves the academy, that her happiness is their most important concern, and that they will continue to support her no matter what she chooses to do.

A commitment to the condition of freedom means, then, that you cannot control the end result of the process of presentational speaking. You enter the situation inviting others to explore a subject with you, and you trust that what you create together will be beneficial for everyone involved. You are willing to live with and even to appreciate the "creative, messy, unfolding"[7] of perspectives that your presentation engenders because you are committed to the freedom of the others with whom you are interacting to make their own choices for their lives.

Value

The external condition of value honors the intrinsic or inherent worth of each individual. It communicates that each participant is a significant and critical part of the interaction because each individual's perspective is unique. To gain a full understanding of an issue, everyone's perspective must be heard and appreciated. If some perspectives are privileged and others are ignored or devalued, comprehensive understandings cannot emerge. When value is created in a speaking situation, audience members feel they have something important to contribute and that the speaker cares about and appreciates those contributions.

One way in which you can convey that you value your listeners is by inviting and encouraging all participants in the interaction to be heard. By structuring opportunities for discussion into your presentation and using question-and-answer sessions, for example, you demonstrate that you value the views of all audience members and want those views to be included in the conversation.

At times, the task you face in terms of value is not figuring out how to get the shy or reticent audience members to share their perspectives but how to prevent one person from doing all the talking. You undoubtedly have been in situations where one person dominates the interaction, apparently believing that his perspective is more valuable than those of the others in the room. In such a case, your task is to limit this person's input without devaluing him. You can say things like, "We have a pretty good understanding of your perspective, Jason. Let's see if anyone would like to share some ideas we haven't heard about yet." Or you could say something like, "I appreciate how willing you are to help us understand and develop that particular perspective, Anna. I wonder if others have suggestions that we may not have considered yet?" (Chapter 2 also offers suggestions for ensuring that all parties are heard.)

Sonja recently attended a colloquium of faculty members at her university, where the speaker presented a paper and asked the audience for ideas about how to revise it to give it a stronger conceptual framework. Sonja took the speaker's request seriously and offered a suggestion for such a framework. The speaker nodded and went on talking about her experience of writing the paper. Sonja and the other audience members got the message very clearly that the speaker really did not want suggestions for revision and did not value those that were offered, and the colloquium soon ended.

⬥ ANALYZING THE SPEAKING ENVIRONMENT

In the ideal speaking situation, you want the conditions of safety, openness, freedom, and value to be present. To create such conditions, you must assess your speaking environment to discover the elements that are available to you. If your analysis of the speaking environment reveals that certain factors are likely to facilitate a transformative environment, you will organize your presentation to emphasize these factors. If other factors in the situation appear likely to be obstacles to transformation, you want to adjust them or neutralize their impact so that they do not hinder the creation of the conditions of safety, openness, freedom, and value.

The four primary components of the speaking environment to consider when creating the external conditions for transformation are: (1) setting; (2) audience; (3) speaker; and (4) subject. Below are lists of questions to stimulate your thinking about each of these components. Your goal is to discover the factors that are likely to facilitate or hinder your creation of the conditions of safety, openness, freedom, and value. These questions are only starting points. The details of your particular speaking situation undoubtedly will suggest other factors that you will want to consider.

Setting

Date

What is the date on which you are speaking? Is there anything unusual or significant about it for either you or your audience? If you are speaking on September 11 in the US, audiences are likely to expect some kind of reference to the events of 2001.

Hour

At what time of day are you speaking? Is it early in the morning or late in the evening, after the audience has had a full day of other speakers or activities? Are you a morning or an evening person? If the hour is not the best for either you or your audience, you will need to pay extra attention to how you can encourage audience members to listen, to engage various perspectives, and to contribute.

Meeting place

What are the characteristics of the place in which you are speaking? Is it indoors or outdoors? What is the shape and size of the space? Are there acoustical problems? Is the room a comfortable temperature, or is it too hot or too cold? What kind of lighting is available in the room? What is the noise level? Are there features of the room that might function as distractions for the audience? Will the audience be standing or sitting in rows of chairs, at tables, or on the floor?

Size of audience

How large is your audience? Are you speaking to one person? To a small group? To a large group? Can the space accommodate your audience comfortably?

Purpose for gathering

What is the purpose of the event, meeting, or interaction at which your presentation will be given? To conduct business? To socialize? To solve a problem? To reinforce community ties?

Order of events

What or who precedes and follows your presentation? Are other presentations planned? On what subjects? How long has your audience been listening to presentations before yours? Are food and refreshments to be served and, if so, when?

Time constraints

How much time do you have for your presentation? Is there enough time for you to accomplish your interactional goal(s)?

Presence of an interpreter

Will someone be translating your presentation into another language? Will that translation be simultaneous or sequential? If it is not simultaneous, your presentation will take twice as long as usual, so you will need to plan carefully so you have time to develop your perspective fully. Will someone be signing your presentation for deaf members of your audience? If so, do you need to adjust your presentation so that audience members relying on the interpretation feel safe, comfortable, and able to contribute? Do you need to make adjustments so that the presence of the interpreter does not distract other audience members?

If an analysis of your **setting** tells you, for example, that you will be speaking following dinner at a conference that has been going on all day, you can assume that your audience members probably will be tired of sitting, tired of listening to speakers, and tired of thinking. Consequently, they are not likely to be as interested in engaging in the sustained listening necessary to follow a presentation and to allow it to serve as a catalyst for transformation. Instead, they are likely to stick with their current ways of thinking because they are interested in other things—perhaps joining friends for after-conference partying or going home to bed. To convert this obstacle into a dimension that facilitates transformation, develop your topic in ways that will connect particularly strongly with your audience. Think about ways to involve your listeners in a discussion of the subject rather than simply presenting your ideas to them. Keep your presentation short. In general, select as communication options those that prevent the setting from becoming an obstacle to the presentation of your perspective.

Audience

Knowledge of subject

How much do your audience members know about the subject of your presentation?

Interest in subject

Do your audience members care about your subject? To what degree? Those who care a great deal may have developed strong views about it, while those who are unfamiliar with it or do not think it is very important will be more neutral.

Perspective on subject

What are the perspectives of your audience members on your subject? If the subject is controversial, what positions do your audience members hold on it? What experiences of audience members are likely to influence the perspectives they hold? What demographic variables of the audience—age, sex, economic status, religious affiliation, political affiliation, or cultural identity, for example—are likely to influence the audience's perspectives?

Receptivity to change

How committed are your audience members to their perspectives? To what degree are they willing to alter their perspectives?

Homogeneity

To what degree are your audience members homogeneous? Are they the same age, for example? The same sex? Members of the same political party?

Cultural/personal identities

What cultural identities are important to audience members? Race? Ethnicity? Class? What are their cultural expectations about speaking situations?

To give you an idea of how your analysis based on **audience** factors might proceed, suppose you have been asked, as the best man, to give a toast at a wedding. Both you and the groom are electrical engineers; you were students together in college. But you know, from your analysis of the audience, that most of the others who will be attending did not go to college and are certainly not familiar with the engineering field. In your toast, then, you probably would not want to make a joke using the specialized jargon from your field because, no matter how funny it might be to the two of you, the others in the audience will be left out. Using engineering terms also might keep others from giving their toasts if they feel intimidated because they do not have the same level of education that you have. The choices you make in terms of the subject on which to focus, your language, and your style of delivery should make your audience members feel safe and free to share their own experiences about the couple following your toast.

Speaker

Position

What is your position, title, or rank? How is it likely to be perceived in this situation?

Attitude toward self

How do you feel about yourself in this speaking situation? Confident? Excited? Tentative? Intimidated? Scared?

Cultural/personal identities

Which of your cultural identities are evident to your audience? Race? Ethnicity? Sex? Sexual orientation? Class? Will you choose to reveal some aspects of your identity that are not readily available? How will these identities affect the audience's perceptions of you and your presentation?

Speaking competencies

What kinds of communication competencies are required in this situation? The ability to explain clearly? To lead a discussion? To generate excitement? How confident are you about your ability to demonstrate these skills? Do you experience communication anxiety that may interfere with your communication competence?

Vulnerabilities

Are there aspects of the speaking situation that make you feel vulnerable? Are they related to your subject? To your communication ability? To your relationship with your audience?

Attitude toward audience

What is the nature of your relationship with your audience? Affection? Respect? Compassion? Irritation? Frustration? Do you have prejudices that may affect your attitude toward your audience?

Previous experience with audience

Are your audience members acquainted with you? From what context? What experiences, if any, have you had with your audience previously that might affect this situation?

Knowledge of subject

How much do you know about the subject about which you will be speaking?

Comfort with subject

How comfortable are you talking about this subject?

Perspective on subject

What is your present viewpoint on the subject?

Receptivity to change

How committed are you to your perspective? To what degree are you willing to shift your perspective? To see it from different vantage points?

In your analysis of the factors that you as the **speaker** bring to the speaking situation, think about your strengths, weaknesses, and degree of comfort as a speaker. You may find that you are less comfortable with particular forms of communication. Give some thought to how you can reduce your uneasiness in certain speaking situations. If you feel removed and distant from your audience when you stand behind a lectern, walk around the room as you speak and encourage your audience members to ask questions during your presentation. Conversely, if you feel you lack the skills to lead a discussion well, you probably will not be comfortable incorporating a great deal of discussion into your presentation. Your discomfort will prevent you from modeling a feeling of safety for your audience.

Subject

Comfort level

Is the subject a comfortable and easy one for your audience members to listen to and discuss?

Complexity

How complex is the subject?

Nature of evidence

What sources of information or evidence about the subject are allowed or privileged? Scholarly research? Personal experience? Testimonials from others?

Controversial nature

How controversial is the subject? Are there likely to be opposing perspectives on it?

Interactional goal

What is the interactional goal guiding your presentation? Will your effort to invite transformation assume the form of asserting individuality? Building community? Articulating a perspective? Seeking adherence? Discovering knowledge and belief? What expectations and constraints are generated by your goal?

Your analysis of **subject** dimensions suggests how to proceed as you develop and deliver your presentation. Perhaps your analysis suggests that the subject you will be discussing is a highly controversial one. By selecting communication options that encourage receptivity, you can create conditions of safety, openness, freedom, and value despite the difficult topic. For example, you could select as your interactional goal articulating a perspective rather than seeking adherence. This goal will allow full presentation of multiple views and convey to participants that they are being heard. Incorporate into your presentation self-disclosure about your own background and the influences that led you to adopt the perspective you hold, helping other participants understand the context for your perspective. Be careful, as you lead the discussion or answer questions, not to belittle or devalue any opinions that others contribute.

Each of the questions concerning setting, audience, speaker, and subject from the lists above can help you identify the elements that will contribute to or detract from your ability to create the conditions of safety, openness, freedom, and value. As always, these elements are cocreated with your audience—no matter how carefully you have considered your options, your audience members may have different ideas.

⟶ RE-SOURCEMENT: MANAGING DIFFICULT ENVIRONMENTS

The creation of the conditions of safety, openness, freedom, and value is not always easy, even if the members of your audience are inclined to communicate in invitational ways. The process is made much more difficult when you find yourself involved in interactions framed in the conquest or conversion modes of rhetoric. In instances in which you are confronted with conquest or conversion rhetoric and want to create the conditions of safety, openness, freedom, and value, you might want to engage in re-sourcement.

Re-sourcement is a term coined by rhetorical theorist Sally Miller Gearhart that means "going to a new place" for energy and inspiration: "To re-source is to find another source, an entirely different . . . one."[8] Re-sourcement involves choosing not to interact within the original frame of the interaction and using a different source to develop a response. Re-sourcement involves two processes: (1) disengaging from the conquest or conversion frame of the precipitating message; and (2) formulating a response within a new frame.

Disengagement

If the message to which you are responding occurs in the context of a frame such as conquest (in which the speaker is trying to dominate or bully you into agreement), the first step in the process of re-sourcement involves stepping away from that frame. Disengagement means simply that you recognize that you have an option of how to respond, and your response does not have to be in that same conquest or conversion mode. You recognize that if the interaction continues within the original framework, nothing will be gained and, in fact, the relationship and future interactions may be jeopardized.

Sometimes, disengagement itself constitutes the entire process of re-sourcement. You literally might choose to walk away from an encounter rather than continue a negative interaction. Karen's grandson talked to her about having to fight the school bully. He acted very surprised when she suggested he just walk away without fighting. Such responses tend not be valued in our culture because they are interpreted to mean that the person is spineless, a wimp, or a coward. The tendency not even to see disengagement as an option is illustrated in an episode of the comic strip *FoxTrot*, in which Jason Fox, a video-game fanatic, spent a month trying to kill off a particular enemy to get to the next level of the game. When his sister quickly made it to the next level simply by walking past the enemy,

Jason responded: "I spent an entire month trying to kill this one video game foe, and it turns out all I had to do was walk past him! Who knew you weren't supposed to club him or kick him or lob fireballs at his head, just because he's huge and fierce and can squash you at will!"[9]

Disengagement can occur in the daily interactions that mark our professional and personal lives. Sonja once received an e-mail message from a colleague who viciously attacked her for a position she held on a departmental issue. After working very hard to formulate an effective response to the message, Sonja realized that she had another option as well—the option of simply deleting the e-mail message and not responding at all, which is what she did. She heard no more from her colleague on the issue. When you do not participate in conquest or conversion rhetoric, it cannot continue. When someone throws a pillow at you, hoping to engage you in a pillow fight, and you let the pillow fall to your feet and don't pick it up, there can be no fight. Not responding to the message by not taking the bait offered by the speaker can change the dynamics of the interaction and open up a space in which safety, openness, freedom, and value can begin to develop.

Formulating a Response within a New Frame

The second step in re-sourcement is the creative development of an invitational response to the conquest or conversion message being offered. This kind of response is designed to foster understanding, communicate that the speaker and audience are equal, and signal an interest in continuing to interact without denigrating the other's perspective. Often, this second step involves engaging in communication that does not directly argue against or even address the message being offered. It presents a response addressed to a different exigence, need, or problem from the one implicit in the conquest and conversion rhetoric. In other words, by offering a message that is different from the initial message, you help shift the nature of the interaction and enable the conditions of safety, openness, freedom, and value to begin to develop. At the very least, this kind of message makes future interactions possible by preserving enough of the relationship that the parties are willing to interact again.

Author and activist Starhawk describes an incident that demonstrates the process of re-sourcement. It occurred following a protest against nuclear weapons at the Livermore Weapons Lab in California, when she and other activists were arrested and held in a school gym. During their confinement, a woman ran into the gym, chased by six guards. She dove into a cluster of women, and they held onto her as the guards pulled at her legs, trying to extract her from the group. The guards were on the verge of beating the women when one woman in the group sat down and began to chant; the other women did the same. Starhawk describes the reaction of the guards: "They look bewildered. Something they are unprepared for, unprepared even to name, has arisen in our moment of common action. They do not know what to do. And so, after a moment, they withdraw. . . . In that moment in the jail, the power of domination and control met something outside its comprehension, a power rooted in another source."[10]

Another example of the use of re-sourcement as a response to conquest or conversion rhetoric occurs in the movie *The Long Walk Home*. The movie recreates the boycott by African Americans of buses in Montgomery, Alabama, in 1955–1956. The protest was aimed at securing seats on buses on a first-come-first-served basis instead of on the basis of race. As the boycott continued, white women began to drive their black maids to and from their homes, often in defiance of their husbands. In one scene, white men surround a group of white women and their black maids, jeering and taunting them. The men appear ready to attack them. The women respond by joining hands and singing a gospel song, and the men back away without harming them. The men's message was one of anger and conquest, and the women's message in response communicated compassion, respect, and solidarity. They acknowledged the perspective of the men, did not try to change it, and instead enacted feelings of safety and value among themselves.

Linguist Suzette Haden Elgin provides an example of re-sourcement in everyday situations when she suggests a tactic by which individuals can respond to instances of sexual harassment. If a colleague, customer, or supervisor makes a sexual proposal or sexually suggestive remark, Elgin suggests using the Boring Baroque Response. This response involves ignoring the content of the message and responding by telling a long story with many tedious details that does not address the unwanted message.[11] Because this story can be made up as the speaker tells it, no special training, talent, or skill is required. A Boring Baroque Response to an unwanted sexual comment might be something like this:

> I'm reminded of when I was growing up on a farm in South Dakota. I remember sitting on the swing on summer evenings, looking at the sky, watching the wheat—you could almost see it growing—and realizing how much I like summers. I associate summers with wheat, grasshoppers, blue sky, and swing sets, and even today, I can't wait for summer to arrive. I know a lot of people can't stand heat and would much prefer spring or fall or even winter, but not me. Winters are too cold for my taste. I might enjoy one snowy evening, but the rest is just a pain—shoveling snow, frozen pipes, cars that won't start. I'm just a summer person!

This is an example of re-sourcement in action because the speaker refuses to participate in the frame established by the harasser—a frame of conquest—and creatively devises a response that is outside of that frame. The conversation moves to another frame without judging, attacking, causing the instigator to lose face or become defensive, or escalating the interaction.

Re-sourcement is useful in a variety of other situations in which a communicator tries to goad you into participating in conquest rhetoric. Kathy, a friend of Karen's who is a facilitator and trainer, is the daughter-in-law of a prominent politician. In the middle of a training session, one of the participants asked her about her name and whether she was related to the politician. When she learned they were related, the participant said, "That's interesting because your work and your perspectives seem so at odds with his views." Rather than denigrate or defend her father-in-law—the options offered in the framing of the original message as conquest rhetoric—Kathy responded from an invitational frame: "Yes, the work I do is very interesting; it allows me to work with diverse issues and to meet lots of people. I like it very much." By using the participant's own term—*interesting*—differently from how it was intended, she contributed to the creation of the conditions that are the mark of invitational rhetoric.

Another form re-sourcement can take is appreciation. When others attack or criticize, your typical response might be to attack back. In response, the attackers defend themselves and often launch new attacks, creating an exchange that tends to destroy any feelings of safety, openness, freedom, and value that might have existed. Appreciating instead of criticizing sometimes can change the entire nature of the interaction because it deliberately reintroduces and focuses on the conditions desired.

At Sonja's university, there was a period when the mail room was not operating well because of high turnover in staff positions and lack of training of new staff members. As a result, her department consistently received the mail of other departments, and the mail the department sent out was very late in reaching its destination. Sonja's program assistant repeatedly complained to the mail room supervisors about the problems, with no noticeable impact. Sonja and her program assistant then decided to try appreciation. They brought boxes of chocolates to the mail room employees with a note acknowledging how hard the employees worked, how difficult their jobs were, and how much the department appreciated what they did. Mail service to the department improved dramatically. The environment in which the initial interaction was framed was one of opposition and defensiveness, but Sonja and her assistant chose to communicate instead within a frame of appreciation.

Re-sourcement is not limited to creating the external conditions of invitational rhetoric in protest situations. Poet Adrienne Rich demonstrated re-sourcement when she was awarded the National Book Award's prize for poetry in 1974. When she accepted the award, she read a statement she had coauthored with Audre Lorde and Alice Walker, both of whom also had been nominated for the prize. In the statement, the three women announced that they were accepting the award together and would share the prize: "We believe that we can enrich ourselves more in supporting and giving to each other than by competing against each other; and that poetry—if it *is* poetry—exists in a realm beyond ranking and comparison."[12] The message of the award was framed within a context of competition and thus conquest rhetoric. Rich, Lorde, and Walker chose not to respond with a message congruent to that frame, which would have supported the competitive, hierarchical system in which one person wins and the others lose. They responded instead with a message of cooperation, creating a collaborative rather than a competitive frame for the poetry competition with their statement. (Their complete statement is one of the sample presentations included at the end of this book.)

Re-sourcement, then, is a response you can use to communicate invitationally and to create safety, openness, freedom, and value when those around you are communicating noninvitationally. It consists of disengaging from the frame of conquest or conversion in which the message to which you are responding is framed and constructing a response from within a different frame—an invitational one. Re-sourcement enables you to continue to value others because you do not engage them in negative confrontation, and you are able to offer your perspective while remaining invitational. Re-sourcement also opens up possibilities for a greater array of options for communication in the future. Because you have not cut off other communication options for interacting with someone, you may go on to articulate your perspective in more traditional ways, using any of the five interactional goals.

In the ideal environment for invitational rhetoric, the conditions of safety, openness, freedom, and value are present and increase the possibilities that a mutual understanding of perspectives will be achieved and that participants will choose to grow and change. An analysis of the dimensions of the speaking environment—setting, audience, speaker, and subject—reveals which factors are likely to facilitate the creation of a transformative environment and which are likely to obstruct it. If you determine that the creation of these conditions will be very difficult because the interaction is framed as conquest or conversion rhetoric, re-sourcement may create a space in which a wider variety of communication options remains possible. Using re-sourcement, opportunities for transformation may emerge that may have seemed virtually impossible to create at the start of an interaction.

4

———

Focusing

After deciding on your interactional goal; analyzing environmental factors relevant to your speaking situation; and planning how to use them to create safety, openness, freedom, and value, you are ready to begin developing your presentation. Although the various processes involved in developing your presentation—focusing, framing, elaborating, beginning and ending, connecting ideas, and delivering—are treated here as a series of discrete steps, they overlap considerably. For example, when working on elaborating your ideas, you simultaneously will be working on how you are going to connect those ideas to one another and how you are going to express them when delivering your presentation.

Three preliminary processes will help you focus your presentation: (1) developing a thesis statement; (2) generating the main ideas for your presentation; and (3) making use of speaking resources. The processes involved in focusing are those that get you started on a presentation—clarifying where your initial commitments lie, generating and selecting your main ideas, and seeking out resources that will help you throughout the preparation process. By the time you have completed these steps, you will have a good sense of the basic elements of your presentation and will be ready to shape and refine it.

➤ DEVELOPING A THESIS STATEMENT

The first decision to make in the course of focusing your presentation is to develop a thesis statement. This is a statement that summarizes the subject matter or gist of your presentation, offers your initial commitment to a position, and suggests your interactional goal. A thesis statement guides you in developing your major ideas, organizing the ideas you generate, and omitting irrelevant information.

A thesis statement is not the same as a subject or topic. A subject simply names a field, a body of knowledge, or a situation. A thesis statement, in contrast, incorporates your position toward the subject you intend to explore, explain, or support. For example, if the subject is accounting, a thesis statement on the subject could be, "I believe accounting currently offers excellent employment opportunities." This thesis statement signals that you have a perspective regarding the accounting field and that you will be articulating that perspective for your audience. In your thesis statement, then, you should be able to locate the subject of your presentation, your particular perspective on it, and your interactional goal.

The thesis statement represents only a preliminary or initial commitment to a perspective. If you think of your thesis statement as tentative, it serves as a reminder that your position is evolving and that you are willing to be changed as a result of the interaction, just as you hope your audience will be. As a result of interacting with your audience in the course of your presentation, you may change your perspective about something, and the next time you address that issue—whether formally or informally—you will have a different thesis statement. Implicit in the thesis statement, then, is the recognition that the interaction is not complete without the incorporation of the audience's perspective. The audience has a central role to play in the further development of your thinking on the subject.

The function of a thesis statement is not unlike the planning you do when you host a party. The thesis statement is the equivalent of a commitment by the host to have done some initial thinking, planning, and preparation for the gathering—cleaning the house or apartment, decorating, and providing refreshments. Your thesis statement communicates to the audience that you have done some initial thinking about the subject and some preparation concerning how to present the results of that initial thinking. You do not know how the party or the presentation will go, however, and the outcome may be different from what you expect.

In most presentations, you will find yourself incorporating your thesis statement or a slight rephrasing of it directly into your presentation. You will find that how you word your thesis statement varies depending on your interactional goal. Thesis statements usually can be identified by certain words or phrases that indicate to your audience which goal is guiding your presentation.

Thesis statements for the interactional goal of **articulating a perspective** often begin with or imply phrases such as *I believe, my view is, I think*, or *my current understanding is*. Your thesis statement makes clear that your belief or position is of primary importance in this presentation. Thesis statements for articulating a perspective are statements such as:

- Our school system needs to implement a foreign-language requirement.

- I believe that moving to a voucher system in our schools would improve educational opportunities for our children.

- I have a particular perspective on ethics concerning artificial intelligence that I would like to share with you.

When your interactional goal is **asserting individuality**, phrases such as *I am, I have certain qualities,* and *I want to* are included or implied. With this goal, your focus is on certain aspects of yourself that you want to highlight for your audience. Thesis statements for presentations to assert individuality might be worded as follows:

- I am a bilingual speaker and personally understand how valuable knowing more than one language is.

- Because of my extensive experience implementing voucher systems in schools, I am an excellent choice for the position you have open.

- I am delighted to be joining this company and would like to share some of my background in the area of artificial intelligence with you.

When your interactional goal is **building community**, your thesis statement is likely to begin with phrases such as *we can, we share, we appreciate,* and *we value.* Your focus is directed collectively rather than individually, and your language is similarly inclusive. Thesis statements that have building community as an interactional goal typically take the following form:

- As bilingual speakers ourselves, I know we all share the value of speaking more than one language.

- All of us want the best possible education for our children, and a voucher system is the best route to take to improve education in this community.

- All of us here appreciate the critical importance of artificial intelligence to this line of work, and I hope that, after we've talked, the ways that each of us can contribute will be clear.

Thesis statements for the interactional goal of **seeking adherence** often use phrases such as *should, would, could, benefit, best,* and *desirable.* With such thesis statements, you are seeking the assent of audience members to something or asking them to adopt a particular idea or plan. The following thesis statements are examples of statements appropriate for presentations centered around this goal:

- We should adopt a foreign-language requirement for students in our school.

- Our educational system would benefit from the introduction of vouchers, and I urge us to vote to implement the proposed voucher system at this meeting.

- Our organization should develop our resources in artificial intelligence so that we can distinguish ourselves from others in the field.

Discovering knowledge and belief is the fifth interactional goal, and thesis statements associated with it often incorporate words such as *explore, determine,* and *decide* and phrases such as *how can we solve . . .?, I'd like you to help me with . . ., I could use some help with . . .,* and *what ideas do* *we have for . . .?* The focus in these thesis statements is on the exploration process central to this interactional goal. Thesis statements for discovering knowledge and belief assume forms such as these:

- I need your help to figure out when a student is exempt from our foreign-language requirement.
- I would like to explore how a system of educational vouchers might benefit our school district.
- How can we use artificial intelligence to benefit the company?

The thesis statement is central to your presentation. It communicates your general subject matter and reveals your commitments around that subject. Although you may find that you often are asked to speak on the same subject matter—the area of your expertise—your choice of interactional goal affects how you word your thesis statement.

➤ GENERATING THE MAIN IDEAS

Once you have developed your interactional goal (see chapter 2) and your thesis statement, you are ready to move to thinking about the main ideas of your presentation. The main ideas should be ones that clearly relate to and develop your thesis statement and that are consistent with the interactional goal you have selected. Often, the main ideas emerge naturally from the thesis statement. Once you have done the thinking and research necessary to formulate your thesis statement, the main ideas are often obvious. Some sample interactional goals, thesis statements, and main ideas are listed below to show the connections among these components.

Scenario 1

Audience. Manager
Setting. Job interview
Interactional goal. To assert individuality
Thesis statement. I am well prepared for this position
Main ideas.
- Emphasize educational background
- Emphasize experience in similar positions
- Emphasize dependability and creativity

Scenario 2

Audience. City council members
Setting. City council meeting
Interactional goals. To articulate a perspective; to seek adherence
Thesis statement. The noise problem downtown needs to be taken seriously, and I urge the city council to pass a noise ordinance.

Main ideas.
• Noise from downtown bars is excessive and disruptive.
• Passage of a noise ordinance will manage this problem.

Scenario 3

Audience. Web designer
Setting. Meeting to revamp company's website
Interactional goal. To discover knowledge and belief
Thesis statement. I want to explore ways to improve our website.
Main ideas.
• What is effective about the current website?
• How can the website be improved?
• Which of the proposed changes are most cost effective for the company?

Scenario 4

Audience. State legislators
Setting. Legislative hearing
Interactional goal. To seek adherence
Thesis statement. I believe the budget for alcohol-education programs directed at underage drinkers should be increased.
Main ideas.
• A majority of alcohol-related traffic fatalities involve underage drinkers.
• This state traditionally has devoted funds to prosecution rather than to the prevention of alcohol-related traffic accidents.
• Education programs have been found to be effective in reducing traffic accidents involving alcohol in other states.

In all of these scenarios, notice how the main ideas are a natural extension of the thesis statement. Once you have your thesis statement, you are likely to have a good idea of some of the major ideas to develop in your presentation. Locating some sources to help you develop those ideas is very useful at this stage in the process of creating your presentation.

⟶ USING RESOURCES TO DEVELOP IDEAS

Some common speaking resources for developing the ideas in your presentation are print sources, electronic sources, interviews, and personal experience. When you are asked to speak because you have developed a particular perspective on a subject, you probably will rely on speaking resources already at your command such as your current knowledge and personal experience. If you are developing a new perspective on a subject or developing a presentation with a new interactional goal or thesis statement, you probably will want to turn to external resources of various kinds to assist you. Regardless of the extent of your knowledge about a subject, researching the topic will allow you to present the most current information, to take into account how your perspective is evolving, and to analyze alternative viewpoints. Discovering new perspectives, materials, and viewpoints enables you to update and rethink your perspective.

In suggesting some of the speaking resources available to you, our intention is not to instruct you in how to do research. As a college student, you undoubtedly are familiar with how to search the Internet, how your library works, and how to access other useful sources on your campus. If you are a first-term freshman, you still may be learning about these resources, but your campus, if it is typical, offers workshops, tours, and programs for new students to become acquainted with the library and its services. Our intent here, then, is simply to remind you of some of the major speaking resources available to you when preparing a presentation.

Print Sources

Traditional sources for finding the materials you need for your presentation are those available in print—books, newspapers, journals, and magazines. Each of these sources is valuable for different reasons. Although books are the least current source of information due to the extensive time required to write and publish a book, they provide historical information and more in-depth analyses than offered by publications devoted to current events. Newspapers and magazines provide up-to-date information, with magazines usually providing more in-depth coverage than newspapers simply because their deadlines are not as immediate. A newspaper story reports daily information about an incident, while a weekly news magazine can provide an overview of the story from start to finish.

Journals or scholarly periodicals are another useful print source. The journals published by academic disciplines provide current research findings on various topics. In the discipline of communication, for example, there are journals that specialize in areas such as media studies, communication theory, applied communication, women's studies in communication, and intercultural communication, as well as many journals that are not topic specific but publish articles about all aspects of the communication field. You can find research in these journals on such diverse topics as the process of compliance gaining in interpersonal communication, religious communication, public relations campaigns, organizational communication, and analyses of television programs and films.

Internet Sources

The Internet has changed how research is conducted, and you are now able to find massive amounts of material on virtually every subject through Internet searches. When you use the Internet as a source for your presentations, you must deal with two primary problems—how to find relevant information and how to find reliable information. You may find that a search on a particular subject produces many screens and includes hundreds or thousands of items. Deciding which Internet sources are most valuable for your project requires patience and practice.

Although you may be able to find much of what you need by searching various websites on your own, numerous databases exist that can assist you with specialized information relevant to your topic. The LexisNexis database (lexisnexis.com), for instance, catalogs legal material, newspapers, and public records and may provide you with more detailed information than you could find in a more random search. Other databases focus on an issue, such as education or government; an example is WorldCat (worldcat.org) or Academic Search Complete (academicsearchcomplete.com). Google Scholar (scholar.google.com) is an excellent source for academic articles in all disciplines.

The Internet offers other resources as well that can be very helpful for discovering information. Web directories are one such resource; they employ editors to organize links to websites in categories. These directories allow you to browse lists of websites by clicking on topics such as the arts and then narrowing your search by clicking on subtopics such as music, video, or literature. Examples include Open Directory (dmoz.org), Google Directory (directory.google.com), and Best of the Web (botw.org). For government documents, USA.gov (usa.gov), sponsored by the US government, allows you to search online resources of publications by federal agencies and institutions. Electronic mailing lists, newsgroups, discussion forums, blogs, wikis, and social networking sites are other sources that can provide you with opportunities to identify people who share your interest in a topic. By searching such sites, you can identify people who might have knowledge about or expertise on an issue or who have been affected by it. Reference librarians can help you find the most efficient databases for a search on your subject.

In addition to searching for relevant information, a second problem you face in using Internet sources is how to evaluate the quality and legitimacy of the information you find. Because of the democratic nature of the web, there is no oversight body or organization that evaluates the credibility, trustworthiness, and reliability of Internet publications. Anyone can put anything on the Internet, whether it is true or false, accurate or inaccurate. In addition, earlier databases on the Internet were constructed by scanning articles, often leading to imperfect renditions of the documents. Thus, if you are using a document—an article, a poem, or an essay—from several years ago, there may be typographical errors or other problems with the document in terms of accuracy.

A number of documents are available on the web to help you evaluate your sources. If you type *Internet + source credibility* into your search engine, you will find several websites devoted to information reliability and credibility on the web. Elizabeth Kirk identifies five major criteria for evaluating information found on the web:

- Authorship. To find out more about the author of an Internet document, search for the author's name on the web or in Usenet. If the author maintains a home page, it will be listed. If biographical links are available, follow them. Also seek out comments from others about the author's work. Your goal is to establish the author's qualifications for making the claims you want to use.

- Publishing body. This criterion deals with the credibility of the publishing source. The publishing body for an Internet document is the server on which the file is stored, but there is no way for the server to guarantee the reliability of the information it stores. More important than the server's name are any names or logos appearing within the document that represent organizations that may stand behind the document.

- Referral to and/or knowledge of other sources. This criterion has to do with how the document in question treats other sources. You can use two approaches to help you make this judgment—examine the content of the document to see whether it represents other sources fairly and seek out other sources to see if the author has considered a sufficient number of alternative views.

- Accuracy or verifiability. How you establish the accuracy of data you find on the Internet is not very different from how you establish the accuracy of print data, but the special features of hypertext may make your task easier. You often will find a direct link in a document to a source cited in a document. You then can go to that document to see if the author of the document you are reviewing has cited from it accurately.

- Currency. The currency of an Internet document is the history of its publication and any revisions. A document with no dating at all is less reliable in terms of currency than one that lists numerous revisions.[1]

Interviews

Another valuable source of information is personal interviews. If you are working in a particular field, you undoubtedly have or can gain access to a variety of individuals with expertise in that field. Interviewing individuals who are working directly in your area of interest provides you with current information about the issue. If you want technical or specialized information about a subject, interview someone who is an expert in the field. If you want to learn what people in general think about something, interview several people who have been affected by an issue—perhaps employees of the organization for which you work who have been harmed by a particular policy that you will be discussing in a presentation. Interviews also give you the opportunity to learn that different people can hold different perspectives on an issue. In addition, interviewing individuals gives you an opportunity to obtain brochures, reports, and other documents from the organizations with which they are associated, which may be useful sources for your presentation.

Personal Experience

Don't forget your own experience as a resource for your presentation. Thinking through the process of how you came to hold a belief about something can help you articulate the various facets of your perspective and make decisions about how to present it to your audience. Realizing how your own perspective developed also makes you more sensitive to similar evolutions in the perspectives held by members of your audience. You can be more appreciative of the variety of perspectives your audience members hold when you understand the role personal experiences have played in your own thinking about an issue. Finally, thinking about the experiences responsible for your perspective can be a source of stories and other forms of elaboration that you can incorporate into your presentation.

You will make use of print resources, Internet sources, interviews, and personal experience at a number of places in the process of creating your presentation. Such sources are critical in the early stages of your thinking about your presentation as you select your topic and begin to develop your thesis statement and the main ideas of your presentation. You will continue to make use of these sources in other parts of the process as well. When you develop your introduction and conclusion, for example, you may find that some of these sources are useful for providing a beginning or ending to your presentation. When you refine the specific ideas of your presentation, you also will draw on these sources for the forms of elaboration for the main ideas in your presentation.

The processes involved in focusing a presentation—clarifying where your initial commitments lie and pointing you in particular directions for the development of your main ideas—are those that get you started. Formulation of your thesis statement and major ideas leads to a consideration of the frame or structure you will create for your presentation; framing is the subject of the next chapter.

5

Framing

Framing is the process of choosing an organizational pattern for the main ideas of your presentation. Because a frame increases the ease with which your audience members can understand your ideas and allows them to retain information more easily, it communicates to your audience members that you value them. There is no one right way to frame or organize a presentation. To decide which frame works best to show the relationships among your ideas, take into account the preferences and expectations of your audience, the cultural context in which you are speaking, your subject, your interactional goal, and your own personal style.

You do not have to begin from scratch to structure your presentation. Ideas for any presentation tend to sort out into some basic or conventional organizational patterns used by speakers and writers. You probably will discover that many of these frames are familiar and that you automatically use some of them to organize your ideas, even though you may not have known their formal labels.

― OPTIONS FOR FRAMING

This section discusses examples and descriptions of some conventional organizational patterns. The patterns are arranged in alphabetical order because we do not want to privilege some over others. We want to encourage you to consider all possible organizational formats for a presentation rather than selecting one that is familiar or formulaic. In the few cases where a specific pattern is appropriate for only one interactional goal, that goal is noted in the description of the pattern.

Alphabet

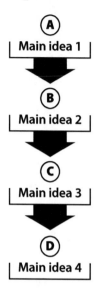

The alphabet pattern involves arranging ideas in alphabetical order. You can organize a presentation on the importance of the arts, for example, around three values that you link to letters of the alphabet: A is for awareness, B is for balance, and C is for creativity. A variation of this pattern is the structuring of a presentation around an acronym that uses letters of the alphabet such as *SAFE* to discuss earthquake preparedness. *S* might stand for securing the environment, *A* for advance planning, *F* for family meeting place, and *E* for emergency supplies.

Category

You can organize ideas around the categories that naturally arise from your subject matter. The major components, types, questions, functions, or qualities of a subject can be used as the categories in this organizational frame. Because almost any subject can be divided into categories, this is a very common organizational pattern. Christine Todd Whitman, administrator of the US Environmental Protection Agency (EPA), used a category pattern when she testified before a Congressional subcommittee about what the EPA was doing to combat bioterrorism. She discussed four categories of actions: (1) undertaking the cleanup of buildings contaminated by anthrax; (2) developing collaborative relationships with other agencies to develop health and safety standards for cleanup efforts; (3) developing a counterterrorism program; and (4) ensuring that the chemicals used to treat anthrax spores are effective and safe.[1]

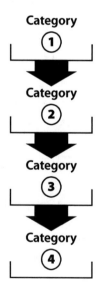

Causal

A causal organizational pattern is structured around a cause or series of causes that account for an effect or effects. In a causal (not *casual*) pattern, you can organize ideas by beginning either with the cause or with the effect. You analyze the conditions that produce a particular effect, or you can discuss the end result first and then trace the links back to the factors responsible for that effect. If your presentation is about the economic crisis, you could begin by discussing the major reasons (causes) for the crisis and the consequences (effects) of those economic behaviors. In a presentation on the condition of the US school system educational consultant David Boaz spent the first part of

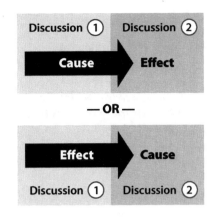

his presentation establishing that schools do not work (the effect). In the second part of his presentation, he established that there is no competition and thus no incentive to improve the school system (the cause).[2]

Circle

In this structure, ideas follow a circular pattern. You develop one idea, which leads to another, which leads to another, which leads to another, which then leads back to the original idea. You might suggest to your coworkers, for example, that greater cooperation is needed to accomplish your unit's goals. To achieve this cooperation, you propose that the members

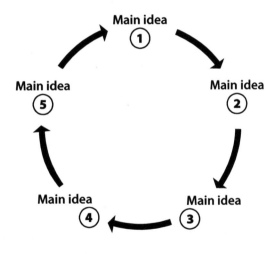

of the unit establish a goal of being honest with one another. You then discuss how honesty can contribute to a greater feeling of trust, and trust, in turn, contributes to an environment in which team members are more likely to cooperate.

Continuum

Ideas can be organized along a continuum, spectrum, or range. All of the ideas along the continuum share some common quality or substance, but they differ in the degree or level to which they contain that quality. Using this pattern, you move from one end of the continuum to the other to discuss your ideas. You might organize a presentation using a continuum pattern by discussing ideas from small to large, familiar to unfamiliar, simple to complex, or least expensive to most expensive.

Chapter 1 of this book contains an example of a continuum organizational pattern. In the discussion of different modes of rhetoric, five kinds of rhetoric are organized and discussed in turn along a continuum that moves from conquest rhetoric to conversion rhetoric to benevolent rhetoric to advisory rhetoric to invitational rhetoric. All of the points along the continuum—the different modes of rhetoric—share the quality or substance of being rhetorical modes, but they differ in the degree to which the speaker seeks to change the perspectives of audience members.

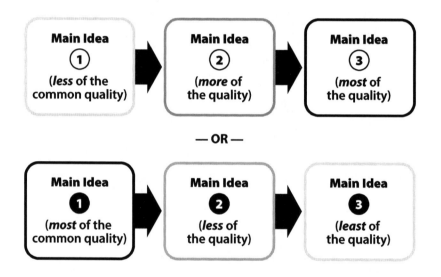

Elimination

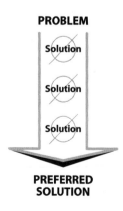

PROBLEM

PREFERRED SOLUTION

An organizational pattern of elimination begins with a discussion of a problem, followed by a discussion of several possible solutions to that problem. You examine each solution in turn and eliminate each one until the one you prefer remains. In a presentation on the state's budget deficit, for example, you might suggest solutions such as imposing an additional tax on cigarettes, implementing a sales tax, cutting state programs, and raising property taxes. You dismiss the first three solutions for various reasons and focus your presentation on advocating an increase in property taxes.

Location

In an organizational pattern of location, ideas are assembled in terms of their spatial or geographic relationships. This pattern only works when you have ideas that can be discussed according to places or locations. In a presentation titled "Asia's Rise: How and When," Hans Rosling discussed major events in 1858 that transformed world cultures and economics. He started with the United States and Great Britain and moved east across the globe to India, China, and Japan, discussing the events that occurred.[3]

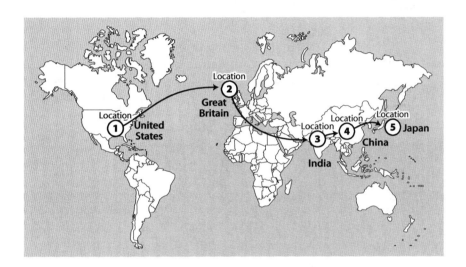

Metaphor

A metaphor is a comparison. When you use this pattern, you compare an item, idea, or experience that is familiar to audience members with one that is less familiar to help them understand the less familiar subject. One example of the use of a metaphor as an organizational pattern was a presentation by Richard R. Kelley, the CEO of Outrigger Hotels Hawaii. He used the metaphor of a cold to organize his ideas on how the company could survive in

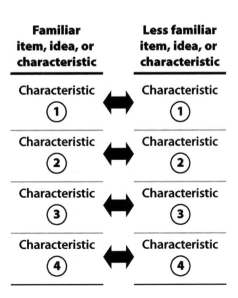

recessionary times in a presentation titled "How to Avoid a Cold When the World is Sneezing."[4]

Motivated Sequence

The motivated sequence is a five-step organizational pattern designed to encourage an audience to move from consideration of a problem to adoption of a possible solution.[5] This pattern is appropriate only for the interactional goal of seeking adherence, although it is not the only pattern that can be used for this goal. The steps are:

Attention

The introduction of the presentation is designed to capture the attention of audience members. In a presentation to high-school students on the sexual transmission of AIDS, for example, you might begin by citing statistics on the number of high-school students who are HIV positive.

Need

In the need step, a problem is described so that the speaker and audience share an understanding of the problem. At this point, you talk about how sexual intercourse is the major means of transmission of the AIDS virus and suggest that there is a need for young people to engage in honest, explicit discussion about sexual practices with their partners.

Satisfaction

A plan is presented to satisfy the need created. You might suggest various ways in which young people can initiate talk about sex with their partners.

Visualization

In visualization, the conditions that will prevail once the plan is implemented are described. Here, you encourage the audience to imagine and anticipate the results of the proposed plan—in this case, the reduced risk of AIDS and more open communication in relationships.

Action

The audience is asked to take action or approve the proposed plan. Here, you ask audience members to use the techniques you have offered to discuss sex more explicitly and openly with their partners.

Multiple Perspectives

An organizational pattern created around multiple perspectives is one in which an idea or problem is analyzed from several different viewpoints. This pattern is designed to generate a full understanding of a subject.

There are several forms this pattern can take. Summarizing different perspectives on an issue is perhaps the most common. Each perspective you discuss is a different lens through which the issue can be viewed or a different way of looking at the problem as a result of different areas of specialty, interest, or expertise. In a presentation discussing whether a proposed mosque should be built within two blocks of the World Trade Center memorial in New York City, for example, you might use this pattern by explaining the various perspectives on the issue—that of the developers, who see it as a way to "foster better relations between the West and Muslims"; that of the family members of those killed in the World Trade Towers, who see it as a "slap in the face"; that of documentary filmmaker Michael Moore, who believes the mosque should be built at Ground Zero itself to demonstrate America's commitment to freedom of religion; and that of Pastor Fred, who planned (but later canceled) a "Burn the Koran Day" on September 11, 2010, to protest the building of the mosque.[6] All of these perspectives are considered a part of the dialogue about this issue, and in your presentation, you would represent and not dismiss any of them.

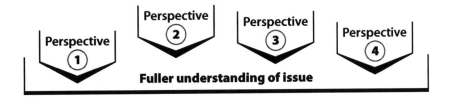

When the perspectives you are choosing to present are in opposition to each other, your analysis might take the form of comparison and contrast—pointing to the differences and similarities among the perspectives. You also might choose to highlight the common ground that exists among the perspectives instead of focusing on the differences among them; you would point to potential points of unity between the two conflicting viewpoints.

If you are a supervisor who is meeting with a work group to try to resolve a conflict about how to determine salary increases, you might use an organizational pattern of multiple perspectives to begin the meeting. You would summarize the perspective of those members who believe that the supervisor should deter-

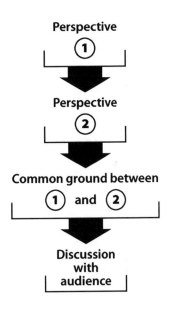

mine the pay increases, then summarize the perspective of those who believe that a committee should make the decision, and conclude with a discussion of what the two perspectives have in common. Both perspectives, you might suggest, are designed to make sure salaries are determined fairly, both would use the same evaluation forms on which group members would report their accomplishments, and both focus on quality of work rather than length of time employed. You then would want to ask your colleagues to join you in trying to resolve the conflict.

Narrative

In a narrative organizational pattern, ideas are structured in the form of a story using characters, settings, and plots. The story may be a true story or one you invent, but it is used to convey information about or illuminate a subject matter in a way that is easy for the audience to grasp. Author Ursula Le Guin, in a speech to the National Abortion Rights League, told of her own abortion by framing it as a story about a princess and a prince who, though "wealthy, well fed, well educated, and well beloved" and knowledgeable about "how babies are made," did not know "how to *keep from making babies.*"[7] She used the story to discuss the controversy surrounding abortion.

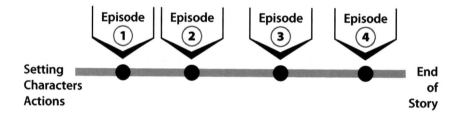

Narrative Progression

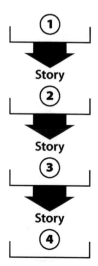

A variation of the narrative pattern is narrative progression, where you tell several stories, one after another. Each story leads into the next and arrives at an overall point you want to make. In a commencement speech at Stanford University, Apple cofounder Steve Jobs offered three stories. In the first story, he told about a calligraphy class he took in college that later would prove the inspiration for the fonts on Mac computers. In the second, he told about getting fired from and then rehired by Mac, which taught him what he really loved in life. The third story was about his brush with pancreatic cancer and what it taught him about living. He concluded with the advice on the back of the final edition of the *Whole Earth Catalog*: "Stay hungry, stay foolish."[8]

Problem/Solution

A problem/solution organizational pattern begins with a discussion of a problem and concludes with your suggestion for a solution or solutions. In a speech to the Economic Club of New York, Ben Bernanke, chair of the US Federal Reserve, used a problem-solution approach in regard to the economy: "The problems now evident in the economy and the markets are large and complex, but, in my judgment, our government now has the tools it needs to confront and to solve them."[9] In the body of his speech, he detailed the various causes and what the government was doing to manage them.

Spiral

A spiral pattern is an organization of ideas that begins at a broad level and moves to an in-depth explanation of those ideas. You begin by talking about something at a general level and wind down into the particular, focusing in greater detail on the subject. You move or proceed toward greater specificity as you develop your ideas.

In your self-presentation on a first date, for example, you tend to use a spiral pattern to organize your ideas. You reveal something about yourself in broad, general terms—perhaps

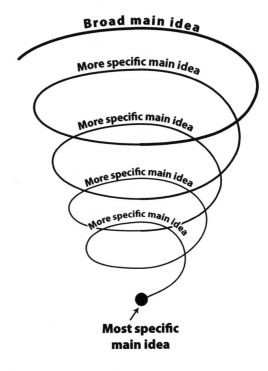

that you enjoy music. If your date is interested in this topic and asks you to tell more about your interest in music, you go into more depth. You might explain that you like many different kinds of music, that you particularly like alternative country, that you have an iTunes collection of many alternative country musicians, and that you would like to play in a band someday.

Thinking Things Through

In this pattern, you lay out the actual thought processes you followed while trying to answer a question or solve a problem. You take your audience on the journey you took in thinking something through, helping the audience understand how you came to the point at which you are now in your thinking. Sometimes, this means that you have arrived at a particular decision, which you share with your audience. At other times, you emphasize that you have not yet finalized your thinking on the matter. This is a good organizational pattern to use for the interactional goals of discovering knowledge and belief and articulating a perspective because it helps others in the interaction understand how you are thinking about an issue under discussion.

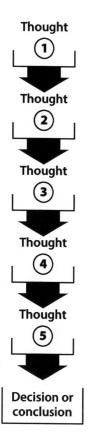

Let's assume that you are on a search committee to hire someone for a position that is open in your organization. At the meeting to select the person for the job, you can use the thinking-things-through pattern to explain why you are leaning toward one candidate over the others. You might tell the other committee members, for example, that you began by thinking about the position and the skills it requires, which led you to think about the differences in skills among the candidates interviewed. You decided that the skills of candidate A are adequate for the organization's needs, although perhaps not as strong as those of candidate B. But then you thought about how each candidate would fit into the organization, and you sense that candidate A, who seems very community oriented, would work hard to fit into the organization. Continuing to reveal your train of thought, you explain that you next remembered experiences you've had with people who didn't fit into the organization and how they tend to leave the organization fairly quickly after they are hired. That's why you have ended up concluding that you probably favor candidate A, who fits in, even though she doesn't have the same level of skill as candidate B. You might conclude your presentation by saying that this is where you are in your thinking right now, but you certainly are open to hearing others' thoughts on the candidates.

Time

When you present the ideas in a presentation according to their temporal relationships, you are using an organizational pattern of time. Ideas presented in this form are structured chronologically from past to present or from present to past. The units also can be time periods or steps in a process. If you are orienting a new employee, you might use a time pattern when you explain the process of getting a company ID card. You would explain the first step, which is to bring a driver's license, Social Security card, and contract to the organization's fiscal officer. The second step is to have the fiscal officer make copies of these documents and complete an ID form. Next, all of these documents must be taken to Human Resources for verification before a picture is taken. After completing these steps, the ID card will be ready.

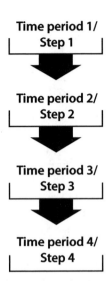

Web

A web organizational pattern revolves around a central or core idea. Other ideas branch out from the core, with each branching idea a reflection and elaboration of the core. In the web form, you begin with the central idea and then explore each idea in turn, returning to the core idea and going out from it and returning to the core again until all of the ideas have been covered. The web structure is especially useful when you really want to emphasize a core or primary idea in your presentation, allowing you to restate that idea frequently.

This pattern is very close to a category organizational pattern in that both patterns address different aspects or categories of a subject. In a web pattern, you return to the core idea and explicitly reference it between your discussions of each of the main ideas, but in the category pattern, you explore various ideas sequentially without explicit reference to the core idea. The web pattern is also similar to the circle pattern, where each idea leads to the next. Rather than simply moving around the circle with the points you want to make, however, you move out from and then back to the main idea when using the web pattern.

A web structure could be used by a manager to explain to her new program

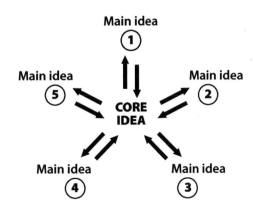

assistant how she will be evaluated each year. The core of the job, she might emphasize, is customer service—treating the clients with respect and helping them solve their problems. She discusses the other aspects on which the program assistant will be evaluated—managing the budget, providing support to the team members, completing the paperwork when new employees are hired, processing the mail, and maintaining the organization's website. The primary function of the job, though, is customer service, and the manager would keep coming back to that point and its importance to the job between her discussions of each of the other duties.

The way you choose to frame your major ideas is an important step in helping your audience understand your perspective. Although we have provided you with a rather lengthy list of potential patterns, the list is by no means comprehensive. Framing is a creative act, and there are an almost infinite number of ways to organize a presentation. Now that you have the main ideas of your presentation and a framework that effectively organizes them, your next task is to elaborate on the main ideas.

6

Elaborating

Elaborating is the process of developing the ideas that emerge as you begin to construct your presentation. In the process of elaboration, you work out the specific details that will support, expand on, and give presence to the main ideas that comprise your presentation. You make a presentation come alive for your audience through examples, figures of speech, facts, statistics, stories, or other forms of elaboration. Enlivening your presentation helps your audience understand your perspective.

The particular combination of forms of elaboration that you select for a presentation depends on your interactional goal; your personal and cultural preferences; and the nature of your audience, setting, and subject. As is the case with all communication options, you naturally will prefer some forms of elaboration over others. If you are uncomfortable sharing highly personal information with a particular audience, you probably will not choose to use personal narrative in a presentation. Similarly, an audience not used to discourse with a strong pattern of rhythm and rhyme might be baffled or even irritated if you incorporate it into a presentation. If you are attempting to build community, you probably do not want to use forms of elaboration that are highly individualistic. Instead, you would choose forms such as myths, participation, and proverbs that bring audience members together.

In this chapter, we discuss possible forms of elaboration to develop your main ideas. These forms are designed to serve as starting points for thinking about how to discuss and extend your ideas for your specific audience. As with the organizational patterns in chapter 5, the forms of elaboration are arranged in alphabetical order because we want to encourage you to consider all possible forms of elaboration for a presentation rather than simply selecting those that are most familiar or most obvious.

⮕ Forms of Elaboration

Audiovisual Aids

Audiovisual aids are materials that supplement spoken words by providing visual or audio elaborations. Charts, graphs, photographs, sketches, and cartoons are visual, while audio aids include music, recorded conversations, and other sounds that elaborate your ideas. In all likelihood, you will make considerable use of formats that combine the visual and audio—video clips and slides accompanying a verbal presentation, for example. Audiovisual aids are dealt with more extensively in chapter 9, so be sure to review that chapter if you plan to use audiovisual aids as one of your forms of elaboration.

Comparison and Contrast

In comparison and contrast, you develop an idea by discussing something unfamiliar through the lens of a concept or experience that is familiar to your audience.

Comparison

Comparison is the process of showing the similarities between the familiar and the unfamiliar. In a presentation about fashion, for example, you might suggest that the 1920s and the 1970s were similar in how fashion functioned as rebellion.

Contrast

Contrast links items to show their differences. Paul Bremer III, who served as US ambassador to Iraq, used contrast to describe Iraq upon his arrival:

> Now, let me turn, if I can, to Iraq and answer two questions I often get: What was it like? And, how are we doing? What was it like? Well, you will have read that we worked and lived in a palace, one of many dozens of palaces that Saddam Hussein wasted money on. But it was certainly not easy living. We had, when I arrived, no electricity, no running water, no telephones. On the plus side of having no electricity, we had no communications from Washington for some time—which is the good news. The bad news was there was no air conditioning. And when I arrived on May 12th, the temperature was already 115 degrees regularly during the day. And that meant that in the palace, if you were lucky, the temperature was only 100. On June 14th the temperature hit 138, and as a good New England boy this felt kind of warm to me—until an Iraqi friend said, "Wait till summer comes."[1]

Credentials

Providing evidence of your background and experience with a subject shows your audience that your ideas are based on some expertise and accumulated resources. Credentials may include a discussion of your cultural background, years of relevant work experience, or other factors that suggest a personal knowledge of or connection to your topic. Harvey Milk, the first openly gay member of the Board of Supervisors in San Francisco, presented his credentials in his campaign for the office by contrasting himself with his opponent:

> He's been an observer, not a participant, and has never really experienced the daily fight for survival that most of us have to face. I'm not being accusatory here—in some respects, I may be envious. I'm a small businessman and I'm well aware of the uncertainties of the economy, exactly what the "inflationary spiral" means when I'm forced to raise prices to my customers, and how taxes can eat into your earnings.[2]

Definition

With definition, you elaborate by providing the meaning of a word or concept in terms the audience will understand. Writer Ursula Le Guin defined *success* in her commencement address at Mills College in a way that made it undesirable: "Success is somebody else's failure. Success is the American Dream we can keep dreaming because most people in most places, including thirty million of ourselves, live wide awake in the terrible reality of poverty. No, I do not wish you success. I don't even want to talk about it. I want to talk about failure."[3] In this case, Le Guin created her own definition for a term. Several other kinds of definitions are available if you choose to use this form of elaboration, including: (1) definition by authority; (2) definition by display; (3) etymological definition; and (4) operational definition.

Definition by Authority

Definition by authority is a definition offered by an expert on a subject. In the following example, Microsoft CEO Bill Gates offered his definition of the phrase *trustworthy computing*: "Another key element and probably the top priority at Microsoft, even beyond the key stuff we're doing around usability and new capabilities, is what we call trustworthy computing. This is the idea of taking the need for extreme reliability, knowing that when you install a new application that it won't disturb other things, knowing that your privacy and your security settings will be appropriate without your having to become an expert or your having to go out and get the new software updates manually going across the network."[4] As an expert on computing matters, Gates provided his own definition of the phrase. You also could use definition by authority if you quoted Gates and his definition of *trustworthy computing*.

Definition by Display

In definition by display, a word or idea is explained by pointing to something visible. A lawyer might use definition by display when showing a jury the position of stab wounds in the clothing of a crime victim to help define the act of self-defense. An architect who shows a sketch of how a building will look after remodeling also would be using definition by display.

Etymological Definition

An etymological definition explains the history, origin, or derivation of a word. In a presentation about avatars, which today means the use of an iconic instead of a real identity on a website, you might cite the original meaning of the term: a Hindu concept referring to the descent or manifestation of a god to earthly existence, typically as a divine teacher.[5]

Operational Definition

An operational definition explains how something works. The actor Christopher Reeve, in his keynote address to the Democratic National Convention, offered an operational definition of the phrase *family values:*

> And over the last few years we have heard a lot about something called "family values." And like many of you, I have struggled to figure out what that means. And since my accident, I've found a definition that seems to make sense. I think it means that we're all family. And that we all have value.[6]

Dreams

Dreams are considered by many audiences to be powerful sources from which to learn about and understand experience. Dreams can be defined in two ways, each of which can be used as a form of elaboration: (1) thoughts, images, or emotions that occur during sleep; and (2) strong desires, goals, or purposes.

Sleeping Dreams

In some cultures, the dreams experienced when sleeping are considered qualitatively more vital than waking events because they provide the opportunity to communicate with nonhuman and superhuman forms and thus to experience alternative levels of reality. Further, dreams can point to and capture the essence of what is important to an individual or community. Even if you have not considered dreams in this way, you still can appreciate the fact that dreams can highlight and illustrate experiences in significant ways. Activist Sonia Johnson recounted a sleeping dream to illustrate the notion of trust:

> A woman in Missouri told me this dream. She was in a city, standing on top of a tall building, looking out upon other buildings as far as she could see. She was a country woman, uneasy amid all the concrete and steel, and longing for home.
>
> Gradually she became aware that to get home she would have to leap off the edge of the building. Looking down at the miniature cars creeping along the miniature street far, far below, she said to herself, "But that's ridiculous! I'll kill myself if I jump off here!" Still, the

feeling persisted that if she didn't jump, she would never get home again. And the grief that overwhelmed her at the thought of being exiled forever from the grass and trees and fields of home became so much stronger than her fear of dying that she leapt.

As she began to fall, a rope appeared before her; she reached out, grabbed it, and swung way out over the street. At the end of its arc, she knew that if she didn't let go, she would swing back to where she had been before and not be any closer to home. So she let go. As she began to fall again, another rope appeared. Grabbing it, she swung out to the end of its arc, and let go again.

Trusting herself, letting go, reaching out, swinging out over the abyss, trusting, letting go, reaching out, she found her way home.[7]

Life Dreams

A future goal or desire is a second kind of dream, and the dreams or goals that you or others have can be important sources of inspiration. Martin Luther King Jr.'s famous "I Have a Dream" speech is probably the best known example of the use of this kind of dream in a presentation.[7] In his remarks upon retiring from baseball, Orioles player Cal Ripken Jr. also used this kind of dream as a form of elaboration:

> As a kid I had this dream. And I had the parents that helped me shape that dream. Then, I became part of an organization, the Baltimore Orioles, to help me grow that dream. Imagine, playing for my hometown team for my whole career. And I have a wife and children to help me share and savor the fruits of that dream. . . . To be remembered at all is pretty special. I might also add that if, if I am remembered, I hope it's because by living my dream, I was able to make a difference.[8]

Emotions

Although the emphasis on logic in contemporary Western culture often discourages speakers from considering emotions as a possible form of elaboration, emotions can be a powerful way to develop ideas. Human beings respond with their feelings as well as with logic to what happens in their lives. Emotions are aroused indirectly through means such as narration, vivid description, and display. Telling a story, describing something in great detail, and displaying an emotion yourself all invite identification with the emotion you want your audience to experience. Mountain climber Gwen Moffat invoked the emotion of fear in the following story:

> Once I was climbing with my partner on the summit of an ice and rock ridge 10,000 feet up. Suddenly I heard a sound like singing. It was the metal head of my ice axe humming with electricity. My hair began to rise and I realized we were in the middle of the storm. It became absolutely still and we were surrounded by black clouds. In the next moment we heard a series of strikes of simultaneous thunder and lightning like one enormous explosion, which lasted several

hours. There was absolutely nothing we could do, except either stand there and literally wait to be struck or keep on moving. We went on moving.[9]

Exaggeration

Overstating a point can serve to elaborate an idea by making it striking and memorable. Exaggeration often is used in humorous presentations, after-dinner speeches, roasts, or other ceremonial occasions. Exaggeration, as it is used in these settings, is not to be confused with the deliberate distortion of information or evidence. As a form of elaboration, exaggeration does not deal with actual facts as much as with the interpretation of ideas in a light-hearted way. "I'm so tired I could sleep for a year" is an example of exaggeration.

Example

The example is a short illustration of a point. It is a specific illustration of a category of people, places, objects, actions, experiences, or conditions that shows the nature or character of that category. Actor Charlton Heston, who served as president of the National Rifle Association, used a series of examples to illustrate his thesis that "a cultural war is raging across our land":

> For example, I marched for civil rights with Dr. King in 1963—long before Hollywood found it fashionable. But when I told an audience last year that white pride is just as valid as black pride or red pride or anyone else's pride, they called me a racist.
>
> I've worked with brilliantly talented homosexuals all my life. But when I told an audience that gay rights should extend no further than your rights or my rights, I was called a homophobe.
>
> I served in World War II against the Axis powers. But during a speech, when I drew an analogy between singling out innocent Jews and singling out innocent gun owners, I was called an anti-Semite.[10]

Explanation

An explanation is a description of a term, concept, process, or proposal to make it clear and understandable. Tiger Woods, in his apology for his marital infidelities, offered this explanation:

> I stopped living by the core values that I was taught to believe in. I knew my actions were wrong, but I convinced myself that normal rules didn't apply. I never thought about who I was hurting. Instead, I thought only about myself. I ran straight through the boundaries that a married couple should live by. I thought I could get away with whatever I wanted to. I felt that I had worked hard my entire life and deserved to enjoy all the temptations around me. I felt I was entitled. Thanks to money and fame, I didn't have far—I didn't have to go far to find them.[11]

Facts

Facts are statements that generally are accepted as true by a culture. They are pieces of information that are verifiable by direct observation, by reference to scientific findings, or because they are offered by individuals who are granted expert status on an issue. Jessica Lynch, a soldier captured by Iraqi forces and subsequently rescued, gave this list of facts to provide context for her presentation to the House Oversight and Government Reform Committee of Congress:

> As we drove through An Nasiryah, trying to get turned around to try to leave the city, the signs of hostility were increasing, where people with weapons were on roof tops and the street watching our entire move. The vehicle I was riding in was hit by a rocket propelled grenade and slammed into the back of another truck in our unit. Three people in the vehicle were killed upon impact. Lori and I were taken to a hospital where she later died and I was held for nine days. In all, eleven soldiers died that day, six from my unit, and two others were— six others from my unit were taken prisoner, plus two others.[12]

Figures of Speech

Figures of speech are unusual turns of language that can elaborate ideas in particularly vivid ways. Some of the most frequently used figures of speech are: (1) alliteration; (2) antithesis; (3) irony; (4) metaphor; (5) oxymoron; (6) personification; and (7) simile.

Alliteration

In alliteration, initial or middle consonants are repeated in two or more adjacent words. In his acceptance address at the 1992 Democratic National Convention, Bill Clinton incorporated several examples of alliteration when he said: "Somewhere at this very moment a child is being born in America. Let it be our cause to give that child a happy home, a healthy family, and a hopeful future."[13]

Antithesis

Antithesis involves the juxtaposition of opposing concepts or the contrast or opposition of ideas. Hillary Clinton's keynote address to the 2008 Democratic National Convention made use of antithesis: "My mother was born before women could vote. My daughter got to vote for her mother for President."[14]

Irony

Irony occurs when intent and expression are contradictory. A speaker, in other words, says one thing and means another. The speaker who says "that's beautiful" when she finds a dress to be ugly is an example of irony. After surviving a particularly difficult day at work, you might say, "That was a pretty easy way to earn a living."

Metaphor

A metaphor is a comparison in which something is spoken about in terms of something else. President George W. Bush used a metaphor of freedom as a beacon of light in a presentation following the terrorist attacks on September 11, 2001: "America was targeted for attack because we're the brightest beacon for freedom and opportunity in the world. And no one will keep that light from shining."[15] Sarah Palin used a basketball metaphor when she announced her resignation as governor of Alaska:

> A good point guard drives through a full court press, protecting the ball, keeping her eye on the basket . . . and she knows exactly when to pass the ball so that the team can WIN. And I'm doing that—keeping our eye on the ball that represents sound priorities—smaller government, energy independence, national security, freedom! And I know when it's time to pass the ball—for victory.[16]

Oxymoron

An oxymoron is a form of antithesis in which words that normally would not appear together are paired. Putting opposites together in such a tight construction can be an effective form of elaboration. B. B. King's Blues Club in Memphis once used the oxymoron "famous unknowns" as a label for the up-and-coming musicians who appeared in the club, and the phrase *postal service* is jokingly referenced as an oxymoron when complaining about the US Postal Service. Walt Bresette used an oxymoron to close a speech to Green Party members, suggesting that to secure their rights, Native Americans must engage in "nonviolent ass kickin'."[17]

Personification

In personification, the speaker attributes human qualities to nonhuman objects or concepts. Writer Annie Dillard discussed how a book can take over its author, using the figure of personification to give the book agency: "Sometimes part of a book simply gets up and walks away. The writer cannot force it back in place. It wanders off to die."[18]

Simile

A simile involves a comparison introduced by either *like* or *as*. In a speech presented at an arts conference, writer Andrei Codrescu used a simile to compare art to a river: "Trying to restrict its liberty is like damming the Mississippi River. Sooner or later Old Man River gets what it wants by the sheer force of its desire."[19]

Humor

Humor can function not just to entertain and amuse but also to develop and extend ideas. Humor is appropriate as a form of elaboration only when it is relevant to the idea you are developing. Television host Conan O'Brien, himself a graduate of Harvard University, made a humorous point about what lies ahead for Harvard graduates at a commencement address at Harvard:

> You see, you're in for a lifetime of "And you went to Harvard?" Accidentally give the wrong amount of change in a transaction and it's, "And you went to Harvard?" Ask the guy at the hardware store how these jumper cables work and hear, "And you went to Harvard?" Forget just once that your underwear goes inside your pants and it's "and you went to Harvard." Get your head stuck in your niece's dollhouse because you wanted to see what it was like to be a giant and it's "Uncle Conan, you went to Harvard!?"[20]

Myths

Myths are stories that explain the origins of practices, beliefs, institutions, or natural phenomena. They express fundamental social, cultural, and religious values important to a community. In testimony before the Supreme Court in 1915, Chief Weninock of the Yakimas told the story of the origins of Native Americans as a way of developing the idea that Native Americans have legitimate claims to their traditional fishing places:

> God created the Indian Country and it was like he spread out a big blanket. He put the Indians on it. They were created here in this Country, truly honest, and that was the time the river started to run. Then God created fish in this river and put deer in the mountains and made laws through which has come the increase of fish and game. Then the Creator gave us Indians Life; we walked, and as soon as we saw the game and fish we knew they were made for us.[21]

Narratives

When used as elaboration, stories involve telling real or fictional narratives, usually complete with characters, settings, plots, and dialogue. You may use stories told by others or personal narratives, in which you recount your own experiences. This is the kind of narrative Professor Patti P. Gillespie used in a presentation she gave as president of the Speech Communication Association:

> As some of you know, I try to spend part of every other summer camping in Kenya. During my last trip in Amboseli, I was awakened just before daybreak by the sound of furiously pounding hooves that grew closer and closer to my tent. There was a horrible cry that intermingled with growls until both seemed within a few feet of where I was lying. Suddenly the cries and growls stopped, and all I heard was a very deep vibrating sound. . . .
>
> Gradually, as I thought about it, the sequence became clear to me. A zebra had been fleeing a lion, who had caught it just outside my tent and was now feasting on it. The five of us in the camp would remain hostage inside our tents until the heat of the day when the

lion, satisfied and sleepy, would move away from us. Very well, I
thought, I will try to calm down and wait. I waited. I had only begun
to regret my last night's beer when I heard what sounded like human
footsteps—yes, they were human because I next heard the unmistak-
able sound of pots and pans. The cook was out of his tent. Thinking
him slightly mad, I dressed hastily, looked out carefully, and then
joined him hurriedly at the fire. "Where was the lion kill?" I asked in
butchered Swahili. "No lion," he said, "hyena fight."[22]

She continued the story, making the point that, just as with the hyena
fight, things in higher education may not be as they seem.

Participation

Audience participation is an invitation to the audience to respond
verbally during the course of the presentation. This form of elaboration
allows you to use the ideas, comments, or responses of the audience to
develop your ideas. More often, it is simply a way for your audience to
interact with you and engage the presentation. Audience participation
assumes a variety of forms: (1) call/response; (2) discussion; (3) encouragement; and (4) testimonials.

Call/Response

Call/response is a pattern of spontaneous vocal and nonverbal
responses from listeners in reply to a speaker's statements or questions
that testify to the impact of the message. Call/response functions, much
as applause does, as a form of affirmation and support. It tells you when
the audience is with you and when you can move to a discussion of your
next idea. Call/response patterns may be formulaic, or they can rely on
innovation and improvisation, with each exchange generating new meanings. Football fans engage in call and response when cheerleaders call out
the letters *D, E, F, E, N, S, E* and the audience repeats each letter in turn.
Denver Broncos fans use call and response when one group in the sta-
dium yells *Go!* and another group answers *Broncos!*

Discussion

Discussion is the consideration of a question through informal
exploration by at least two individuals. If your goal is discovering knowledge and belief, discussion is a necessary form of elaboration—although
it can be part of any presentation. Most interviews and informal conversations naturally take the form of a discussion, with all participants sharing ideas and responding to the thoughts of others. Managing a
discussion is described in greater detail in chapter 2 in the discussion of
the interactional goal of discovering knowledge and belief.

Encouragement

Although you cannot rely on your audience offering encouraging
remarks, such encouragement can function as a powerful form of elabo-

ration and affirmation of your ideas if it happens. Participants at a campaign rally, for example, might call out "I hear you" to signal their agreement with the candidate. They might urge a speaker to continue in a particular direction by shouting "take your time," "speak on it," "work it," "amen," "hallelujah," or "right on!" Nonverbally, audience members might offer encouragement by waving their hands in the air, whistling, jumping up and down, or clapping their hands.

Testimonials

You can elicit another form of audience response to develop ideas by asking audience members to offer examples from their own lives. Stories told by participants in meetings of Alcoholics Anonymous or other support groups, for example, constitute testimonials. Religious revivals sometimes make use of testimonials to help secure new converts, and the testimony of witnesses in courts of law is another example of this form of elaboration.

Poetry

Poetry is the use of meaning, sound, and rhythm in language, chosen and arranged to create a concentrated image of a particular condition or experience. You could use William Shakespeare's poetry about the world as theater to elaborate on the idea that humans live in dramas of their own making:

> All the world's a stage,
> And all the men and women merely players:
> They have their exits and their entrances;
> And one man in his time plays many parts.[23]

Prayers

Prayers are entreaties, supplications, or requests directed at a force the audience acknowledges as a supreme being. The speaker who prays for wisdom for those about to make an important decision, for example, is using prayer as a form of elaboration. Football player Tim Tebow, speaking at the annual presidential prayer breakfast in 2010, incorporated a prayer to provide support for his beliefs:

> Lord we pray for the people all over the world that are hurting right now.
>
> The verse that comes to mind is James 1: 2-4, "Consider it all joy, my brethren, whenever you encounter various trials, knowing that the testing of your faith produces endurance. And let endurance have its perfect result, that you may be perfect and complete lacking in nothing."
>
> And we pray for the people in Haiti right now Lord, that you make them perfect and complete because you love them and have a plan for their lives, just as you do with our lives now.[24]

Proverbs

Proverbs are succinct cultural sayings that express obvious truths and capture audience members' experiences. In a sermon, Barbara Brown Zikmund cited a Yoruba proverb to develop her idea that each person is an important part of God's creation: "There is an old Yoruba proverb told among the indigenous tribes of Nigeria in West Africa that expresses the same message: 'The hand of a child cannot reach the ledge; the hand of the elder cannot enter the gourd: both the young and the old have what each can do for the other.'"[25]

Puns

Puns are plays on words based either on different words that sound alike or on various meanings of the same word. In a presentation about her work, visual artist Janet Hughes used puns to describe what her selection for inclusion in an art exhibition meant to her. One portion of her presentation included puns on the word *read*. (Hughes's presentation is one of the sample presentations at the end of the book.)

> She was well read.
> She became widely read.
> She painted the town
> the picture
> and her lips.
> Her lips were read.
> Her lips were red.[26]

Questions

Questions can be used to develop an idea by encouraging listeners to think about the idea and to become mentally engaged in the subject matter. Three common kinds of questions are: (1) rhetorical questions; (2) substantive questions; and (3) questions of facilitation.

Rhetorical Questions

Rhetorical questions are those a speaker asks and wants the audience to answer mentally. They are designed to stimulate audience members to think about the subject. Actor Bill Cosby, in his address to the National Association for the Advancement of Colored People, used a series of rhetorical questions to challenge his audience to do more: "I'm telling you Christians, what's wrong with you? Why can't you hit the streets? Why can't you clean it out yourselves? It's our time now, ladies and gentlemen. It is our time."[27]

Substantive Questions

Substantive questions are those that you as speaker both ask and answer or ones you expect your audience to answer. Author Alice Walker, in a speech to the Midwives Alliance of North America shortly after the terrorist attacks of September 11, 2001, used a substantive question to talk about those who would engage in such acts: "What is the story whose fiery end I am witnessing?" She answers her own question:

> This was an act by a man who did not believe in the possibility of love, or even common sense, to transform the world. I can easily imagine there will be thousands like him born in our time, that from the roots of this one man's story, they will come to birth practically every minute, and our government will not be remotely able to "smoke" all of them "out of their holes."[28]

Questions of Facilitation

Questions of facilitation help manage group interactions. They are used to enable all perspectives to be heard by keeping the discussion on track and preventing any single individual from monopolizing the conversation. A more complete discussion of the use of these questions in offered in chapter 2 in the discussion of the interactional goal of discovering knowledge and belief.

Quotations

When a quotation is used as a form of elaboration, a speaker uses the words of others to develop and extend an idea. A quotation may draw its effectiveness from the content of the quotation or from the reputation or expertise of the person who is quoted. Maya Angelou's eulogy at the funeral service for Coretta Scott King quotes both herself and King:

> Many times on those late . . . evenings she would say to me, "Sister, it shouldn't be an 'either-or,' should it? Peace and justice should belong to all people, everywhere, all the time. Isn't that right?" And I said then and I say now, "Coretta Scott King, you're absolutely right. I do believe that peace and justice should belong to every person, everywhere, all the time."[29]

Repetition and Restatement

In repetition, words or phrases are repeated exactly. In restatement, an idea is repeated using different words. Both forms of elaboration function to reinforce an idea. Presidential candidate Barack Obama, in his speech about the Reverend Jeremiah Wright, repeated the phrases "not this time" and "this time":

> Or, at this moment, in this election, we can come together and say, "Not this time." This time, we want to talk about the crumbling schools that are stealing the future of black children and white children and Asian children and Hispanic children and Native-American children. This time, we want to reject the cynicism that tells us that these kids can't learn—that those kids who don't look like us are somebody else's problem. The children of America are not "those kids"—they are our kids, and we will not let them fall behind in a

21st-century economy. Not this time. This time, we want to talk
about how the lines in the emergency room are filled with whites and
blacks and Hispanics who do not have health care, who don't have
the power on their own to overcome the special interests in Washington but who can take them on if we do it together.[30]

Rhythm and Rhyme

In rhythm and rhyme, words and phrases are chosen for their sound
effects. In this form of elaboration, the sounds of the words develop the
idea the speaker wants to convey. Many forms of elaboration, such as
alliteration and repetition, rely to some degree on the sounds of words,
but in rhythm and rhyme, the sounds of the words are emphasized as
much as—if not more than—their content.

Rhythm

Rhythm is the arrangement of words to achieve a regular recurrence
of beat or accent. Civil rights activist Jesse Jackson used rhythm in a
speech to the Democratic National Convention:

> I told them in every slum, there are two sides. When I see a broken
> window, that's the slummy side. Train that youth to be a glazier,
> that's the sunny side. When I see a missing brick, that's the slummy
> side. Let that child in the union, and become a brick mason, and
> build, that's the sunny side. When I see a missing door, that's the
> slummy side. When I see the vulgar words and hieroglyphics of desti-
> tution on the walls, that's the slummy side. Train some youth to be a
> painter, an artist—that's the sunny side.

Rhyme

Rhyme involves words that correspond with one another in terms of
ending sound. Jackson, of course, is using rhyme as well as rhythm in his
speech to the Democratic National Convention. The commencement
address of Theodor Seuss Geisel, better known as *Dr. Seuss*, at Lake Forest College, provides another example. His presentation consisted
entirely of a series of rhyming statements:

> My uncle ordered popovers
> from the restaurant's bill of fare.
> And, when they were served,
> he regarded them
> with a penetrating stare.
> Then he spoke great Words of Wisdom
> as he sat there on that chair:
> "To eat these things,"
> said my uncle,
> "you must exercise great care.
> You may swallow down what's solid
> BUT
> you must spit out the air!"

And
as you partake of the world's bill of fare,
that's darned good advice to follow.
Do a lot of spitting out the hot air.
And be careful what you swallow.[31]

Ritual

Rituals are set forms or systems of rites in which members of a community participate. Often handed down from generation to generation, rituals and ceremonies function to connect community members to their heritage, their community, their country, or the cosmos. Through that connection, they generate feelings of power and wholeness. Author Diane Stein often uses rituals in her workshops designed to create changes in consciousness. In her "Croning" ritual, for example, a woman who is undergoing a transition—menopause, retirement, or her last child's departure from home, for example—is given tangible or verbal gifts by each of those present.[32] A speaker who asks listeners to join her in reciting a familiar credo or a pledge is also using ritual as a form of elaboration.

Sensory Images

Sensory images are words or phrases that communicate feelings and perceptions through one or more of the five senses—sight, smell, sound, taste, and touch. Author Barbara Kingsolver used olfactory images to help capture the idea of a rainstorm:

That was when we smelled the rain. It was so strong it seemed like more than just a smell. . . . I don't know how a person could ever describe that scent. It certainly wasn't sour, but it wasn't sweet either, not like a flower. . . . To my mind it was like nothing so much as a wonderfully clean, scrubbed pine floor.[33]

Songs

When a speaker sings a song or asks the audience to join in the singing of a song, an idea can be elaborated in a particularly vivid and powerful way. A speaker might ask an audience of union members to join in the singing of "I Dreamed I Saw Joe Hill Last Night" to remind them of the strength and tenacity of labor movements. Likewise, "We Shall Overcome" often is sung at civil rights events to suggest the perseverance and determination of those involved in the struggle. Musician Billy Joel's song, "We Didn't Start the Fire," which details the history of the United States from 1949 to 1989, could be used to chronicle the important events of the mid-twentieth century. The singing of "Amazing Grace" or "Danny Boy" at funerals is another example of songs as forms of elaboration.

Statistics

Statistics are numerical data designed to show relationships between or among phenomena. The relationship expressed can emphasize size or magnitude, establish trends such as increases or decreases in a particular population, or make comparisons. In a presentation about homelessness, a statistic might be used to show a change in the configuration of the homeless population: "In contrast to the usual conception of the homeless as hard-core unemployed, 1 in 5 residents of shelters now holds a full- or part-time job."[34]

Understatement

In understatement, the speaker states an important point in a restrained style. The low-key nature of the understatement highlights its importance. Holden Caufield, the protagonist in the novel *The Catcher in the Rye*, uses understatement in his announcement, "It isn't very serious. I have this tiny little tumor on the brain."[35] In her speech to the Democratic National Convention, Michelle Obama used understatement to open her speech: "As you might imagine, for Barack, running for President is nothing compared to that first game of basketball with my brother Craig."[36]

Visions

Visions are valuable sources of power, energy, and insight that may be used to elaborate ideas. Visions are of two types: (1) religious or spiritual visions; and (2) visionary statements about the future.

Spiritual Visions

A vision in the spiritual sense is a mystical experience of seeing something supernatural or prophetic. In this context, visions function as vehicles through which special powers or insights are made available to those who experience them. An example is the story of how the Lady of Guadalupe, also known as the *Virgin of Guadalupe*, appeared to Juan Diego near Mexico City in December 1531. As proof of her presence, she made red roses appear for him to pick, and when he brought them to the bishop, her image was visible on Diego's cloak. In certain cultures, sharing a vision of this type is an especially meaningful form of elaboration because of shared beliefs about the power of the source.

Secular Visions

In secular contexts, visions capture and embody the ideals or desired future state of an individual, group, or nation. You might decide to write a personal vision statement about where you want to be in five years, and a company might engage in a "visioning" process to decide what changes to make for the next decade. State-of-the-union addresses envision a country's future for the year to come. Professor Mary Catherine Bateson envisioned a particular kind of future—a future of complementarity—in the following excerpt:

> The visions we construct will not be classic pioneer visions of struggle and self-reliance. Rather, they will involve an intricate elaboration of themes of complementarity—forms of mutual completion and enhancement and themes of recognition achieved through loving attention. All the forms of life we encounter—not only colleagues and neighbors, but other species, other cultures, the planet itself—are similar to us and similarly in need of nurture, but there is also a larger whole to which all belong. The health of that larger whole is essential to the health of the parts.[37]

The list in this chapter provides some suggestions for ways to elaborate the ideas of your presentation. Your own processes of invention will generate others as you work to develop the main ideas of your presentation. Your next task is to develop an introduction and a conclusion that complete the frame of your presentation.

7

Beginning and Ending

Now that you have selected the basic structure of your presentation and the forms of elaboration by which to amplify your main ideas, your next step is to develop an introduction and a conclusion. Because your ideas often change extensively as you work to put them into an organizational structure, you want to wait until you have prepared the body and main ideas before you decide how you want to introduce and end your presentation. The organizational format and the forms of elaboration you choose for the presentation also may suggest possible directions for your introduction and conclusion.

⟶ THE INTRODUCTION

The introduction is a critical part of your presentation because it is where you have your first opportunity to invite your audience to see the world as you see it. You offer your audience a glimpse of your perspective and how you will be framing it. By the end of your introduction, your audience should know the subject of your presentation and your interactional goal(s). Your audience also will have begun making assessments about you as a speaker, and you want them to see you as someone with whom they want to continue to interact.

The introduction not only gives the audience information about you and your topic but also begins the process of establishing the conditions of safety, openness, freedom, and value for your audience. Everything you do in your introduction should communicate to your audience members that you want them to feel comfortable and free to choose whether and how to make use of new ideas that emerge from their interaction with you. Communicating genuine warmth as part of an introduction is likely to put your audience members at ease and encourage them to continue listening. Similarly, when you are energetic about different ideas, you communicate that you value diverse perspectives. If the four speaking conditions are met, your audience will want to continue to be part of the interaction that you have initiated with your introduction. Carefully considering how you introduce your presentation is important, then, because it makes a difference in how the entire presentation is received.

You may have been told that introductions should be dramatic and exciting or that you should tell a joke to get the attention of audience members. By using such openings, you signal to your audience members that you do not believe they are interested in your topic or are able to be attentive listeners and thus need to be startled, cajoled, or humored into listening to you. We have seen presentations where students began by pulling out a gun and pointing it at the audience, riding a motorcycle into the classroom, or jumping out of a second-story window. In every case, these actions only scared audience members and left them unable to focus on the topic of the presentation itself. Similarly, a joke, especially if it is unrelated to your topic, takes audience members' attention away from the subject of your presentation.

Even interested audience members, however, may not be fully present mentally for a variety of reasons as you begin your presentation. There also will be times when you must speak to a captive audience—one that is required to be there for some reason. A supervisor may have required the members of your audience to attend a seminar in which they personally are not very interested, or your audience members may be attending a conference and discover that a particular presentation is not what they thought it would be. Perhaps you are speaking about drug addiction to a group of inmates required to attend such classes, or you may be giving a history lecture to seniors in their final week of high school. In these instances, we still do not recommend a startling statement or a joke for your introduction. The most effective introduction in this situation is one that connects the topic to the audience in a way that is engaging, specific, and perhaps personal. Telling a story in some detail, for example, about something that happened to you that is directly relevant to audience members might be a good way to begin in these instances.

There are many different ways to begin a presentation. Below are descriptions of some commonly used types of introductions. You do not need to select your introduction only from this list; often, your subject matter will suggest an introduction unique to your presentation. You also might find that there are times when a combination of several different types of introductions would be best to open your presentation.

Narrative

In a narrative or story that functions as an introduction, you describe a particular incident, furnishing specific details about the characters, actions, and settings involved. For example, Supreme Court Justice Sonia Sotomayor's opening statement at her confirmation hearing began with a narrative about her life:

The progression of my life has been uniquely American. My parents left Puerto Rico during World War II. I grew up in modest circumstances in a Bronx housing project. My father, a factory worker with a third grade education, passed away when I was nine years old. On her own, my mother raised my brother and me. She taught us that the key to success in America is a good education. And she set the example, studying alongside my brother and me at our kitchen table so that she could become a registered nurse.

We worked hard. I poured myself into my studies at Cardinal Spellman High School, earning scholarships to Princeton University and then Yale Law School, while my brother went on to medical school. Our achievements are due to the values that we learned as children, and they have continued to guide my life's endeavors. I try to pass on this legacy by serving as a mentor and friend to my many godchildren and to students of all backgrounds.[1]

Poem

When you use a poem to introduce your presentation, the concentrated imagery and rhythmic use of language combine to evoke a powerful introduction to the main idea of the presentation. An excerpt from the poem "Introduction to Poetry" by Billy Collins could be used, for example, in a presentation to English teachers about teaching poetry:

I ask them to take a poem
and hold it up to the light
like a color slide
or press an ear against its hive.
. . .
But all they want to do
is tie the poem to a chair with rope
and torture a confession out of it.
They begin beating it with a hose
to find out what it really means.[2]

Presentation of Basic Theme

You may decide that explicitly stating your primary idea or theme is the best way to introduce your presentation. Jessica Jackley, cofounder of the lending agencies Kiva and Profounder, uses this kind of opening in her presentation, "Poverty, Money—and Love": "The stories we tell about each other matter very much. The stories we tell ourselves about our own lives matter. And, most of all, I think the way that we participate in each other's stories is of deep importance."[3] (Jackley's presentation is one of the sample presentations at the end of the book).

Question

Questions can function as introductions, just as they can serve as forms of elaboration. An introduction that features questions can consist of: (1) a rhetorical question or questions; or (2) a substantive question or questions.

Rhetorical Question

Rhetorical questions are ones you expect your audience to answer mentally. Such questions require audience members to engage the material by answering the questions for themselves. A welcoming presentation to camp counselors, for example, could begin with this series of rhetorical questions:

> So why do we do it?
> What *good* is it?
> Does it teach you anything
> Like determination? Invention? Improvisation?
> Foresight? Hindsight?
> Love?
> Art? Music? Religion?
> Strength or patience or accuracy or quickness or tolerance or
> Which wood will burn and how long is a day and how far is a mile
> And how delicious is water and smoky green pea soup?[4]

Substantive Question

Your presentation can begin with an actual question you expect the audience to answer. In a presentation about the drawbacks of technology, you might ask your audience members to raise their hands if they have upgraded a computer within the last year or purchased a flat-screen TV. By answering your questions, they become involved in your subject and begin to anticipate your presentation.

Quotation

When a quotation is used to start a presentation, you use a statement made by someone who has addressed your topic in a particularly eloquent way.[4] As speaker of the House of Representatives, Nancy Pelosi incorporated Helen Keller's language to begin a speech at the unveiling of a statue of Keller in the Capitol Rotunda: "As Helen Keller said: 'My sympathies are with all who struggle for justice.' In her lifetime, Helen Keller worked for opportunity for people with disabilities, for racial equality, and for the rights of women."[5]

Reference to Speaking Situation

Another way to begin a presentation is by mentioning or referring to any of the components of the speaking situation: (1) audience; (2) occasion; (3) place; (4) speaker, or (5) previous speaker.

Reference to Audience

When beginning with a reference to your audience, you focus on special attributes that characterize your audience. When Dan Rather retired as a CBS newscaster, he opened his sign-off with a reference to his audience:

We've shared a lot in the 24 years we've been meeting here each evening, and before I say good night, this night, I need to say, "thank you." Thank you to the thousands of wonderful professionals at CBS News, past and present, with whom it's been my honor to work over these years. And a deeply-felt thanks to all of you who have let us into your homes, night after night. It has been a privilege, and one never taken lightly.[6]

Reference to Occasion

A reference to the occasion uses the purpose for gathering as a shared starting point. The Reverend Al Sharpton began his eulogy for Michael Jackson with a reference to the occasion: "All over the world today, people are gathered in love vigils to celebrate the life of a man that taught the world how to love."[7]

Reference to Place

Referring to the site where you are presenting is another possibility for your introduction. Tom Delay, in his retirement address from the House of Representatives, referred to the capitol building as well as the city of Washington, DC, in his introduction:

What a blessing this place is, Mr. Speaker. What a castle of hope this building is, this institution is for the people of the world. It's one of those things in political life that you always know but seldom notice. The schedules we're forced to keep during our days in Washington are not always hospitable to sitting back and reflecting on the historical significance of our surroundings.[8]

Reference to Self

You may decide to begin your presentation with a reference to yourself as the speaker. You might discuss yourself as a representative of a particular category of individuals whom you will discuss in your presentation, or you might highlight a quality or experience you bring to the speaking situation. English professor Karen Carlton used a reference to herself to begin a commencement address at Humboldt State University: "Exactly 30 years ago, I graduated from a small, liberal arts college in southwest Texas and prepared to live in a world I knew and understood. Roles were defined for me: I was engaged to be married; I would teach school so that my young husband could proceed with his studies; we would have children and live happily, safely ever after."[9]

Reference to Previous Speaker

In an introduction that refers to the previous speaker, you recall a major idea developed by someone else earlier in the interaction and relate it to your presentation. At a Medal of Honor ceremony for Richard Etchberger, General Norty Schwartz made a reference to the previous speaker as his introduction when he said:

Chief Roy, thank you very much for that stirring account of Chief
Etchberger's heroism. I think that we can all agree: such singular
valor can never be retold too many times. Stories like this inspire the
efforts of those who serve today, and legends like Chief Etchberger
serve as role models for an entire new generation of everyday Airmen
performing extraordinary deeds.[10]

The introduction to your presentation is critical because it not only
introduces your audience to your topic and your perspective on it but
also establishes the tone of the entire presentation. As a result of what
you say in the introduction, your audience members will decide whether
to continue listening, whether they want to continue interacting with
you, and whether they feel safe and valued and able to discuss and consider a variety of perspectives.

⏤ THE CONCLUSION

The conclusion of your presentation provides a final opportunity to
leave your audience members with your perspective clearly in mind. This is
one last place in which to communicate the overall vision of your presentation. The primary function of the conclusion, then, is to reemphasize the
main idea or gist of your presentation. To accomplish this function, your
conclusion needs to be consistent with the tenor of the rest of the presentation—using the same tone to enact the qualities and conditions you have
been seeking to create. Changing tone drastically at this point is jarring for
the audience because it is unexpected. For the same reason, the conclusion
is not the place to introduce new ideas. Doing so can detract from audience
members' understanding and retention of your central idea. Think of the
conclusion as a place for summarizing, emphasizing, and highlighting the
main ideas you've offered in the body of your presentation.

A second function of the conclusion is to convey to the audience
what you would like to have happen next in the interaction. If you want
to convey a sense of finality and signal that there will not be questions,
conclude in a way that communicates closure. Quotations and poems
often are used as endings when a speaker wants to conclude with finality.
You would not call for questions if time is limited, if the group is
extremely large, or if a call for questions is inappropriate for the occasion—a toast at a wedding or a eulogy at a funeral, for example.

On the other hand, if you want to encourage the participation of
audience members following your presentation, signal that now is the
time for them to speak by using a conclusion that is open and tentative.
At the end of your prepared remarks, pause briefly and then call for questions. If you want the audience to do something specific—sign a petition
or gather in small groups, for example—this is the time to make that
request or, if already made, to reinforce that request.

Conclusions assume a variety of forms. Some of the most common types are listed below. As with the options for introductions to a presentation, these are only some of the kinds of conclusions possible. We hope they will stimulate your thinking so that you construct conclusions that effectively meet the needs of your speaking situations.

Call to Action

With some interactional goals, a challenge to the audience to take some kind of action is an appropriate conclusion. Billy Joel, in his commencement address to the Berklee College of Music, ended with a call for the students to make better music:

> But consider this: have you listened to the radio lately? Have you heard the canned, frozen and processed product being dished up to the world as American popular music today? What an incredible opportunity for a new movement of American composers and musicians to shape what we will be listening to in the years to come. While most people are satisfied with the junk food being sold as music, you have the chance and the responsibility to show us what a real banquet music can be. You have learned the fine art of our native cuisine—blues, jazz, gospel, Broadway, rock and roll and pop. After all this schooling, you should know how to cook! So cook away and give us the good stuff for a change. Please. We need it. We need it very, very much. Congratulations and good luck![11]

Narrative

Just as a story can serve as an organizational pattern or an introduction to a presentation, it can also enhance the conclusion of your presentation. Pete Geren, Secretary of the Army, concluded with a narrative in his "Salute to the Military":

> Let me continue with the story of Paul Ray Smith—his story did not end with his death. He died a hero—he left behind a hero.
>
> David Smith is his 12-year-old son. Earlier this year, David and his mother were interviewed at Fort Stewart by CBS's Katie Couric.
>
> They walked together down the Warrior's Walk, alongside the trees planted to honor the fallen heroes of the 3rd Infantry Division, the Dog Face Soldiers, as they call themselves, those killed in the Global War on Terror. They walked by the tree honoring David's father.
>
> Ms. Couric asked David if it wasn't hard to talk about his father's death. David, standing tall next to his mother, said simply, and these are his words, "I am doing this to help out all the kids who have lost a father or mother in the war. When I speak out and I go on the news, they probably see me—that I have lost my father. Then they will feel better because they'll see that they're not the only one who's lost somebody."[12]

Pledge

A pledge is a promise that something will happen or a commitment to undertake certain actions. Concluding your presentation with a pledge can signal your dedication to a proposal or a cause. Chief Dan George of the Coast Salish tribe ended his presentation commemorating Canada's 100th birthday with a pledge:

> Oh, God! Like the Thunderbird of old I shall rise again out of the sea; I shall grab the instruments of the white man's success—his education, his skills—and with these new tools I shall build my race into the proudest segment of your society. Before I follow the great Chiefs who have gone before us, oh Canada, I shall see these things come to pass.[13]

Poem

Poems serve as well in conclusions as they do in introductions. In her March 8, 2010, speech commemorating International Women's Day, former U.S. Secretary of State Madeleine Albright ended with a poem. She introduced it this way: "To illustrate, I'd like to offer a poem, written by the granddaughter of a community organizer from America's Midwest. Her name is Marge Piercy and the poem begins with questions." She continued:

> What can they do
> to you? Whatever they want.
> They can set you up, they can
> bust you, they can break
> your fingers, they can
> burn your brain with electricity,
> blur you with drugs till you
> can't walk, can't remember, they can
> take your child, wall up
> your lover. They can do anything
> you can't blame them
> from doing. How can you stop
> them? Alone, you can fight,
> you can refuse, you can
> take what revenge you can
> but they roll over you.

She read the complete poem, which makes the point that two or more people working together can have an impact. The poem and Albright's speech ended in this way:

> It goes on one at a time,
> it starts when you care
> to act, it starts when you do
> it again after they said no,
> it starts when you say We
> and know who you mean, and each
> day you mean one more.[14]

Question

Questions can function as conclusions, introductions, or forms of elaboration. Both rhetorical and substantive questions can serve as conclusions to a presentation.

Rhetorical Question

A rhetorical question—a question you expect your audience to answer mentally—is a good conclusion because it leaves the audience thinking about the subject of the presentation. Swimmer and environmentalist Lewis Pugh uses a rhetorical question to begin the conclusion in his presentation about a swim under the summit of Mt. Everest: "What radical tactical shift can you take in your relationship to the environment which will ensure that our children and our grandchildren live in a safe world and a secure world and, most importantly, in a sustainable world?"[15] (Pugh's presentation is one of the sample presentations at the end of this book.)

Substantive Question

A presentation also can conclude with an actual question that the audience is expected to answer. Al Pacino, giving a pep talk as the coach of a football team in the movie *Any Given Sunday*, ends with a substantive question: "Now, what are you gonna do?" The team responds with cheers of affirmation to answer the question. (Pacino's presentation is one of the sample presentations at the end of this book.)

Quotation

You can use an eloquent statement made by someone else as a conclusion, just as you can use it as an introduction. Oprah Winfrey, speaking at a commencement at Stanford University, ended her presentation by quoting Martin Luther King Jr.:

> So let me end with one of my favorite quotes from Martin Luther King. Dr. King said, "Not everybody can be famous. . . . But everybody can be great, because greatness is determined by service." Those of you who are history scholars may know the rest of that passage. He said, "You don't have to have a college degree to serve. You don't have to make your subject and verb agree to serve. You don't have to know about Plato or Aristotle to serve. You don't have to know Einstein's theory of relativity to serve. You don't have to know the second [law] of thermodynamics in physics to serve. You only need a heart full of grace and a soul generated by love."[16]

Reference to Introduction

A reference back to the introduction of your presentation provides a sense of completeness to the main ideas you have developed. Christine D. Keen, issues manager for the Society for Human Resource Management, began a presentation with a reference to a Chinese proverb: "The Chinese have a curse: 'May you live in interesting times.' And these certainly are interesting times. American business and American society are undergoing dramatic changes, and human resources sits right at the crossroads of these changes." To close, she referred back to her opening proverb: "For at least the next decade, then, we will all live in interesting times. And it's up to us to determine if that's a curse or a blessing."[17]

Reference to Speaking Situation

You can conclude your presentation by reminding audience members of the structure and main ideas of your presentation by referencing: (1) audience; (2) occasion; (3) place; or (4) self.

Reference to Audience

A reference to the audience in a conclusion highlights the importance of the audience to the interaction. When Steve Spurrier left his position as football coach at the University of Florida, he acknowledged the Gator fans in the conclusion of his presentation: "Again, I thank the 'Gator Nation' for the overwhelming support of our teams for 12 years. The seven SEC championships and the 1996 national championship are memories of a lifetime that we will all share together."[18]

Reference to Occasion

If the occasion on which you are speaking is significant, referring to that occasion leaves your audience with a clear sense of the significance of your presentation in relation to that event. When tennis player Pete Sampras was inducted into the International Tennis Hall of Fame, he began by referencing the occasion:

> Good afternoon, everyone. I'd like to thank you all for being here today to celebrate this day. It's truly an honor to be officially inducted into the Hall of Fame. I'd also like to congratulate my fellow inductees as well for taking a timeless place in the history of tennis, which is really special.

In closing, he referenced the Hall of Fame again:

> So as I take my place among the greatest players of all time here in the Hall of Fame, I stand before you both humbled and grateful. I'm a tennis player: nothing more, and nothing less. It's more than enough for me. It always has been. I thank you."[19]

Reference to Place

A reference to place is an appropriate ending to a presentation given at a significant location. Speaking in New Orleans following hurricane Katrina, US President George W. Bush concluded with a reference to place:

> In this place, there's a custom for the funerals of jazz musicians. The funeral procession parades slowly through the streets, followed by a band playing a mournful dirge as it moves to the cemetery. Once the casket has been laid in place, the band breaks into a joyful "second line"—symbolizing the triumph of the spirit over death. Tonight the

Gulf Coast is still coming through the dirge—yet we will live to see the second line.[20]

Reference to Self

In a case where you were selected as the speaker because of certain accomplishments, a reference to self is an appropriate conclusion. US President Barack Obama, speaking on Father's Day, ended with a reference to himself as a father:

> Over the course of my life, I have been an attorney, I've been a professor, I've been a state senator, I've been a U.S. senator—and I currently am serving as President of the United States. But I can say without hesitation that the most challenging, most fulfilling, most important job I will have during my time on this Earth is to be Sasha and Malia's dad.[21]

Summary of Basic Theme

In a conclusion that summarizes the main idea, you emphasize the primary idea of the presentation. Reese Witherspoon, accepting the Oscar for best actress for her role as June Carter in *Walk the Line*, summarized her main point in her conclusion:

> People used to ask June how she was doin'. And she used to say, "I'm just tryin' to matter." And, I know what she means, you know. I'm just trying to matter and live a good life and make work that means something to somebody. And you have all made me feel that I might have accomplished that tonight. So, thank you so much for this honor.[22]

Summary of Main Ideas

In this type of conclusion, you reiterate your major ideas rather than restate the overall theme of your presentation. You list the main points of your presentation so that your audience members can remember them easily. Julius Genachowsky, FCC chair, summarized the three main ideas he had offered about the advantages of a national mobile broadband plan: "If we get it right, broadband will be an enduring engine for creating jobs and growing our economy, for spreading knowledge and enhancing civic engagement, for advancing a healthier, sustainable way of life. This is our moment. Let's seize it."[23]

The conclusion, like the introduction, is crucial to the overall impact of your presentation. Your conclusion offers your audience a reminder of the gist of your message and its main ideas and provides you with a final opportunity to create an environment of safety, openness, freedom, and value. The conclusion also indicates to your audience that you are closing. It either provides a sense of finality or suggests that now is the time for the audience to assume a larger role in the interaction. You are now ready to develop the transitions that will enable you to move from one part of your presentation to the next and from one idea to another.

8

Connecting Ideas

The process of connecting ideas involves the use of transitions that enable you to communicate to your audience how you see the frame or form of your presentation. The frame you have created is "the organization of an entire personal world,[1] as literary critic Umberto Eco puts it, and your task now is to communicate the personal world you have created to the audience by providing guideposts as you move from one idea to the next.

You cannot assume that your listeners will grasp the frame of your presentation that you see so clearly. As your listeners decode your ideas, they are engaged in a number of processes that work against their coming to the same understanding of your frame as you have. They are forgetting much of what you say simply because the short-term memory can handle only a limited number of new inputs at one time. They are consolidating information into manageable and retainable chunks. They are fitting your new information into a context or framework with which they are already familiar, and it may not be the one you envision. They are developing expectations and making predictions about what will come next in your presentation. They are drawing inferences or developing new ideas from the ideas you discuss. In general, then, they are hard at work using your ideas to build an idea structure of their own. If your presentation does not help them build that structure, what they construct may have little resemblance to your structure. You can increase the possibility of a common structure by using transitions to provide explicit cues about the frame of your presentation.

Some speakers concentrate so hard on preparing each segment of a presentation—the introduction, the body, and the conclusion—that they forget to think about how they will move from one of these sections to the next. Consequently, their transitions are rough or nonexistent. If you haven't made decisions about how to move from one point to the next, you might find yourself saying *uh* and then launching into your next point. You also might end up using the same transition over and over, such as *another point is* or *next*. You want to think deliberately about your transitions—and perhaps even to write them out in your notes—so that they help promote rather than detract from the perspective you are offering in your presentation.

⟶ FUNCTIONS OF TRANSITIONS

The use of transitions is the process of linking the various parts of your presentation so your audience can easily follow the frame for the perspective you are offering. Just as builders frame a house, providing its broad structure, so you want to provide your audience with guideposts to the general form of your presentation. The connections you construct direct your audience from one part of the presentation—one area of the house—to another. These internal indicators are structural guideposts that orient listeners to your frame and direct them to the next point or section in your presentation. The connections or transitions in a presentation fulfill three major functions: (1) remind and forecast; (2) keep listeners on track; and (3) communicate safety, openness, freedom, and value.

Transitions Remind and Forecast

A significant function of transitions is to remind and forecast. Use a transition to summarize or restate the point you have just discussed and to preview what will happen next in the presentation. Transitions let your audience know where you've been and where you're going. Consequently, they orient audience members to where you are in your larger organizational structure.

Transitions Keep Listeners on Track

A second function of transitions is to help your audience stay on track. Transitions help reorient audience members who may have become so focused on a specific idea that they've missed part of your presentation. Other listeners might have become distracted by something else happening in the room and stopped listening. Transitions provide a means for these audience members to rejoin the presentation and to begin attending to it again.

Transitions Communicate Safety, Openness, Freedom, and Value

Transitions serve a third function—helping you create the kind of speaking environment in which everyone can consider all perspectives fully. Transitions help an audience feel safe because you are providing clear signals about the structure of your presentation and its progression. Audience members will not be surprised by where you are going if you offer frequent internal indicators of your structure. They also will feel valued because you have taken the time to include connections that will make listening easy for them.

The use of transitions enhances the conditions of freedom and openness. Transitions demonstrate to your audience that you truly want them to understand the perspective you are offering and to be able to consider it as a viable option. If audience members are confused about what you are proposing because you have not taken the time to make the connections among the ideas in your presentation clear, they will be unable to give your presentation complete consideration. When you make deliberate choices about your transitions, the audience is more likely to perceive, understand, and appreciate the presentation and the coherence you have given it.

⌐ FORMS OF TRANSITIONS

Transitions can assume a variety of forms, including: (1) paragraphs; (2) sentences; and (3) words and phrases. In each case, transitions assist your listeners in following your structure or frame as you move from one idea to the next in your presentation.

Paragraphs

Paragraphs are the longest kind of transition or connection in a presentation. They most often are used in two places. One is between the major sections of the presentation—between the introduction and the body and between the body and the conclusion. Transitional paragraphs also are used between main ideas within the body of the presentation itself. In each case, the paragraph contains some combination of summarizing and forecasting.

At times, your transition paragraph will consist primarily of a summary and a short forecast or preview. This transitional arrangement most often is used when the ideas offered are complicated or new to the audience, and a summary of them is necessary if audience members are going to be able to move with you to the next set of ideas. Perhaps you have been discussing the virtues and limitations of various security systems for the networked computers in your office. Because the systems are complex, a summary of the strengths and weaknesses of each system will be helpful to your audience before moving to the need to make a decision about security quickly, which is your next main idea. A transition that focuses on summary also could be used when the ideas you are offering are novel for an audience. If you are discussing reasons why audience members should consider sending their children to a new charter school—something they have not considered before—reiterating the benefits of this kind of education may be the most helpful transition for your audience of parents.

In other cases, the paragraph of connection consists of a short summary and a much lengthier forecast. This kind of transition paragraph is used when you are most concerned with focusing your audience's attention in a new direction. If you are using the organizational pattern of elimination, for example, you might choose this kind of transition from your introduction to the body of your presentation to alert listeners to the fact that you will be describing various solutions, ending with the one you believe is most desirable. Similarly, if you are describing multiple perspectives in your presentation, you might want to devote the bulk of your transition paragraph to forecasting to ensure that your audience members understand that this is the approach you will be taking.

Sometimes, the transition paragraph is fairly balanced between restatement and forecasting. You might use a couple of sentences to summarize and a couple of sentences to preview where you are heading next. In a presentation to the International Consumer Electronics Show, Microsoft CEO Bill Gates used a transition paragraph balanced between summary and forecast to move between the introduction and the body of his presentation: "So what are the fundamental hardware trends? You know, consumer electronics historically have been mostly about hardware. How is that changing? Well, first and foremost we have the continued truth of Moore's Law. It may not last forever, but for the next decade we're certainly going to get this doubling in power every 18 months to two years."[2] He then went on to discuss the impact of Moore's Law on the computer industry.

Sentences

When sentences serve as transitions, they most often are used to move between major segments of a presentation and between main ideas in the body of a presentation. This kind of transition can be a single sentence or a couple of sentences. The sentence that moves between segments of a presentation contains both a reference to the previous section and a preview of what will follow in the next section. President Barack Obama used such a sentence transition in a speech on immigration at American University when he said, "Immigration reform is no exception." The great challenges of contemporary times were the focus of the previous section of his speech, and immigration reform was the focus of the subsequent section.[3]

A sentence moving between main ideas also contains both restatement and forecast, making clear the connection between the two. In a presentation about an upturn in the economy, you could use a sentence as a transition to move from the main idea that financial indicators point to growth in the nation's economy to the main idea that such growth can be seen in your own city: "But indicators of growth at the national level are impersonal and abstract. We can also see evidence of the economy's recovery in the story of our own city."

Rhetorical questions often are used as sentence transitions because the question format invites audience members to consider possible answers, which are the subject of the next section. Bill Gates frequently uses rhetorical questions to move from one idea to another. In the presentation at the International Consumer Electronics Show mentioned above, he asked, "So what's driving the opportunity?" His next sentence provided the answer to the question and also served as a preview of where he was headed next: "The smart devices where the hardware costs are coming down and the intelligence is going up."[4]

Your thesis statement can serve as a transition sentence because it fulfills the summarizing and previewing functions of a transition. The thesis statement is often placed at the end of the introduction of a presentation, where it leads from the preliminary material to the body of the presentation. For a presentation on the need to reevaluate the importance parents place on athletics in elementary school, you might begin with the story of the father who was beaten to death at his son's hockey game.[5] Your thesis statement would move your audience from that story into the body of your presentation: "Although most parents do not come to blows at their children's sporting events, I believe parents are placing too much emphasis on competitive sports at the elementary school level."

Phrases or Single Words

Phrases or single words also can function as transitions. Because these are brief, they most often are used to move between forms of elaboration that develop a main idea to suggest relationships among them. Transitions that make comparisons include words such as *similarly, likewise,* and *in comparison.* To move between two examples of overspending in a company, you might say, "Similarly, we can see another instance of overspending in the parts department."

Some transitions indicate a causal relationship between forms of elaboration, indicated by phrases such as *therefore, as a result,* and *consequently.* With the topic of overspending, you might move from making a point about bad accounting practices—an explanation—to a metaphor by means of a transition that stresses a causal connection: "As a result of bad accounting practices, we now find ourselves in hot water."

Other transition words or phrases focus on summary. Words such as *finally, in summary,* and *as we have seen* are examples of transitions of this type. For a presentation in which you have offered a problem-solution approach, for example, you might begin your conclusion by saying, "As we have seen, the problem of overcrowding in schools will not be fixed overnight."

As a speaker, you might be tempted to overuse certain transitions because they are familiar. Consequently, they have lost much of their impact. Many speakers use *next, furthermore,* or numbers (*first, second, third*) as transitions. They also use *in conclusion, I would like to say* as a way to move into their conclusions. Rather than serving as effective transitions, these do little more than tell your audience that you didn't take the time to think of a transition that effectively allows you to move from one idea to another. Saying *I see that my time is up* is equally unimpressive. Rather than assisting your audience in moving between segments of your presentation, you let time—or, more precisely, the lack of it—provide your transition. Transitions should be designed carefully to assist your audience in moving with you among the segments, main ideas, and forms of elaboration of your presentation. They should not be fillers you insert because you did not take the time to do the kind of planning your audience deserves.

Transitions provide your audience with crucial cues about the world you are creating with your presentation. As you incorporate explicit cues about the frame or structure into your presentation, you encourage your listeners to understand your perspective fully. In finalizing your transitions, the process of developing your presentation is complete, and you are ready to work on the most effective way to deliver it.

9

Delivering

Delivering your presentation is the final step in the process of preparing a presentation. Delivery means using your body and other presentational aids to help express the ideas that comprise the content of your presentation. The various components of delivery—mode of presentation, speaking notes, time limits, practice, bodily elements, and presentational aids—can be thought of as tools to facilitate the full presentation of your perspective and to provide opportunities for transformation to your audience.

⟶ FUNCTIONS OF DELIVERY

The elements of delivery perform two primary functions for your presentation. Delivery assists you in the creation of an environment of safety, openness, freedom, and value. When your posture, gestures, and facial expressions communicate warmth and a genuine interest in audience members rather than combativeness, aloofness, or superiority, for example, you are more likely to create an environment in which transformation is possible. When you use projection aids thoughtfully and carefully, you communicate that you value audience members and their capacity for understanding.

A second function of delivery is that it offers an additional means for you to give full expression to your perspective. The more attractive and appealing your perspective is because of how it is delivered, the more likely it will be accorded full consideration by others. Many elements of delivery communicate your message to your audience visually and thus reinforce what you are saying verbally. Audience members are able to remember your perspective more easily because they have been able to process it using more than one sensory channel.

⟶ COMPONENTS OF DELIVERY

Factors to consider in delivering your ideas include: (1) mode of presentation; (2) speaking notes; (3) time limits; (4) practice; (5) bodily ele-

113

ments; and (6) presentational aids. You have a great deal of freedom in how you combine the various components of delivery, but you always want to be guided by your interactional goal; your audience; and your desire to create an environment of safety, openness, freedom, and value.

Mode of Presentation

One of the first choices you make when considering how best to use the delivery options available to you is mode of presentation. The three options available to you are: (1) extemporaneous mode; (2) manuscript mode; and (3) impromptu mode.

Extemporaneous Mode

The mode of presentation you are likely to use for most formal speaking situations is the extemporaneous mode. In this mode, you speak from notes of some kind, and not everything you plan to say is written out in those notes. Each time you give the presentation, it will be different as you spontaneously create the presentation from your notes. This mode of presentation allows you to present your ideas in a careful and thoughtful way but also to be conversational in tone and to adapt readily to the verbal and nonverbal responses of the audience.

Manuscript Mode

Sometimes, you will choose to write your presentation out completely and to read from a text. The manuscript mode is used if there are strict time limits within which you must speak or when the wording of the ideas in your presentation is critical. This mode has the advantage of allowing you to present your ideas exactly as you have planned, using the precise language you intended. Generally, however, the disadvantages of this mode outweigh its advantages. Because your entire presentation is written out in advance, your ideas are more likely to be phrased in a written style, which is more formal and less conversational than your natural oral style. You also cannot adapt to your audience as easily during the presentation. Whatever happens in the course of the interaction, your inclination is to continue reading your manuscript no matter how the audience is responding.

If you choose to use a manuscript, begin by converting the written style into a conversational one, which will help you sound as though you are speaking during your presentation rather than reading. Read the manuscript out loud and change formal language such as *do not* to more conversational constructions such as *don't*. Change passive voice to active voice—*I researched this topic extensively* rather than *research has shown*. Make your presentation, in other words, sound like you talk. As you practice speaking from the manuscript, think about your ideas as you say them and remind yourself of the feelings and emotions that led you to express ideas in particular ways. Don't be afraid to deviate from the manuscript if something occurs to you or you want to respond to the audience during the presentation.

Impromptu Mode

Impromptu speaking is the mode of presentation you use most often—when you speak in class; offer your ideas at a staff meeting; or explain, in response to a question from your supervisor, how your current project is progressing. In this mode, you speak with little or no planning or preparation, forming your presentation at the time that you speak. There will be times, however, when you are asked to speak impromptu in more formal situations—to give a toast at a wedding, to say a few words at a memorial service, to accept an award, or to introduce someone, for example. Remember that you have been asked to speak because of your expertise or special connection to the occasion, so responding appropriately probably will not be too difficult in these situations. If you have time, find a quiet place to think for a few minutes and develop a few main points that can serve as the basic structure for your presentation. You then can elaborate on each of those points as you speak, using a story, fact, example, or other form of elaboration.

Speaking Notes

Your choice of notes is an important element in creating a situation in which you feel comfortable presenting your ideas. Although you may have been told at some time to use note cards, they often are not practical for an extensive presentation where you need to present a great deal of information. You may find that you prefer to use one or two sheets of paper rather than note cards so that you aren't creating a distraction for your audience by shuffling many cards. Another advantage of larger sheets of paper over note cards is that, if you are using a lectern, an 8½" × 11" sheet of paper will sit higher on the stand than will a note card, making it is easier for you to read. Do not display your notes on your laptop computer, propped on a table in front of you. You will not be able to maintain eye contact with your audience because your eyes will be on the screen, and your frequent clicking to scroll to the next page will be distracting to the audience.

You will find that certain approaches to your notes work better for you than others. Your notes may consist of a list of key ideas, major points of elaboration, and transitions; a formal outline; or a visual diagram. Whatever format you choose, your notes should be easy for you to read. Typing your notes rather than handwriting them, double or triple spacing them, and using a large and bold font can make them easy to see as you glance back and forth between the notes and your audience.

You also might find that writing notes to yourself about aspects of delivery you want to be sure to remember is helpful. If you tend to talk fast during presentations, for example, you might want to write *SLOW DOWN* in bold, colorful letters at the top of each page of notes. Write *MOVE* on your notes to encourage you to move out from behind the lectern and to use appropriate gestures. If you have a tendency to play with your hair, use a notation such as *HAIR* to remind yourself to manage problematic elements of delivery.

Time Limits

When you are asked to speak, you most likely will be given a length of time for your presentation. Perhaps you are speaking at a luncheon meeting and are scheduled to talk for 20 minutes, or perhaps you are lecturing to a class that meets for 50 minutes. Staying within the time frame available is critical because time limits create expectations on the part of the audience, and audience members can become irritated and restless if you violate those limits. Acceptance speeches at the Academy Awards ceremony are examples of a presentational situation in which maintaining strict time limits is important if the ceremony is to end at a reasonable hour. By staying within the time limits you are given, you will be communicating that you are considerate of your audience members' needs and interests.

Paying close attention to time constraints also means you must be able to fit your perspective on your subject into whatever time is available for your presentation. You need to consider carefully what to leave in and what to take out. When you refuse to omit aspects of your perspective, you are forced to talk very fast or go overtime to get all of your ideas into your presentation. This approach works against accomplishing your goal of giving full expression to your perspective. Attending to time limits, then, not only communicates to your audience members that you are respectful of their time, but it also helps you focus your perspective so that you can offer it as fully as possible in the time available.

Practice

For presentations other than impromptu, practice facilitates the full articulation of your perspective and the creation of an environment of safety, openness, freedom, and value. Try to practice under the most realistic conditions possible. You may find that practicing in front of real people—someone such as your roommate or partner—is helpful. The feedback of a live audience better approximates what you will experience in front of your audience during the actual presentation. If you will be standing to give your presentation, stand up to practice it. Each time you practice, deliver your presentation all the way through without stopping. If you stumble over a word or idea, don't start the presentation over. Instead, think about what you would do if that happened in front of your actual audience, and go on from there. We suggest practicing in front of a mirror a time or two and, if possible, recording a practice session. Both of these types of practice will show you the general impression created by your presentation and, in particular, whether you have gestures or mannerisms that distract from the presentation of your ideas.

Practice, then, is a major factor in your ability to create a potentially transformative environment and to ensure that your perspective is presented fully. For a major presentation, practice your talk at least once and even twice a day for the week or so before the presentation. Even short presentations of four or five minutes deserve at least five or six practice sessions. The more times you give your presentation, the more familiar and comfortable you are with it, and the more confident you can be that your delivery will enhance rather than detract from the full articulation of your perspective.

Bodily Elements

Elements of your body that contribute to or detract from the delivery of your presentation include voice, movement, and personal appearance and dress. **Voice** includes the factors of volume, rate, pitch, and pausing. Volume is the degree of loudness or intensity of sound, and rate is the speed at which you speak. Pitch is the tone or register of vocal vibration, and pausing is the length of time between words or sentences.

Various other aspects of your body also can assist you in offering your perspective. **Movement** involves posture, gestures, facial expressions, and general bodily movement. Posture is how you carry your body, and gestures are movements of the hands, arms, body, and head. Facial expressions are the use of the face and eyes to communicate, and movement includes the general actions of your body, such as when you walk, stand, or sit.

Personal appearance is another way in which your message is delivered. Personal hygiene concerns issues of health, cleanliness, and neatness. For many audiences, body odor, dirty or unkempt hair, a scruffy beard, and wrinkled clothing detract from delivery. Hairstyle, clothing, jewelry, accessories such as scarves or ties, and tattoos are other aspects of personal appearance available for decorating your body.

Offering specific guidelines for every bodily element of delivery is not possible because what is appropriate in one situation is inappropriate in another. For example, many audiences in the United States expect eye contact. It is a primary way to communicate that you sincerely want your audience members to understand your ideas and that you are interested in their responses to your perspective. If your audience members are from cultures in which direct eye contact is regarded as insulting or disrespectful, however, efforts to create an environment in which they feel safe and valued would need to assume a different form. In that case, you might choose to sit in a circle with audience members, where you can look down easily and naturally while others are talking.

Presentational Aids

Presentational aids are any audiovisual aids you use to supplement the content of your presentation, and many options are available for this purpose. You can show objects to your audience that illustrate some feature of your presentation. If you choose to show a fossil to explain plant life in an earlier geologic period or a quilt made by your grandmother in a presentation on sewing, you are using an object as a presentational aid. A three-dimensional representation of something such as a building makes use of a **model** and might be used in a presentation about architecture or the revitalization of a neighborhood. **Diagrams** show how something works, and you might choose to use them in a presentation about how information travels in an organization or how the computers in your office could be networked.

Graphs and charts show information in numerical form. **Graphs** often are used to show relationships among components. For a presentation on water conservation, you might use a graph that shows how conservation has reduced water use over the past five years. **Charts** also organize information in a visual format. To discuss where layoffs may occur in a company, an organizational chart would be useful in your presentation. **Maps** display geographical areas. You could use a map of the United States in a presentation about college recruitment to show how your university draws students from all 50 states. **Pictures,** which include paintings and photographs, are two-dimensional representations of people, places, and things. A photograph of a street scene in Beijing could be used to illustrate the increase of auto traffic in China, or painted self-portraits by several renowned artists could serve as aids in a presentation about the artistic genre of self-portraits. With many of these visual aids, you have a choice not only about what kind of visual aid to use but also how to present or display it. Diagrams or graphs, for example, can be displayed via computer-generated slides, flip charts, chalkboards, whiteboards, posters, or handouts.

Many other forms of presentational aids are available to you. **Audio and visual clips**—short recordings of music, sounds, and speech or excerpts from movies, television, and radio—are another option for presentational aids. Playing a segment from the movie *Babies* to demonstrate child-rearing techniques in the United States is an example of the use of an audiovisual clip as a presentational aid. Don't forget that you also can use members of your **audience** as visual aids—you can ask audience members to join you at the front of the room and use their clothing, height, or other characteristics to illustrate points in your presentation, or you can line audience members up in a certain way or ask them to hold up signs you have created as visual aids. Of course, you never want to force any audience members to serve as visual aids for you if they are shy or reluctant to do so.

Regardless of the kind of visual aid you select for your presentation, your aids should be supplemental. They should elaborate on ideas in the presentation but should not constitute the presentation itself. If you discover that your video clip consumes over half of your presentation, you need to cut it down so that it becomes a form of elaboration and not the presentation itself. Likewise, a presentation that consists solely of showing PowerPoint slides and reading each one aloud is a presentation in which the aid has become the presentation. You also need to be prepared in case your audiovisual aids fail or are not available. Perhaps the computer does not work, or you accidentally leave your handouts at home. If you can give the presentation without any aids at all and it still makes sense, you will be prepared for any contingency and will be confident that your presentation is more than just a visual display.

Presentational Software

Despite the abundance of different media available for presenting audiovisual aids, most speakers use only one form—PowerPoint software. The typical presentation today consists of a speaker presenting slides with bulleted lists illustrated by clip art. These kinds of Power-Point presentations are so universal that you might think using presentational software is the only way to give a presentation. Because of the pervasiveness of this mode of presentation, we want to spend more time on it than on other kinds of visual aids.

Think about when you are in an audience and a speaker is using PowerPoint in the standard way—showing slides with bullet points and clip art and reading the slides to the audience. If you are like many audience members, you find such presentations to be "mind-numbingly dull"[1] and something to be endured rather than invitations to understand the speaker's perspective. You are not alone in your assessment of Power-Point presentations. General David H. Petraeus, whose military work has included overseeing the wars in Iraq and Afghanistan, says that sitting through many PowerPoint briefings is "just agony."[2] Seth Godin, author of *Really Bad PowerPoint*, says that "almost every PowerPoint presentation sucks rotten eggs."[3]

Audiences often react negatively to PowerPoint presentations because they have been exposed to so many routine, uninspired examples. As a speaker, then, you are faced with a dilemma. You may be expected to use PowerPoint (or believe it is expected of you), but, at the same time, you know that you risk losing the attention of the audience during PowerPoint presentations. In the next section, we'll consider some of the problems with Power Point and some ways to address them.

Problems with PowerPoint Software. The fact that using Power-Point software may encourage audiences not to pay attention to your presentation is a major difficulty. There are other problems as well: (1) PowerPoint software is presenter oriented rather than audience oriented; and (2) PowerPoint software contains biases that may not enable you to present your perspective effectively.

PowerPoint software is presenter oriented rather than audience oriented. When speakers use PowerPoint, they often feel they don't need to prepare, practice, or use notes for their presentation because they can read the slides they are showing. Relying on PowerPoint also allows the speaker to avoid discovering how to deliver a presentation in an engaging way—the software dictates the delivery. None of these so-called *advantages* for the speaker benefits the audience. In fact, what could be perceived as benefits to the speaker are likely to make the audience less interested in learning about and understanding the speaker's perspective.

PowerPoint software contains biases. PowerPoint also has biases that affect not only the nature of your presentation but the kind of thinking and understanding that audience members can achieve as a result of the presentation. As artist and musician David Byrne explains, PowerPoint appears to be a neutral tool, "unbiased and free of any leanings one way or another."[4] But, he explains, PowerPoint has

> been designed assuming, a priori, a specific world view. The software, by making certain directions and actions easier and more convenient than others, tells you how to think as it helps you accomplish your task. Not in an obvious way or in an obnoxious way or even in a scheming way. The biases are almost unintentional, they are so natural and well-integrated. . . . You are thus subtly indoctrinated into a manner of being and behaving, assuming and acting, that grows on you as you use the program.[5]

Rhetoric professor Jens E. Kjeldsen explains the issue in this way: "The problem lies in *PowerPoint's cognitive style*, for the software forces us to speak and think in particular ways. Like all tools—and media—it has constraints, certain possibilities and limitations."[6] Edward Tufte, a former professor of political science, statistics, and computer science at Yale University and the author of books such as *Envisioning Information*, makes the same point: "PowerPoint comes with a big attitude."[7]

Several biases that make us think in particular ways are inherent in PowerPoint software. A major one is that it does not allow you to present detailed or sophisticated information to your audience. As Kjeldsen explains, "The software makes us think and speak in isolated blocks, instead of in coherent context, totalities, narratives or linear reasoning."[8] PowerPoint short circuits the capacity to think in sophisticated ways because of a number of its features. The lists of short phrases it requires—the power points—do not allow you to develop a complicated argument. The fact that PowerPoint breaks up narratives and data into bullet points, slicing and dicing "the evidence into arbitrary compartments," also makes complex reasoning difficult.[9] In addition, because PowerPoint software organizes all content into lists, you are not able to present complex relationships among items.

PowerPoint also diminishes audience members' ability to reason in sophisticated ways because it does not allow for the presentation of extensive data in graphics and tables. Extensive graphs and tables must be broken up and spread over many different slides, making their use for analysis and evaluation difficult. These problems are magnified because PowerPoint design style does not give you much space with which to work. Only about 40% of a slide is available for you to use for your content, and the remaining space is devoted to bullets, frames, clip art, and branding.[10] The result of these built-in biases of PowerPoint, according to many studies, is superficial, simplistic thinking and the stifling of "discussion, critical thinking and thoughtful decision making."[11]

Using Presentational Software Effectively.   Let's assume you have thought carefully about the problems inherent in PowerPoint presentations and have decided that you still want to use this presentational software. Various options are available to you to circumvent some of the problems inherent in PowerPoint: (1) develop your ideas before using the software; (2) pay attention to design principles; (3) check the quality of projection; (4) keep the focus on you; (5) develop a back-up plan; and (6) consider options other than PowerPoint software.

Develop your ideas before using the software.   Develop your key ideas before you touch your software. You might be tempted to make the software your major concern in the preparation process for your presentation, jumping right into the software and starting to lay out slides. When you do this, though, you tend to "get bogged down in what the presentation looks like much too soon," and the templates and wizards can take you in directions you may not want to go.[12] As Nancy Duarter, CEO of a presentation-design firm, explains, "Presentation software was never intended to be a brainstorming tool or drawing tool. The applications are simply containers for ideas and assets, not the means to generate them."[13] Your focus should not be on your slides at this point in the process: "As speakers, we should not be thinking of how to fill in a template. We should be thinking of purpose, goals and means. What do we want to achieve? How can we best achieve it?"[14]

Turn off your computer as you plan your presentation. Use some system other than PowerPoint software to create the ideas for your presentation. Brainstorm as many possible ideas for your presentation as you can, letting the ideas flow and capturing them using words, diagrams, and images on paper, a whiteboard, a blackboard, large sheets of paper, or Post-It-Notes. If you must use your computer, both PowerPoint and Keynote have outline views that allow you to develop the structure of your presentation in plain text without being concerned about what the slides are going to look like. If you like to use mind maps, concept maps, or idea webs to outline your ideas visually, a good tool is Inspiration software (Inspiration.com). At the end of this brainstorming session, identify the one key idea that is central from the point of view of the audience and go from there to develop the main ideas that you will use to elaborate on that idea. This is the process outlined in chapter 4, the chapter about focusing.

Pay attention to design principles.   After you have worked out the ideas around your one key idea, you can begin to design images to help your audience understand those ideas. This is the point where you design your slides. Many books are available that will help you develop slides that meet criteria for good presentation design, including *The Non-Designer's Presentation Book* by Robin Williams and *Presentation Zen* by Garr Reynolds. At the very least, however, you'll want to pay attention to two key design principles—the signal-to-noise ratio and the picture-superiority effect.

The **signal-to-noise ratio** is the ratio of relevant to irrelevant elements in a slide or other display. You want to have a high signal-to-noise ratio in your slides, which means communication "with as little degradation to the message as possible."[15] To achieve a high signal-to-noise ratio, make sure everything on your slides clearly supports and develops your message, and remove anything that compromises it. One of the biggest mistakes that speakers make is to use every inch of space on a slide, "filling it up with text, boxes, clip art, charts, footers, and the ubiquitous company logo."[16] The more irrelevant items you add to slides, the more those items take attention away from you—and the more trouble your audience has mentally sifting through the pieces and combining them into a coherent whole. The more you include in your slides that has nothing to do with your presentation, the more you distract from what you want your focus to be. To have no graphics at all is better than showing irrelevant words, lines, shapes, symbols, and logos that take the viewer's mind in the wrong direction.

Another way to be sure that you have an appropriate signal-to-noise ratio is to make your photographs and video clips relevant. Don't use them just because you think they are cool or beautiful or funny. Be careful, too, with animation or movement on your slides. Movement creates a focal point and calls attention to itself, so only animate when you have something special on which you want the audience to focus. Some good advice regarding relevance is this: "Away with everything just meant to be a little amusing and diverting. Away with irrelevant pictures and dingbats, disturbing animations and sounds without function."[17]

A second key design principle, the **picture-superiority effect**, says that pictures are remembered better than words, especially when people are exposed to information for a short amount of time. As much as possible, use images on your PowerPoint slides to improve your audience's understanding of your perspective. Replace words with photographs or other appropriate images or graphics whenever possible. A PowerPoint presentation is not a document, so your slides should not resemble printed matter. Your projected slides should be as visual as possible and support your points quickly, efficiently, and powerfully, with the verbal content of your presentation coming primarily from your spoken words.

Because you are emphasizing visuals in your PowerPoint slides, be sure to use good images instead of cheesy clip art. There are a number of places where you can get free or inexpensive professional level illustrations and photographs. The following sites offer free images, but, as you know, options available on the web are constantly changing, so watch for other good sources of images:

- Dreams Time Stock Photos: www.dreamstime.com
- Everystockphoto search engine: www.everystockphoto.com
- Image After: www.imageafter.com
- Morgue File: www.morguefile.com
- Stock.xching: www.sxc.hu
- Wikimedia Commons: www.commons.wikimedia.org

Here are sites where you can find images at low cost:

- Stock Images and Photos: www.stockphotos.com
- Dreams Time Stock Photos: www.dreamstime.com
- Fotolia: www.fotolia.com
- Veer Creatives: www.Veer.com
- ShutterMap: www.ShutterMap.com

Check the quality of projection.   When the time comes to deliver your presentation using PowerPoint, be sure to check the quality of projection. After spending all those hours designing your PowerPoint presentation, you want your images to show up. Power is measured for LCD projectors in lumens, or light output. The typical portable projector that many organizations own puts out around 1,200 lumens, which is suitable for an audience of 30 to 40 people. If you are speaking to an audience of 100 or more, you need a projector with a minimum of 2,500 lumens and a screen that is at least 10 feet by 10 feet. Before you arrive to give your presentation, talk to your contact person and make sure you have the right amount of lumens needed to show your slides properly.[18]

Keep the focus on you.   As you deliver your presentation, keep the focus on you. If audience members are not engaged with you, they are less likely to understand the perspective you are presenting, and your opportunity to understand the perspectives they offer is diminished. The focus will not be on you if you are glued to your laptop and continually look down to change your slides or if you walk back to the computer to change slides every few minutes. To keep the audience's focus on you, use a remote control. It doesn't have to be anything fancy—all you need is the ability to go forward, go back, and turn the screen black. A remote allows you to move closer to your audience and to walk around to address different parts of the audience.

Another way to keep the focus on you is to keep the lights on in the room when you are speaking. You've undoubtedly had the experience, when a presentation is about to begin, of someone shouting, "Could you get the lights, please?" The room goes dark, except for the light reflecting off the screen, and the presenter disappears. The more lights you can keep on during your presentation, the better. Connecting with the audience is very difficult if your audience members can't see you. Much of your message comes from your nonverbal behavior, so the audience must not only hear you but also see you. Early projectors were not very bright, so turning the lights off made more sense, but today, even inexpensive business projectors are usually bright enough for a small room, so there is no good reason to turn off all the lights.

You also have available to you a device in the PowerPoint program to focus audience members' attention on you. Given the choice of looking at the speaker or a slide, audiences usually will choose the slide. To bring audience members' attention back to you, use the letter B key. Press it once while in VIEW SHOW mode, and the screen will go black. Audience members will turn their attention to you. Press it again, your slide will reappear, and the audience will focus attention back on the screen.

Develop a back-up plan.   Don't forget to have a back-up plan. If you are bringing a presentation on your laptop, have a copy on a CD or portable drive with you as well. If you send your presentation in advance, bring an extra copy in case the presentation was corrupted in the transfer or if there are compatibility issues with the equipment in the room where you are presenting. If the technology in the room fails completely, be prepared to give your presentation without any visual support.

Consider options other than PowerPoint software.   PowerPoint slides are not your only option for including visual material in your presentation. Many other options are available, and new software is being developed all the time. One alternative is Prezi (Prezi.com), a free presenting application that allows you to zoom in and out of images and to create presentations that flow like a movie. Prezi is free, and students and professors have access to the educational version, which has slightly better features than the basic free edition. You also have the option of using a word-processing or page-layout software capable of capturing, editing, and publishing text, tables, data graphics, images, and scientific notation. Replacing PowerPoint with Microsoft Word, for example, allows you to present more sophisticated intellectual content and analysis.

Although Microsoft's PowerPoint or Apple's Keynote is the first thing many people think of when they are asked to give a presentation, not all information is suited to digital presentations. Don't forget that presentational aids can include many different kinds of visual formats. Think about the other alternatives that you have available so you can select the best method for presenting your information. The method you choose depends on factors such as the number of people in the audience, the size of the room, how much time you have, and whether you want to engage your audience in a discussion.

Handouts are one alternative. When they have a handout, audience members can easily follow along with your presentation, and they can take notes on the handout and bring it home with them. As presentation designer Robin Williams notes, "What the audience members see on the overhead screen is temporary, and there is no guarantee they will remember it correctly; what you give them to take back to the office is permanent."[19] If you are speaking in a large room, some people might not be able to see your slides, or perhaps the projection system is poor. A handout is the perfect solution to both of these problems. Handouts can range from an outline of key points in your presentation to a table of data that is difficult to present in PowerPoint to a more detailed document. A handout also allows you to provide your audience with your contact information, additional resources, or web addresses.

You might have heard the rule that you should never pass out handouts because audience members will read the handout and not pay attention to you. Certainly, if you give people a handout, they will read it the first moment they are bored with your presentation. Remember, though, that your audience members already have all sorts of ways to distract themselves other than with your handout. Their iPhones and BlackBerries give them access to the Internet, e-mail, and Twitter. Their laptops give them access to their work responsibilities, school assignments, and movies. They also probably have notepads and pens, with which they very well may be making a grocery list or doodling. They also can distract themselves simply by thinking about things unrelated to your presentation. A handout at least keeps the audience focused temporarily on your topic.

To prevent your handout from being too much of a distraction, distribute it at the moment in your presentation when you want to make use of it (you might ask someone in the audience to help you pass it out) or distribute it at the end of your presentation as a summary of your major points. Timing the distribution of your handout helps keep audience members focused on you and provides them with one less potential distraction. When event organizers ask you to send your handouts ahead of time so they can incorporate them into a conference notebook, just say, "That's okay. I'll distribute them myself."[20] Williams summarizes the benefits of a good handout: "Your thoughtfully created handout tells me you respect me enough to have created it for me, and that in turn makes me pay a little more attention."[21]

Remember, too, that you don't have to choose between slides and handouts—consider using a mixture of both. You can use slides for most of your presentation but occasionally stop to distribute handouts with more detailed data. Another option—one that works particularly well for a presentation where your interactional goal is to discover knowledge and belief—is to begin with a short briefing paper or technical report that everyone reads at the beginning of your presentation (people can read three or four times faster than presenters can talk). Following the reading period, you can provide a guided analysis of the briefing paper and then lead a discussion on the material in the document.[22]

⟿ TWIRKS

Although there are no absolute rules for the use of elements of delivery, there is a category of elements or conditions called *twirks* that can interfere with delivery. *Twirk* is an arcane word that linguist Suzette Haden Elgin discovered and uses to refer to *"a feature of language behavior which attracts so much attention to itself that it outweighs both the content and the form of the speech."*[23] According to Elgin, a twirk is anything that provokes a reaction not based on the content of your presentation. Elgin offers the following example of a twirk:

> Suppose you make an interesting, rational, and compelling speech, and you do that while wearing a purple velvet floppy hat with rabbit ears and scarlet satin roses. Then that hat is a *twirk*—and it will seriously interfere with the manner in which your speech is heard and understood by your audience. You could be the greatest orator since Demosthenes, and that hat would still undercut you and cancel out the power of your words and all the nonverbal communication that went with them.[24]

The purple hat—or whatever the object or condition that constitutes a twirk—is not in itself good or bad, positive or negative. But certain elements associated with delivery have the potential to interfere with the full presentation and reception of your perspective. Analyze all aspects of your planned delivery to recognize and eliminate the twirks that could hinder the transformative possibilities for your particular audience.

Any element that is sustained constitutes a twirk. If any aspect of your delivery is repeated over and over again, it is sustained and, in all likelihood, will dominate audience members' attention and make fulfilling the functions of your presentation difficult. If you use one gesture repeatedly or pace back and forth in the front of the room, for example, those sustained elements distract the audience from the goals you have for your presentation. Running back and forth between your computer and the lectern is another instance of a sustained activity that is detrimental to the presentation of your message. Any element that is repeated to this degree calls attention to itself rather than to your perspective and thus is a twirk.

While some twirks develop from communication behaviors that are sustained, others take the form of elements that in themselves function as distractions for the audience. Some that are most likely to affect a speaking presentation involve: (1) communication anxiety; (2) language; (3) clothing and adornment; (4) permanent physical conditions; and (5) presentational aids.

Communication Anxiety

When you become so nervous that it interferes with your ability to present your perspective effectively, you are experiencing communication anxiety or stage fright. When you perceive that you are in a challenging, frightening, or new situation, your body responds by producing adrenaline. Adrenaline sets you up to respond by "fight or flight," but in a communication situation, of course, you can do neither, so the adrenaline in your body seeks some kind of release. Manifestations of adrenaline take the form of the symptoms often associated with communication anxiety, such as shaking hands and knees, a dry mouth, butterflies in the stomach, an accelerated heartbeat, or blushing. If these symptoms are obvious to your audience as you are speaking, they may function as twirks for you.

Some degree of anxiety about communicating is normal; in fact, there are many legitimate reasons why you might feel anxious. One reason is that there is the expectation, when you are asked or choose to speak, that you will offer a perspective or viewpoint that, if not novel, is somewhat interesting and of value to the audience. You also may not be entirely confident that your perspective will be accepted and appreciated by your audience.

A lack of preparation also may trigger feelings of anxiety. If you are not as ready as you would like to be for a speaking situation—you have not had adequate preparation time, did not know you would be asked to speak, procrastinated in preparing your presentation, or did not practice your presentation very much—you probably will find yourself experiencing some anxiety.

Even when you are well prepared, you still may experience anxiety because of uncertainties related to your presentation. Perhaps you are planning a presentation with an interactional goal of discovering knowledge and belief. You have prepared fully for the discussion, but it is a mode you do not use very often, and thus it generates anxiety for you. Perhaps your perspective itself is undergoing major shifts, and you feel a natural anxiety about articulating it in its changing form to an audience. Perhaps you are experiencing anxiety because you feel you have nothing to contribute to the interaction. This feeling may be the result of having been silenced in the past, of feeling devalued in a group, or of not having the communication tools to express your perspective adequately. All of these feelings are legitimate and may provoke feelings of anxiety before and during your presentation.

There are other sources of anxiety, however, that are irrational and consist of exaggerated or needless fear. Most irrational concerns arise not because of fear of possible physical harm or injury but because of an "*over-concern for what someone thinks about you*."[25] This kind of anxiety is self-defeating because the worry and fretting themselves are usually far worse than the actual event. If you experience anxiety of this sort, you are likely to exaggerate the possible outcomes of a speaking situation, and the worry itself increases the likelihood of something unexpected occurring.[26] You may worry, for example, about tripping on the way to the lectern and falling flat on your face. That this will occur is extremely unlikely, but stewing about it—focusing on it—will not keep it from happening.

Whether your anxiety has a legitimate basis or is largely irrational, it can be managed. You may have been given all sorts of advice for dealing with communication anxiety. Not all of it, however, helps create an environment of safety, openness, freedom, and value. You may have been told, for example, to look over the heads of your audience members; to imagine them sitting before you in their underwear; or to say over and over to yourself before you speak, "I'm a better person than they are." All of these techniques create just the opposite conditions from the ones you are attempting to foster. They require you to see yourself as superior to your audience rather than as a participant in an interaction in which everyone's perspective is welcomed and valued. They also assume that you are facing a hostile audience, which is probably not the case.

Some ways of managing communication anxiety do allow you to contribute to the creation of the conditions of safety, openness, freedom, and value. One is simply to deal with the symptoms you tend to experience so that your discomfort with or embarrassment about them does not interfere with your efforts to communicate. If your mouth tends to be dry when you speak, bring water with you to sip throughout your presentation. If your neck turns red when you speak, wear a turtleneck or a scarf that covers it. If shakiness is your body's preferred symptom of speech anxiety, try to engage in some physical activity before your presentation to rid your body of excess energy—take a walk, breathe deeply, or move your head and arms. Once you know that you have addressed your body's symptoms of communication anxiety, you will feel more comfortable and can concentrate on creating the kind of environment you desire.

Practicing your presentations also can lessen your communication anxiety. As you listen to yourself speak, your perspective will become increasingly clear, and you will become more confident about expressing it. If you are uncertain about what you are going to say and are aware that your presentation is not flowing smoothly, your anxiety level is sure to increase.

Voicing your perspective whenever you get the opportunity is another way to decrease communication anxiety. Whenever you are given the chance to present your ideas, take it. The first several or perhaps the first hundred times you accept the opportunity to share your perspective, you might be uncomfortable and might experience symptoms of anxiety. Gradually, however, they will begin to disappear. You will feel more comfortable with the process of presenting ideas orally, will discover that you have good ideas to contribute, and will find that others appreciate your input into various interactions. This certainly was the case for us. We were incredibly shy, so when we had to give a presentation, we wrote every word on note cards. We turned bright red, our hands and knees shook, and we hated all of those eyes staring at us. Even talking with one other person we didn't know well was hard for us. But we kept giving presentations, and, eventually, we got pretty good at them. If we can go from our starting point of extreme nervousness to becoming communication majors, teaching communication, writing a book about speaking, and being able to give presentations easily, we are confident you can make progress, too.

If your stage fright is irrational because it assumes the form of exaggerated and needless worry, rational self-talk might be your best response. Recognizing the degree to which you can control how you interpret a situation can be a first step toward reducing irrational anxiety. Rather than reinforcing anxiety by dwelling on and worrying about the things that might go wrong in a presentation, you can minimize or even dispel anxiety by focusing your attention elsewhere and making positive statements about your performance and your presentation. One of the ways to do this is to put the presentation in perspective. It is only a presentation, and if it does not go perfectly, it is not the end of the world. The notion that perfection is not the goal of the presentation might be one statement to make part of your positive self-talk. You also might turn your attention to the presentation itself and construct messages to yourself that reinforce the positive features of the presentation—how much you enjoy the opportunity to discuss the subject, how exciting it will be to hear others' perspectives on the same issue, or how delighted you are to have the opportunity to talk to a particular audience. Don't forget, too, that spending your time preparing for your presentation rather than worrying about it will focus your attention where it will do some good.

Just because you have addressed your speech anxiety, however, does not mean you can eradicate it entirely or forever. Even the most veteran speakers may experience some symptoms of anxiety in particularly difficult or challenging speaking situations. By understanding why the anxiety is surfacing and reminding yourself of what you have going for you in your presentation, how much you have practiced, and how much you want to give expression to your perspective, those anxieties will dissipate and probably disappear.

Language

Twirks of language relate to how something is said and include pronunciation, grammar and usage, jargon, obscenities, and fillers. **Pronunciation** associated with a particular dialect often functions as a twirk. The way of pronouncing a certain vowel can be a twirk if the pronunciation is different from that of the dialect of your audience members. Dropping the endings of words—*workin'* instead of *working*—or eliding words—*gonna* instead of *going to*—can be twirks for some audiences.

Grammar and usage also function as potential twirks, usually when violations of standard grammar and usage occur. Saying *ain't* instead of *isn't* or using the double negative—*I don't have no money*—are examples of such violations. For some cultural groups, grammatical errors interfere with the creation of an environment of safety, openness, freedom, and value. **Jargon** might be seen as the opposite of poor grammar in the sense that it involves language that exceeds conversational standards and norms. Jargon is the use of a highly technical vocabulary characteristic of one field of activity. Virtually every discipline or field has its jargon, but use of that vocabulary with an audience not familiar with that field is a twirk. In a presentation about the military to a nonmilitary audience, for example, discussing *Batts, gunnery sergeants, master petty chief officers,* and *midshipmen* without defining those terms would constitute jargon.

Obscenities or swear words also function as twirks for many audiences. Some audiences are accustomed to hearing such language, but for others, obscenities are offensive and violate norms for polite or appropriate speech. If you are not sure how an audience will respond to an obscenity, err on the side of caution and don't use it. For many audiences, obscenities are major detractors from the content of the presentation and affect audience members' attitudes toward you as a speaker. When an audience dismisses you because of your use of obscenities, your perspective is not given a full hearing, and your audience does not feel safe and valued.

Fillers are words that are inserted between phrases or sentences to avoid silence. Some common fillers are *you know, I mean, uh, um,* and *like.* Because these are natural elements in informal conversation, they are not twirks for most audiences unless they appear so frequently that they become distracting. When this occurs, audience members may start waiting for the next filler to occur instead of listening to the content of the presentation itself. One of Karen's students had a professor who said *actually* a lot as he lectured. One day, the student decided to count each instance of *actually* the professor said and became so focused on this task that he did not hear when the professor called on him. The professor walked over to his desk, asked what he was doing, and discovered the tally marks. Until that moment, the professor had no idea that he overused *actually,* and he made a concerted effort after that to excise it from his vocabulary.

Linguistic twirks are among the most manageable because, with awareness, you can make changes in your language so that particular aspects of your presentation do not become twirks. You can practice your presentation, for example, so that many of your fillers disappear and, with vigilance, you can catch and change grammatical errors. Recording your presentation or asking for feedback from those who hear you practice also can help you become aware of twirks. Language is the vehicle through which your presentation is offered. If you can prevent your language from producing twirks, your audience will be more likely to hear your perspective.

Clothing and Adornment

Your clothing and other forms of adornment can become twirks if they are unacceptable, unusual, or inappropriate for your audience. Clothing becomes a twirk when it is outside the clothing norms of a particular group. Speaking in a short-sleeved shirt and khakis when everyone else is wearing a suit is a twirk, just as is presenting in a suit when everyone else is in shorts and T-shirts. For a formal presentation, the norm is that a speaker should be dressed at or slightly above the dress level of the audience; major discrepancies in clothing between you and your audience tend to make you and your audience uncomfortable. Personal hygiene can become an issue, too, if your deodorant has failed or if you have not taken a shower recently or washed your hair before your presentation.

Bodily adornments in the form of tattoos and body piercings are twirks for some audiences. The tattoo on your hand—no matter what the image—may keep some employers from taking you seriously at a job interview no matter how well you present your ideas. Any tattoo that cannot be covered is a potential twirk, as is an eyebrow ring, tongue stud, nose ring, or pierced lip. Earrings on men are considered inappropriate by some audiences and would function as twirks in those settings.

At times, hair style or hair color can function as a twirk. Hair that is dyed an unusual color—pink, purple, or green, for example—is a twirk if it is all the audience members can see and think about during your presentation. An unusual hairstyle or dated style—a beehive, for example—might keep an audience from focusing on what you are presenting. Long strands of hair combed over a man's bald spot can be a twirk because such a hairstyle typically encourages audience members to spend their time wondering why the speaker thinks the few strands of hair are hiding anything.

Twirks relating to clothing and adornment also can include temporary conditions that affect appearance such as spinach between your front teeth, lipstick on your teeth, a loose hem, spaghetti sauce spilled on a blouse, a tie that has inadvertently flipped over, a collar that is up instead of down, or an unzipped zipper. If you become aware of temporary quirks while presenting, fix them unobtrusively so that they do not remain twirks for very long.

Conditions related to clothing and appearance that can become twirks usually can be managed with some forethought. Talking with the person who asked you to speak about the kind of dress appropriate for the occasion can be helpful. If your analysis of the speaking situation tells you that adornments such as earrings, piercings, and tattoos will constitute twirks for your audience, remove or cover them for your presentation, if possible. Checking yourself in a mirror immediately before a presentation to make sure there are no temporary problems is also a good idea.

Permanent Physical Conditions

There are also twirks that are permanent features, and these can function as distractions for the audience when you give a presentation. Such physical conditions include being in a wheelchair; having a large birthmark on your face; or being hard of hearing, deaf, blind, or cerebral palsied. Weight (for example, an obese or severely anorexic speaker) may constitute a twirk for some audiences if it distracts from the content of the presentation. Speaking in a strong foreign accent also can be perceived as a permanent twirk. Although accents can be changed, adults often have difficulty eliminating an accent entirely. If an audience cannot understand you and focuses on that difficulty, your accent has become a twirk.

The best way to manage permanent physical twirks is directly. You may want to explain to the audience near the beginning of your presentation, for example: "I have cerebral palsy" or "I am a stutterer" or "I don't hear well." You then can let your audience know how to handle the situation: "Because this may interfere with our communication, please feel free to ask me to repeat or explain whenever necessary. I won't be offended, and I appreciate your patience."[27] By dealing with the twirk directly, you reduce the discomfort of your audience, make the condition something that can be addressed explicitly, and, as the interaction proceeds, encourage audience members to think less and less about it. Instead of spending their time wondering whether to ask if you need help with your wheelchair or whether they can ask you to repeat something they missed because of your accent, you have made the condition something that can be talked about. Audience members then can turn their attention to the presentation itself rather than worrying that something they do or say will offend you or make you uncomfortable.

Your sex constitutes another potential permanent twirk because the expectations for speaking are different for the sexes. Although gendered associations with sex vary greatly across cultures and time periods, biological sex can be a twirk in some situations. Just over 100 years ago, women were not even allowed to speak in public. Not only was speaking considered unladylike for a woman, but it generally was considered a physical impossibility. Women were not believed to have the stamina or temperament required to manage public speaking.[28]

Although women now speak in every kind of context, there are some audiences that might begrudge a woman a position of power or influence or who might perceive the same statement from a man and a woman in different ways. A man who reveals emotion might be seen as sensitive; a woman who does so might be viewed as hysterical or emotional. A man who is assertive might be seen as commanding, while a woman who is assertive might be viewed as bitchy. Whether you are a woman or a man, then, may function as a twirk for certain audiences, especially if you are speaking on subjects that have not been typical for members of your sex or if you are violating gender norms in some way. If you are a woman, dressing in a particular way—wearing a revealing, low-cut blouse, for example—may increase an audience's perception of inappropriateness, especially if audience members believe that your topic is not something a woman should be discussing.

Another permanent condition that can become a twirk is an extraordinary appearance—the opposite of the physical impairments and conditions that engender uncomfortable responses in many audiences. Being spectacularly beautiful, having magnificent green eyes, or having an unusually resonant voice can be so distracting that audience members don't hear what you are saying. Although these kinds of conditions may not seem as if they could be twirks, they may function as twirks if the striking characteristics distract audiences from the content of the presentation.

If you do have a feature that is especially striking, you may make a deliberate decision not to call attention to it and perhaps even to minimize it. If you are a woman with an especially good figure, you might choose a long, loose-fitting dress and jacket rather than a short, fitted suit. Karen once worked with a teaching assistant who was particularly attractive and highlighted her figure by wearing extremely short miniskirts and fitted tops. She wondered why her students did not take her seriously. You can make choices that almost guarantee that such features do or do not become twirks for a given audience.

Presentational Aids

Sometimes, twirks result from the misuse of an aspect of delivery that typically would be considered useful in a presentation. Presentational aids can become twirks when they are of poor quality, are overused, and take too much attention away from the speaker. These conditions were discussed in the earlier section on presentational aids, but they are so important that they deserve discussion again.

If, because of poor quality, an aid does not fulfill its function—to *aid* in the understanding of the content of the presentation—it becomes a twirk. The chart that is too small to be seen or LCD projectors that do not have enough light output to project your images adequately are some situations in which presentational aids function as twirks. Rather than assisting in the full articulation of your perspective, these aids are likely to irritate your audience members and to decrease their attention to the perspective you are offering.

The overuse or excessive use of presentational aids also constitutes a twirk. When an excerpt from a movie consumes the time allotted for your entire presentation, your audiovisual aid is functioning as a twirk. Similarly, when you give audience members handouts that duplicate the screens of your PowerPoint presentation, you are overusing aids, and they lose their impact. Even using PowerPoint because "everyone else does" may be too much of a good thing when one speaker after another gives presentations that are very much the same in terms of graphics, layout, color schemes, and outlining formats. As a result, the presentational software not only loses its effectiveness but functions as a twirk.

The delivery of your presentation is more than the means by which your ideas are expressed. It is an additional resource available to you for creating an environment of safety, openness, freedom, and value and for enhancing the articulation of your perspective. Attention to the various components of delivery and how they can become twirks creates a presentation that helps your audience members both understand and remember your presentation.

10

Assessing Choices

You now have made decisions about all aspects of your presentation in terms of focus, frame, forms of elaboration, introduction and conclusion, transitions, and delivery. Your final task, before the actual delivery of your presentation, is to write your speaking plan. The speaking plan is an assessment tool you can use to evaluate the decisions you have made about your presentation. It summarizes what you plan to do in your presentation. As a representation of your understanding of your presentation, the speaking plan encourages you to think carefully about all of the components of your presentation. One way to think about this plan is as a path through your understanding of your ideas. Obviously, there are many presentations you give when you do not have the opportunity to write a speaking plan. If you are able to complete this step, however, it will tell you if what you have planned for your presentation will accomplish your interactional goal and if it will create the environment of safety, openness, freedom, and value required for transformation.

⌐ CREATING THE SPEAKING PLAN

Your speaking plan should include the 11 basic components of the process of creating a presentation:

1. **Audience**. Identify your audience.

2. **Setting**. Identify the setting for your presentation.

3. **Interactional goal**. State your interactional goal for the presentation. (Review pages 22–37.)

4. **Thesis statement**. Write a thesis statement that captures the perspective on your subject that you plan to develop in the presentation. (Review pages 55–58.)

5. **Organizational pattern**. State the organizational pattern you are using to organize your major ideas. (Review pages 66–76.)

6. **Major ideas.** State the major ideas you will develop in the presentation. This section is the most extensive part of your speaking plan because it includes the major and supporting ideas of your presentation. Many different formats exist for depicting the major ideas and the relationships among them. One way is to outline them. Translate your major and minor ideas into key words or phrases and arrange them hierarchically in groups of points and subpoints. Your major ideas are major headings, and the elaborations of them—the minor ideas—are subpoints under them in the outline.

   Sometimes, you will find that an outline form cannot capture the vision you have for your presentation because an outline requires that your ideas be structured in a linear, hierarchical way. In such a case, a visual diagram will serve you better than an outline to present your major ideas, their elaborations, and the relationships among them. A visual diagram involves summarizing your major ideas with key words and phrases and laying them out in the structure in which you see them related. Lines and arrows indicate the relationships among the ideas. Both forms of presenting major ideas are illustrated in the sample speaking plans that follow.

7. **Major forms of elaboration.** List the names of the forms of elaboration you use to develop your major ideas. (Review pages 78–93.)

8. **Introduction.** Indicate the type of introduction you are planning to use. (Review pages 95–100.)

9. **Conclusion.** Indicate the type of conclusion you are planning to use. (Review pages 100–105.)

10. **Transitions.** Write out the paragraph, sentence(s), or words you will use to move from the introduction to the body and from the body to the conclusion of your presentation. You will want to plan other transitions for moving between the main ideas and the forms of elaboration in the body of your presentation, but these do not need to be included in your speaking plan.

11. **Delivery.** List major strengths and weaknesses you bring to the delivery of your presentation. Strengths are aspects of your delivery that you believe will facilitate the accomplishment of your goals for the presentation and the creation of the conditions of safety, openness, freedom, and value. For example, you may see as strengths the audiovisual aid you have prepared, the amount of time you practice your presentations, and your ability to think on your feet to adapt to what is happening in the audience. Weaknesses are aspects of your delivery you want to eliminate or neutralize in your presentation because they make achieving your goals for your presentation more difficult. For example, you

may see as weaknesses your tendency to speak too softly, your speech anxiety, and the twirk of using *um* frequently.

⟶ SAMPLE SPEAKING PLANS

Below are seven sample speaking plans. They show different interactional goals, different styles of presenting major ideas, and a variety of organizational patterns and forms of elaboration.

Speaking Plan for "Who Is a True Friend?"

1. **Audience**. Junior-high-school students
2. **Setting**. Sunday school class
3. **Interactional goals**. To discover knowledge and belief, to articulate a perspective
4. **Thesis statement**. Let's develop a definition of friendship and see in what ways God can be a friend.
5. **Organizational pattern**. Multiple perspectives
6. **Major ideas**.
   I. Audience's perspectives on friendship
   II. My definition of friendship
      A. Someone who will respect what I say
      B. Someone who is there for me
   III. What the Bible says about friends
      A. Proverbs 18:24
      B. Proverbs 27:10
   IV. How we can be true friends
      A. Keep secrets
      B. Be trustworthy
   V. God is a trustworthy friend
7. **Major forms of elaboration**. Participation (discussion), comparison and contrast, definition, exaggeration, examples, questions (substantive)
8. **Introduction**. Reference to speaking situation (audience), questions (substantive)
9. **Conclusion**. Summary of basic theme
10. **Transitions**.
    I. **Transition from introduction to body**. These are all excellent ideas about friendship. I hold a similar perspective to yours on friendship.

    II. **Transition from body to conclusion.** At the beginning of my presentation, you shared with me your perspectives on friendship. I hope you can see how God can be a friend in much the same way to you.

11. **Delivery.**

    I. **Strengths.** I know the people in the audience well, so I'll feel comfortable asking them questions and presenting my perspective.

    II. **Weaknesses.** I tend to experience speech anxiety; frequent use of *um* is a twirk for me.

This speaking plan was adapted from one developed by Christa C. Porter at Ohio State University. The presentation for which this speaking plan was developed is included in the presentations at the end of the book.

Speaking Plan for "The Pre-Season Presentation"

1. **Audience.** Thirty soccer players, ranging in age from 16 to 18 years old

2. **Setting.** First day of school, August 20

3. **Interactional goal.** To build community

4. **Thesis statement.** If we work together, we can build an excellent team this year.

5. **Organizational pattern.** Category

6. **Major ideas.**

    I. We are getting better in all aspects of the game

        A. Practiced hard all summer

        B. Several experienced players

        C. Cohesive team

    II. My expectations for the team

        A. Play with a sense of urgency

            1. Anticipate and play with intensity

            2. Make each other better players

        B. Communicate on the field

            1. Let each other know where you are

            2. Move without the ball

        C. Special responsibilities for the seniors

            1. Step up and take responsibility

            2. Set an example

      III. Team goals for the season

        A. Improve individual scoring

        B. Place in regional tournament

        C. Have fun

7. **Major forms of elaboration.** Explanation, repetition, and restatement

8. **Introduction.** Reference to speaking situation (occasion)

9. **Conclusion.** Summary of main ideas

10. **Transitions.**

    I. **Transition from introduction to body.** We can have a winning season this year if we are willing to develop as a team in three areas: Play with a sense of urgency, communicate on the field, and expect our seniors to do a bit extra.

    II. **Transition from body to conclusion.** I have outlined some ambitious goals for the season, but I am confident that we can accomplish them.

11. **Delivery.**

    I. **Strengths.** Feel comfortable giving presentations; use lively bodily movement and gestures naturally

    II. **Weaknesses.** Have a tendency to go over my time limit; get so excited about my ideas that I sometimes forget to pay attention to my audience members and their perspectives

This speaking plan was adapted from one developed by Wes Zunker at the University of New Mexico.

Speaking Plan for "Violations of the Covenants"

1. **Audience.** Homeowners and representatives from Grubb and Ellis (Grubb and Ellis regulates the homeowner association for my subdivision)

2. **Setting.** A meeting for concerned homeowners to voice concerns to Grubb and Ellis

3. **Interactional goals.** Articulate a perspective, seek adherence, build community

4. **Thesis statement.** In my opinion, unintended and uncorrected violations of the covenants allow for the deterioration of the subdivision, and we should all work to see that these violations are corrected.

5. **Organizational pattern.** Metaphor

6. **Major ideas.**

    I.   Broken windows as metaphor for decline in neighborhood

    II. Explanation of broken-windows theory

    III. Examples of broken-windows theory

    IV. Violations of covenants in neighborhood as "broken windows"

7. **Major forms of elaboration.** Figure of speech (metaphor), sensory images, explanation, participation (discussion)

8. **Introduction.** Reference to speaking situation (audience)

9. **Conclusion.** Call to action

10. **Transitions.**

    I.   **Transition from introduction to body.** Unintended and uncorrected violations of the covenants allow for the deterioration of the subdivision, as the broken-window theory of community development suggests.

    II. **Transition from body to conclusion.** The broken-window theory suggests that broken windows are a metaphor for the decline of neighborhoods. So, too, the violations of the covenants of our community, if left unchecked, can lead to the decline of our community.

11. **Delivery.**

    I.   **Strengths.** I have a style of delivery that many people see as warm and friendly

    II. **Weaknesses.** My hair color may distract the audience; I tend to talk too fast

This speaking plan was adapted from one developed by Joanne Villa at the University of New Mexico.

Speaking Plan for "First Day of Class"

1. **Audience.** College students in an Anthropology 101 class

2. **Setting.** The first day of the semester

3. **Interactional goal.** Assert individuality, seek adherence

4. **Thesis statement.** I want to communicate my goals, assignments, and policies for Anthropology 101.

5. **Organizational pattern.** Web

6. **Major ideas.**

7. **Major forms of elaboration.** Definition, example, explanation, humor, audiovisual aids, credentials

8. **Introduction.** Questions (substantive), reference to speaking situation (audience, occasion)

9. **Conclusion.** Summary of main ideas

10. **Transitions.**
    I. **Transition from introduction to body.** I'd like to go over the syllabus now to see if you have any questions about the course and my expectations for you in this course.
    II. **Transition from body to conclusion.** These are my plans and expectations for the course.

11. **Delivery.**
    I. **Strengths.** I am able to speak conversationally while giving presentations; I move around the room to make my presentation lively
    II. **Weaknesses.** The fact that I'll be going over a syllabus may keep me too tied to this handout, diminishing my movement and eye contact

This speaking plan was adapted from one developed by Madalena Salazar at the University of New Mexico.

Speaking Plan for "Creating an Educational Foundation"

1. **Audience.** Crownpoint High School students
2. **Setting.** Student assembly
3. **Interactional goal.** To articulate a perspective

4. **Thesis statement**. It is important to create a firm educational foundation in preparation for college.

5. **Organizational pattern**. Problem-solution

6. **Major ideas**.

    I. Problem: Native Americans sometimes have difficulty in college

      A. Different values

      B. Lack of adequate preparation

      C. Lack of role models for success in college

    II. My perspective on education

      A. Education has always been important to me

        1. To set a good example for my younger sister and older brother

        2. To prove to my parents that I could do it

        3. To get a good job

    III. Solution: It's important to get a good education

      A. Take pride in who you are

      B. Don't let school get in the way of your education

      C. Approach each situation with a positive mind

      D. Do more than you are expected to do with any assignment you are given or any task you face

7. **Major forms of elaboration**. Examples, explanation, narratives

8. **Introduction**. Reference to speaking situation (self)

9. **Conclusion**. Call to action

10. **Transitions**.

    I. **Transition from introduction to body**. I once held the same view of education that most of you do. I've since developed a new perspective and would like to suggest that it's important to create a firm educational foundation in preparation for college.

    II. **Transition from body to conclusion**. I did the best I could when I was in high school to make good use of what my teachers had to offer, but I know now there were many other things I could have done. Taking pride in who you are, refusing to let school get in the way of your education, approaching each situation with a positive mind, and doing more than expected at any task are ways that anyone can create a firm educational foundation for college.

11. **Delivery.**

    I. **Strengths.** I'm enthusiastic about my subject, which should come out in my gestures and voice; I practice my presentations a lot so they flow easily

    II. **Weaknesses.** I don't have much vocal variation.

This speaking plan was adapted from one developed by Tracy J. Tsosie at the University of New Mexico.

Speaking Plan for "Medical School Interview"

1. **Audience.** Interviewers at medical school asking the question, "What influenced you to want to become a doctor?"

2. **Setting.** Office/small meeting room at medical school

3. **Interactional goal.** Assert individuality, seek adherence

4. **Thesis statement.** I want to share how my life experiences have led me to want to become a pediatrician.

5. **Organizational pattern.** Narrative progression

6. **Major ideas.**

    I. Babysitting

        A. Story about babysitting sick nephew

    II. Past volunteer work

        A. Story about work at Camp Fire day camp

        B. Story about volunteering at hospital

    III. Summer job

        A. Story about life guarding at swimming pool

    IV. Religious experience

        A. Story about experience at hospital chapel

    V. Education

        A. Story about fifth-grade science project

        B. Story about internship in college

    VI. Current volunteer work

        A. Story about work with Doctors Without Borders

7. **Major forms of elaboration.** Stories, questions (substantive)

8. **Introduction.** Reference to speaking situation (occasion)

9. **Conclusion.** Summary of main ideas

10. **Transitions.**

    I. **Transition from introduction to body.** What I hope to convey to you in the short time I have here is how my life experiences have led me to want to become a pediatrician.

    II. **Transition from body to conclusion.** I've told you a number of stories of various experiences I've had that show how my interest in becoming a pediatrician developed.

11. **Delivery.**

    I. **Strengths.** I know my stories well and have told them many times, so I should be able to tell them in a way that suggests my passion and excitement for my topic.

    II. **Weaknesses.** I have a tendency to keep going once I start, so I need to watch the time and pay attention to the response I'm getting from the interviewer as I tell the stories.

This speaking plan was adapted from one developed by Cuoghi Edens at the University of New Mexico.

Speaking Plan for "Increased Funding for the Colorado Council on the Arts"

1. **Audience.** Representatives in the Colorado legislature
2. **Setting.** Hearing room in state capital
3. **Interactional goal.** To articulate a perspective, to seek adherence
4. **Thesis statement.** There should be an increase in the legislature's appropriation to the Colorado Council on the Arts.
5. **Organizational pattern.** Circle
6. **Major ideas.**

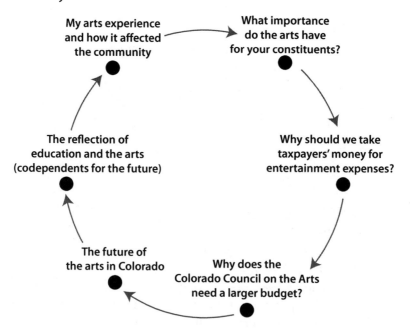

7. **Major forms of elaboration.** Explanation, examples, stories, audiovisual aids

8. **Introduction.** Narrative

9. **Conclusion.** Call to action.

10. **Transitions.**

    I. **Transition from introduction to body.** Why am I suggesting that the budget of the Colorado Council on the Arts be increased? Because of the importance of the arts for your constituencies.

    II. **Transition from body to conclusion.** I've suggested many reasons why the arts are important in our communities. That's why I'm asking for your support for an increase in the legislative appropriation to the Colorado Council on the Arts.

11. **Delivery.**

    I. **Strengths.** Visual aid provides a clear summary of the budget, so the audience will be able to understand my perspective easily; I practice my presentations a lot

    II. **Weaknesses.** I will experience speech anxiety because this is a very important presentation, and I've never testified before the legislature before. My hands tend to shake and my face turns red when I experience stage fright.

This speaking plan was adapted from one developed by Jason Renak at the University of Colorado Denver.

⁓ ASSESSING YOUR SPEAKING PLAN

Your speaking plan allows you to assess the results of your process of developing a presentation and to discover whether how you have planned the presentation matches up with the mental vision you have for it. It also allows you to do a final check of whether the options you have selected facilitate or impede the creation of an environment in which transformation may occur—whether they contribute to the creation of safety, openness, freedom, and value in the interaction. The following questions will help you determine if the various decisions you have made about your presentation create or inhibit possibilities for transformation. If a check of your speaking plan reveals any problems, this is the time to revise it. Do not be afraid to change or abandon parts of the plan and to change your presentation if you discover that some of the decisions you have made about your presentation do not contribute to the accomplishment of your goals for the interaction.

Audience. How carefully have you considered the characteristics of your audience members, their interest in this interaction, and their willingness to be changed as a result of it?

Setting. What have you done to minimize distracting environmental factors that might inhibit or negate your efforts at establishing the conditions of safety, openness, freedom, and value?

Interactional goal. Does your interactional goal promote the creation of conditions that maximize possibilities for transformation? If your audience members' interactional goals are at odds with creating a transformative environment, do you attempt to reshape their expectations, encouraging them to join you in working to create such an environment?

Thesis statement. Do you convey to audience members your willingness to yield your tentative commitments as a result of your interaction with them? Do you suggest that you are willing to follow the interaction wherever it goes and to be transformed in the process? In communicating your thesis statement, do you suggest that you value the commitments of audience members if they are different from yours?

Organizational pattern. Does your organizational pattern open or restrict the terms of the interaction? Does it enable audience members to participate, if they wish, in the interaction? Do you provide sufficient unity and coherence in your presentation so your audience members can follow you without difficulty and understand your perspective easily?

Major ideas. Do your major ideas communicate the essence of your perspective so that your audience members can understand it?

Forms of elaboration. Do your forms of elaboration provide sufficient development of your ideas so your audience members are able to understand your perspective? Are your forms of elaboration relevant to the ideas they develop so that the audience can understand those ideas? Are the feelings you evoke through your choice of forms of elaboration ones that facilitate or impede the possibility of transformation? Do your forms of elaboration silence other participants because they are presented, for example, in technical jargon? Do the forms of elaboration you have chosen encompass sufficient variety so that they maintain audience members' interest in hearing about your perspective?

Introduction. Does your introduction function to orient your audience to your topic and begin to establish the conditions of safety, openness, freedom, and value?

Conclusion. Does your conclusion function to reemphasize your main idea and convey what you would like to have happen next in the interaction?

Transitions. Do the transitions you are planning for your presentation move you from the introduction to the body and from the body to the conclusion so that audience members can follow your ideas and thus understand your perspective easily?

Delivery. How do you plan to use the strengths you've identified concerning your delivery to facilitate your goals for your presentation? How are the weaknesses you've identified likely to have negative impacts on your presentation? What can you do to ensure that you minimize them as much as possible?

You now have the basic information you need to create and deliver a presentation that invites your audience members to consider your perspective and that facilitates your understanding of their perspectives. You know the characteristics of the invitational mode of rhetoric in which to frame your presentation; the options you have for interactional goals in presentations; and how to create a speaking environment of safety, openness, freedom, and value. You know how to develop your thesis statement, how to form your ideas into an organizational frame, and how to elaborate those ideas in various ways. You have completed the frame of your presentation with an introduction and a conclusion and know the importance of transitions to disclose the frame of your presentation to your audience. If your choices in these areas contribute to the creation of safety, openness, freedom, and value, the interaction that results as your audience members respond to your invitation will enable everyone involved to understand one another better and to consider choosing to change. The result will be further conversations that produce greater understanding, more creative solutions to problems, and ever more opportunities for transformation.

Sample Presentations

Asserting Individuality

Retailing Clothing and Cosmetics:
Response to an Interview Question

Liz Stroben
Student, Ohio State University

In this presentation, Liz Stroben is responding to a question as part of an interview for a position with a retail firm that sells clothing and cosmetics. The question is: "What inspired you or led you to pursue a career in women's fashion and cosmetics?"

When I think back over my life and my experience, three specific times in my life come to mind that have emphasized my interest in a career in retail. First, when I was about five years old, my mom took me to an antique shop owned by a friend of hers. As you know, antique stores are often small and have lots of objects in them—lots of glass, lots of plates, lots of things that are breakable. As you can imagine, my mom was watching me closely so I didn't run around too much. But I was mesmerized by one table, and as my mom and her friend were talking, they realized that I had started to arrange the different items on the table. They didn't say anything to me because I was being very careful in moving the things around and doing so very slowly. When I was done, they asked me, "Liz, why did you rearrange that table?" And I said, "Well, I like it this way." My mom's friend looked at it and said, "I like it, too—but I can't believe a five-year-old is merchandising my antique store."

This presentation was given at Ohio State University, Columbus, Ohio, spring 1993. Used by permission of Liz Stroben.

She led me around that day to different tables, and I got to arrange them as well. From the age of five through high school, then, I went twice a month to her store and did all of her displays as well as some designs for her customers who wanted ideas for how to arrange their furniture and antiques. This experience really helped me later on as I moved into my official retailing career, where I did floor plans and rearranged stores to help customers find things more easily and to help sales. That was my start in the retailing business.

Around the age of 12 or 13—the age when a lot of young women get into clothing and make-up—my friends and I were no different. Every Friday, we'd go to a different person's house, and we'd do what we called *fashion show*. We'd all bring our suitcases with a bunch of clothes, and we'd mix and match them and play fashion show. I was the person who would create the different outfits for everybody. So, again, I learned how to put things together—colors and textures—and I also learned something that really helped me later. I learned that I really like working with people, and I like helping clients choose things for themselves. That's what helped me later on when I worked in various stores. I really enjoy customer contact and the positive feedback from the people I've helped. This experience, then, pretty much solidified the fact that I was going to stay in retailing.

The most recent experience—and probably the most important experience that confirmed my interest in fashion retailing—was my work with Calvin Klein. This was an official working position. It wasn't playtime or me at the age of five. And what I learned in this position was that you really can combine clothing and cosmetics in a single business because, as you know, they have a couture line, a sportswear line, and a cosmetics and fragrance line. At Calvin Klein, I also learned that clothing is not just an outer shell. When you see someone, you think, "Oh, they have a sweater on," or "Oh, they have a T-shirt on." But clothing and cosmetics are not just a superficial way of expressing your personality. They are really an expression of you; they are not just something superficial. Most women and most men don't do clothing for someone else—they do it for themselves—as a way to express their personalities.

Obviously, my most recent experience has been with you as a summer intern, and this work has had the most impact on my career thus far. It has been an incredible learning experience because it has been my first time working in a corporate setting instead of in the store setting with clients. The personnel have been incredible; they are really, really supportive; they've helped me any time I've asked; and they answered any questions I had, no matter how trivial; and they made me feel important. Your company image is very much in keeping with the image that I have for the kind of place in which I'd like to work. Not only do you have a clothing line, but you have also added a new division—a cosmetics and body-care line.

One of the questions you asked me earlier and that I'd like to incorporate into this answer as well is, "Would I be the right person for this job?" I believe that I've explained how, from a very early age, I've had the inclination and the desire to design, to arrange things, and to sell things. These have been very important to me, and I'd like to keep doing them as part of your company.

Exhibiting With Pride

Janet K. Hughes
Artist

This presentation was given as part of a panel discussion of artists whose work had been selected for inclusion in the Missouri Visual Artists' Biennial. The artists were asked to discuss their work prior to the opening of the exhibition.

She's an exhibitionist
She exhibits with pride
She exhibits her work in the Missouri Visual Artists' Biennial.

She collected her thoughts
    dust
    and her award.

She means what she says
She means well
She now has the means to continue and expand her work.

For her it was a time of renewal
She renewed her spirit
    an old acquaintance
    and her contract at Indiana State University.

She moved from private to public
and enjoyed the exposure.
The exposure was wide.
She exposed herself.
She was well read.

She became widely read.
She painted the town
    the picture
    and her lips.
Her lips were read.
Her lips were red.

She moved from the margin
Into the center
And preferred the view.

This presentation was given at the University of Missouri, Columbia, Missouri, March 5, 1993. Used by permission of Janet K. Hughes.

I am a Man, a Black Man, an American

Clarence Thomas
Justice, US Supreme Court

Thirty years ago, we all focused intently on this city as the trauma of Dr. King's death first exploded, then sank into our lives. For so many of us who were trying hard to do what we thought was required of us in the process of integrating this society, the rush of hopelessness and isolation was immediate and overwhelming. It seemed that the whole world had gone mad.

I am certain that each of us has his or her memories of that terrible day in 1968. For me it was the final straw in the struggle to retain my vocation to become a Catholic priest. Suddenly, this cataclysmic event ripped me from the moorings of my grandparents, my youth and my faith and catapulted me headlong into the abyss that Richard Wright seemed to describe years earlier.

It was this event that shattered my faith in my religion and my country. I had spent the mid-'60s as a successful student in a virtually white environment. I had learned Latin, physics and chemistry. I had accepted the loneliness that came with being "the integrator," the first and the only. But this event, this trauma I could not take, especially when one of my fellow seminarians, not knowing that I was standing behind him, declared that he hoped the SOB died. This was a man of God, mortally stricken by an assassin's bullet, and one preparing for the priesthood had wished evil upon him.

The life I had dreamed of so often during those hot summers on the farm in Georgia or during what seemed like endless hours on the oil truck with my grandfather expired as Dr. King expired. As so many of you do, I still know exactly where I was when I heard the news. It was a low moment in our nation's history and a demarcation between hope and hopelessness for many of us.

But three decades have evaporated in our lives, too quickly and without sufficient residual evidence of their importance. But much has changed since then. The hope that there would be expeditious resolutions to our myriad problems has long since evaporated with those years. Many who debated and hoped then now do neither. There now seems to be a broad acceptance of the racial divide as a permanent state. While we once celebrated those things that we had in common with our fellow citizens who did not share our race, so many now are triumphal about our differences, finding little, if anything, in common. Indeed, some go so far as to all but define each of us by our race and establish the range of our thinking and our opinions, if not our deeds by our color.

This presentation was given to the National Bar Association, Memphis, Tennessee, July 29, 1998. Available at http://douglass.speech.nwu.edu/thom_b30.htm

I, for one, see this in much the same way I saw our denial of rights—as nothing short of a denial of our humanity. Not one of us has the gospel. Nor are our opinions based upon some revealed precepts to be taken as faith. As thinking, rational individuals, not one of us can claim infallibility, even from the overwhelming advantage of hindsight and Monday morning quarterbacking.

This makes it all the more important that our fallible ideas be examined as all ideas are in the realm of reason, not as some doctrinal or racial heresy. None of us—none of us have been appointed by God or appointed God. And if any of us has, then my question is why hasn't he or she solved all these problems.

I make no apologies for this view now, nor do I intend to do so in the future. I have now been on the court for seven terms. For the most part, it has been much like other endeavors in life. It has its challenges and requires much of the individual to master the workings of the institution. We all know that. It is, I must say, quite different from what I might have anticipated if I had the opportunity to do so. Unlike the unfortunate practice or custom in Washington and in much of the country, the court is a model of civility. It's a wonderful place. Though there have been many contentious issues to come before the court during these initial years of my tenure, I have yet to hear the first unkind words exchanged among my colleagues. And quite frankly, I think that such civility is the sine qua non of conducting the affairs of the court and the business of the country.

As such, I think that it would be in derogation of our respective oaths and our institutional obligations to our country to engage in uncivil behavior. It would also be demeaning to any of us who engaged in such conduct. Having worn the robe, we have a lifetime obligation to conduct ourselves as having deserved to wear the robe in the first instance.

One of the interesting surprises is the virtual isolation, even within the court. It is quite rare that the members of the court see each other during those periods when we're not sitting or when we're not in conference. And the most regular contact beyond those two formal events are the lunches we have on conference and court days. Also, it is extraordinarily rare to have any discussions with the other members of the court before voting on petitions for certiorari or on the merits of the cases. And there is rarely extended debate during our conferences. For the most part, any debate about the cases is done in writing. It has struck me as odd that some think that there are cliques and cabals at the court. No such arrangements exist. Nor, contrary to suggestions otherwise, is there any intellectual or ideological pied piper on the court.

With respect to my following, or, more accurately, being led by other members of the Court, that is silly, but expected since I couldn't possibly think for myself. And what else could possibly be the explanation when I fail to follow the jurisprudential, ideological and intellectual, if not anti-intellectual, prescription assigned to blacks. Since thinking beyond this prescription is presumptively beyond my abilities, obviously someone must be putting these strange ideas into my mind and my opinions.

Though being underestimated has its advantages, the stench of racial inferiority still confounds my olfactory nerves.

As Ralph Ellison wrote more than 35 years ago, "Why is it so often true that when critics confront the American as Negro, they suddenly drop their advance critical armament and revert with an air of confident superiority to quite primitive modes of analysis?" Those matters accomplished by whites are routinely subjected to sophisticated modes of analysis. But when the selfsame matters are accomplished by blacks, the opaque racial prism of analysis precludes such sophistication and all is seen in black and white. And some who would not venture onto the more sophisticated analytical turf are quite content to play in the minor leagues of primitive harping. The more things change, the more they remain the same.

Of course there is much criticism of the court by this group or that, depending on the court's decisions in various highly publicized cases. Some of the criticism is profoundly uninformed and unhelpful. And all too often, uncivil second-guessing is not encumbered by the constraints of facts, logic or reasoned analysis. On the other hand, the constructive and often scholarly criticism is almost always helpful in thinking about or rethinking decisions. It is my view that constructive criticism goes with the turf, especially when the stakes are so high and the cases arouse passions and emotions, and, in a free society, the precious freedom of speech and the strength of ideas. We at the court could not possibly claim exemption from such criticism. Moreover, we are not infallible, just final.

As I have noted, I find a thoughtful, analytical criticism most helpful. I do not think any judge can address a vast array of cases and issues without testing and re-testing his or her reasoning and opinions in the crucible of debate. However, since we are quite limited in public debate about matters that may come before the court, such debate must, for the most part, occur intramurally, thus placing a premium on outside scholarship. Unfortunately, from time to time, the criticism of the court goes beyond the bounds of civil debate and discourse. Today it seems quite acceptable to attack the court and other institutions when one disagrees with an opinion or policy. I can still remember traveling along Highway 17 in south Georgia, the Coastal Highway, during the '50s and '60s and seeing the "Impeach Earl Warren" signs.

Clearly, heated reactions to the court or to its members are not unusual. Certainly, Justice Blackmun was attacked repeatedly because many disagreed, as I have, with the opinion he offered on behalf of the Court in Roe vs. Wade. Though I have joined opinions disagreeing with Justice Blackmun, I could not imagine ever being discourteous to him merely because we disagreed.

I have found during my almost 20 years in Washington that the tendency to personalize differences has grown to be an accepted way of doing business. One need not do the hard work of dissecting an argument. One need only attack and thus discredit the person making the argument. Though the matter being debated is not effectively resolved, the debate is reduced to unilateral pronouncements and glib but quotable clichés. I, for one, have been singled out for particularly bilious and venomous assaults. These criticisms, as near as I can tell, and I admit that it is rare that I take notice of this calumny, have little to do with any particular opinion, though each opinion does provide one more occasion to criticize. Rather, the principal problem seems to be a deeper antecedent offense.

I have no right to think the way I do because I'm black. Though the ideas and opinions themselves are not necessarily illegitimate if held by non-black individuals, they, and the person enunciating them, are illegitimate if that person happens to be black. Thus, there's a subset of criticism that must of necessity be reserved for me, even if every non-black member of the court agrees with the idea or the opinion. You see, they are exempt from this kind of criticism, precisely because they are not black. As noted earlier, they are more often than not subjected to the whites-only sophisticated analysis.

I will not catalogue my opinions to which there have been objections since they are a matter of public record. But I must note in passing that I can't help but wonder if some of my critics can read. One opinion that is trotted out for propaganda, for the propaganda parade, is my dissent in Hudson vs. McMillian. The conclusion reached by the long arms of the critics is that I supported the beating of prisoners in that case. Well, one must either be illiterate or fraught with malice to reach that conclusion. Though one can disagree with my dissent, and certainly the majority of the court disagreed, no honest reading can reach such a conclusion. Indeed, we took the case to decide the quite narrow issue whether a prisoner's rights were violated under the "cruel and unusual punishment" clause of the Eighth Amendment as a result of a single incident of force by the prison guards which did not cause a significant injury. In the first section of my dissent, I stated the following. "In my view, a use of force that causes only insignificant harm to a prisoner may be immoral; it may be tortuous; it may be criminal, and it may even be remediable under other provisions of the Federal Constitution. But it is not cruel and unusual punishment."

Obviously, beating prisoners is bad. But we did not take the case to answer this larger moral question or a larger legal question of remedies under other statutes or provisions of the Constitution. How one can extrapolate these larger conclusions from the narrow question before the court is beyond me, unless, of course, there's a special segregated mode of analysis.

It should be obvious that the criticism of this opinion serves not to present counter-arguments, but to discredit and attack me because I've deviated from the prescribed path. In his intriguing and thoughtful essay on "My Race Problem and Ours," Harvard law professor Randall Kennedy, a self-described Social Democrat, correctly observes that "If racial loyalty is deemed essentially and morally virtuous, then a black person's adoption of positions that are deemed racially disloyal will be seen by racial loyalists as a supremely threatening sin, one warranting the harsh punishments that have historically been visited upon alleged traitors." Perhaps this is the defensive solidarity to which Richard Wright refers. If so, it is a reaction I understand, but resolutely decline to follow.

In the final weeks of my seminary days, shortly after Dr. King's death, I found myself becoming consumed by feelings of animosity and anger. I was disenchanted with my church and my country. I was tired of being in the minority, and I was tired of turning the other cheek. I, along with many blacks, found ways to protest and try to change the treatment we received in this country. Perhaps my passion for Richard Wright novels was affecting me. Perhaps it was listening too intently to Nina Simone. Perhaps, like Bigger Thomas, I was being consumed by the circumstances in which I found myself, circumstances that I saw as responding only to race.

My feelings were reaffirmed during the summer of 1968 as a result of the lingering stench of racism in Savannah and the assassination of Bobby Kennedy. No matter what the reasons were, I closed out the '60s as one angry young man waiting on the revolution that I was certain would soon come. I saw no way out. I, like many others, felt the deep chronic agony of anomie and alienation. All seemed to be defined by race. We became a reaction to the "man," his ominous reflection.

The intensity of my feelings was reinforced by other events of the late '60s, the riots, the marches, the sense that something had to be done, done quickly to resolve the issue of race. In college there was an air of excitement, apprehension and anger. We started the Black Students Union. We protested. We worked in the Free Breakfast Program. We would walk out of school in the winter of 1969 in protest.

But the questioning for me started in the spring of 1970 after an unauthorized demonstration in Cambridge, Mass., to "free the political prisoners." Why was I doing this rather than using my intellect? Perhaps I was empowered by the anger and relieved that I could now strike back at the faceless oppressor. But why was I conceding my intellect and rather fighting much like a brute? This I could not answer, except to say that I was tired of being restrained. Somehow I knew that unless I contained the anger within me I would suffer the fates of Bigger Thomas and Damon Cross. It was intoxicating to act upon one's rage, to wear it on one's shoulder, to be defined by it. Yet, ultimately, it was destructive, and I knew it.

So in the spring of 1970 in a nihilistic fog, I prayed that I'd be relieved of the anger and the animosity that ate at my soul. I did not want to hate any more, and I had to stop before it totally consumed me. I had to make a fundamental choice. Do I believe in the principles of this country or not? After such angst, I concluded that I did. But the battle between passion and reason would continue, although abated, still intense.

Ironically, many of the people who are critics today were among those we called half-steppers, who had [been] co-opted by "the man" because they were part of the system that oppressed us. When the revolution came, all of the so-called Negroes needed to be dealt with. It is interesting to remember that someone gave me a copy of Prof. Thomas Sowell's book, *Education, Myths and Tragedies,* in which he predicted much of what has happened to blacks and education. I threw it in the trash, unread, declaring that he was not a black man since no black could take the positions that he had taken, whatever they were, since I had only heard his views were not those of a black man.

I was also upset to hear of a black conservative in Virginia named Jay Parker. How could a black man call himself a conservative? In a twist of fate, they both are dear friends today, and the youthful wrath I visited upon them is now being visited upon me, though without the youth. What goes around does indeed come around.

The summer of 1971 was perhaps one of the most difficult of my life. It was clear to me that the road to destruction was paved with anger, resentment and rage. But where were we to go? I would often spend hours in our small efficiency apartment in New Haven pondering this question and listening to Marvin Gaye's then new album, "What's Going On?" To say the least, it was a depressing summer.

What were we to do? What's going on?

As I think back on those years, I find it interesting that many people seemed to have trouble with their identities as black men. Having had to accept my blackness in the cauldron of ridicule from some of my black schoolmates under segregation, then immediately thereafter remain secure in that identity during my years at an all-white seminary, I had few racial identity problems. I knew who I was and needed no gimmicks to affirm my identity. Nor, might I add, do I need anyone telling me who I am today. This is especially true of the psycho-silliness about forgetting my roots or self-hatred. If anything, this shows that some people have too much time on their hands.

There's a rush today to prescribe who is black, to prescribe what our differences are or to ignore what our differences are. Of course, those of us who came from the rural South were different from the blacks who came from the large northern cities, such as Philadelphia and New York. We were all black. But that similarity did not mask the richness of our differences. Indeed, one of the advantages of growing up in a black neighborhood was that we were richly blessed with the ability to see the individuality of each black person with all its fullness and complexity. We saw those differences at school, at home, at church, and definitely at the barbershop on Saturday morning.

Intraracially, we consistently recognized our differences. It is quite counter-factual to suggest that such differences have not existed throughout our history. Indeed, when I was on the other side of the ideological divide, arguing strenuously with my grandfather that the revolution was imminent and that we all had to stick together as black people, he was quick to remind me that he had lived much longer than I had and during far more difficult times, and that, in any case, it took all kinds to make a world.

I agree with Ralph Ellison when he asked, perhaps rhetorically, why is it that so many of those who would tell us the meaning of "Negro," of Negro life, never bothered to learn how varied it really is. That is particularly true of many whites who have elevated condescension to an art form by advancing a monolithic view of blacks in much the same way that the mythic, disgusting image of the lazy, dumb black was advanced by open, rather than disguised, bigots. Today, of course, it is customary to collapse, if not overwrite, our individual characteristics into new, but now acceptable stereotypes. It no longer matters when one is from urban New York City or rural Georgia. It doesn't matter whether we came from a highly educated family or a barely literate one. It does not matter if you are a Roman Catholic or a Southern Baptist. All of these differences are canceled by race, and a revised set of acceptable stereotypes has been put in place.

Long gone is the time when we opposed the notion that we all looked alike and talked alike. Somehow we have come to exalt the new black stereotype above all and to demand conformity to that norm. It is this notion that our race defines us that Ralph Ellison so eloquently rebuts in his essay, "The World and the Jug." He sees the lives of black people as more than a burden, but also a discipline, just as any human life which has endured so long is a discipline, teaching its own insights into the human condition, its own strategies of survival. There's a fullness and even a richness here. And here despite the realities of politics, perhaps, but nevertheless here and real because it is human life.

Despite some of the nonsense that has been said about me by those who should know better, and so much nonsense, or some of which subtracts from the sum total of human knowledge, despite this all, I am a man, a black man, an American. And my history is not unlike that of many blacks from the deep South. And in many ways it is not that much different from that of many other Americans. It goes without saying that I understand the comforts and security of racial solidarity, defensive or otherwise. Only those who have not been set upon by hatred and repelled by rejection fail to understand its attraction. As I have suggested, I have been there.

The inverse relationship between the bold promises and the effectiveness of the proposed solutions, the frustrations with the so-called system, the subtle and not-so-subtle bigotry and animus towards members of my race made radicals and nationalists of many of us. Yes, I understand the reasons why this is attractive. But it is precisely this in its historic form, not its present-day diluted form, that I have rejected. My question was whether as an individual I truly believed that I was the equal of individuals who were white. This I had answered with a resounding "yes" in 1964 during my sophomore year in the seminary. And that answer continues to be yes. Accordingly, my words and my deeds are consistent with this answer.

Any effort, policy or program that has as a prerequisite the acceptance of the notion that blacks are inferior is a non-starter with me. I do not believe that kneeling is a position of strength. Nor do I believe that begging is an effective tactic. I am confident that the individual approach, not the group approach, is the better, more acceptable, more supportable and less dangerous one. This approach is also consistent with the underlying principles of this country and the guarantees of freedom through government by consent. I, like Frederick Douglass, believe that whites and blacks can live together and be blended into a common nationality.

Do I believe that my views or opinions are perfect or infallible? No, I do not. But in admitting that I have no claim to perfection or infallibility, I am also asserting that competing or differing views similarly have no such claim. And they should not be accorded a status of infallibility or any status that suggests otherwise.

With differing, but equally fallible views, I think it is best that they be aired and sorted out in an environment of civility, consistent with the institutions in which we are involved. In this case, the judicial system.

It pains me deeply, or more deeply than any of you can imagine to be perceived by so many members of my race as doing them harm. All the sacrifice, all the long hours of preparation were to help, not to hurt. But what hurts more, much more is the amount of time and attention spent on manufactured controversies and media sideshows when so many problems cry out for constructive attention.

I have come here today not in anger or to anger, though my mere presence has been sufficient, obviously, to anger some. Nor have I come to defend my views, but rather to assert my right to think for myself, to refuse to have my ideas assigned to me as though I was an intellectual slave because I'm black. I come to state that I'm a man, free to think for myself and do as I please.

I've come to assert that I am a judge and I will not be consigned the unquestioned opinions of others. But even more than that, I have come to say that isn't it time to move on? Isn't it time to realize that being angry with me solves no problems? Isn't it time to acknowledge that the problem of race has defied simple solutions and that not one of us, not a single one of us can lay claim to the solution? Isn't it time that we respect ourselves and each other as we have demanded respect from others? Isn't it time to ignore those whose sole occupation is sowing seeds of discord and animus? That is self-hatred.

Isn't it time to continue diligently to search for lasting solutions?

I believe that the time has come today. God bless each of you, and may God keep you.

Articulating a Perspective

City Planning as a Career

Andrea Armstrong
Student, Ohio State University

In this presentation, Andrea Armstrong assumed the role of a city planner, speaking to first-grade students on career day.

Hi, I'm Ms. Armstrong, and I'm a city planner for the city of Columbus. I'd like to ask you a couple questions. Do any of you have a favorite city?

Student: Columbus.

Columbus? Anybody else?

Student: Chicago.

Chicago? Yes?

Student: Las Vegas.

What do you all like about Columbus, since that's where we're living right now?

Student: The zoo.

Student: I like the playgrounds.

The playgrounds? Anything else?

Student: It doesn't take long to get anywhere.

Student: The fair.

The fair—the state fair. You like going to the fair? I like going to the fair, too. OK, those are some of the things you like about Columbus, but a long time ago, cities weren't such nice places to be. There were a lot of factories, there was a lot of smoke, cities were crowded, and there weren't very many parks. Kids actually used to have to play in cemeteries because there weren't parks in their neighborhoods to play in—that was the only green space they could find. That was before planning. What planners try to do is to make places nicer for people. They make cities places where people want to live and want to be.

Planners try to make cities better in a lot of different ways. For instance, they try to decide where schools should be. They try to make sure that there are enough parks and playgrounds in neighborhoods for families and friends to play in. They have to make sure there are police and fire services for everyone in the city. They need to make sure that there are enough water lines and sewer lines. They have to make sure that buildings are built correctly.

This presentation was given at Ohio State University, Columbus, Ohio, spring 1993. Used by permission of Andrea Armstrong.

City planners have to know a lot about a lot of things. They have to know about law because they have to know laws that affect where and how things can be built. City planners also have to be good public speakers because they have to explain ideas and plans to people. They need to be architects and engineers—they need to know how things are built and how they can be built. They need to be computer users; they use computers to figure things out. They need to be demographers—they need to know how to use numbers and statistics and to figure out how many people are in cities.

City planners also need to be mapmakers. I've brought along a few of the maps I use at work every day. These are the kinds of maps that planners use and make. The first map is an annexation map. Annexation is how a city grows—how it gets more land. The purple area in this map shows Columbus in 1900; that's all the bigger Columbus was in 1900. If any of you have a grandmother who is 93 years old, that's how big Columbus was when she was born. Today, Columbus is as big as all the areas that are colored on this map. Planners need to know this, and they need to be able to provide services in all these areas. They need to make sure that there are police, fire, water, and roads and everything for all this area.

Your school is in this area, near the river. City planners need to know where the flood plain is for the river. We have something called 100- and 500-year floods. That means that we have a 1-in-100 chance to get a flood or a 1-in-500 chance to get a flood, which means the river will go outside of its banks. We need to know this so we don't build in those flood plains—people lose their houses and belongings if they do. Ohio State University's campus is located right here. It is in part of the flood plain, so part of this land may flood. We need to know that ahead of time.

This map shows flight contours for the airport, which is west of town—Port Columbus Airport. Every line on here is how loud the noise is from the air traffic in the air. We need to know this because nobody wants to live within these noise contours because it's loud, it hurts our ears, it's not good for our health. We need to make sure we don't build in those areas—it's not good for us.

Finally, we need to know where fire stations are located in our city. We need to make sure that if your house catches on fire, there's a fire station nearby that will be able to put the fire out. All the red circles are Columbus fire stations.

There are planning issues going on now that you might have heard about in the news or from your parents. The Tuttle Crossing area is a planning issue in Columbus. This is a mall that's being developed on the north side of town. It involves city planners who are trying to do all the things necessary to make sure the mall is a nice place.

So, planners do a lot of different things in their jobs. They have to know a lot of different things. Planning is a good profession for people who are curious. So, if you're a curious person and like to do a lot of different things, planning might be a profession for you someday.

A More Perfect Union

Barack Obama
US President

Thank you so much. Thank you. Thank you. Thank you so much. Thank you. Thank you. Let me begin by thanking Harris Wofford for his contributions to this country. In so many different ways, he exemplifies what we mean by the word *citizen*. And so we are very grateful to him for all the work he has done; and I'm thankful for the gracious and thoughtful introduction.

"We the people, in order to form a more perfect union." Two-hundred-and-twenty-one years ago, in a hall that still stands across the street, a group of men gathered and, with these simple words, launched America's improbable experiment in democracy. Farmers and scholars, statesmen and patriots who had traveled across the ocean to escape tyranny and persecution finally made real their Declaration of Independence at a Philadelphia convention that lasted through the spring of 1787.

The document they produced was eventually signed but ultimately unfinished. It was stained by this nation's original sin of slavery, a question that divided the colonies and brought the convention to a stalemate until the founders chose to allow the slave trade to continue for at least 20 more years and to leave any final resolution to future generations. Of course, the answer to the slavery question was already embedded within our Constitution—a Constitution that had at its very core the ideal of equal citizenship under the law—a Constitution that promised its people liberty and justice and a union that could be and should be perfected over time.

And yet words on a parchment would not be enough to deliver slaves from bondage or provide men and women of every color and creed their full rights and obligations as citizens of the United States. What would be needed were Americans in successive generations who were willing to do their part—through protests and struggles, on the streets and in the courts, through a civil war and civil disobedience, and always at great risk—to narrow that gap between the promise of our ideals and the reality of their time.

This was one of the tasks we set forth at the beginning of this presidential campaign: to continue the long march of those who came before us, a march for a more just, more equal, more free, more caring, and more prosperous America. I chose to run for president at this moment in history because I believe deeply that we cannot solve the challenges of our time unless we solve them together—unless we perfect our union by understanding that we may have different stories, but we hold common

This presentation was delivered in Philadelphia, Pennsylvania, on March 18, 2008. A video of the presentation can be viewed at http://www.barackobama.com/2008/03/18/remarks_of_senator_barack_obama_53.php

hopes; that we may not look the same and may not have come from the same place, but we all want to move in the same direction: towards a better future for our children and our grandchildren. And this belief comes from my unyielding faith in the decency and generosity of the American people. But it also comes from my own story.

I'm the son of a black man from Kenya and a white woman from Kansas. I was raised with the help of a white grandfather who survived a Depression to serve in Patton's army during World War II and a white grandmother who worked on a bomber assembly line at Fort Leavenworth while he was overseas. I've gone to some of the best schools in America, and I've lived in one of the world's poorest nations. I am married to a black American who carries within her the blood of slaves and slave owners, an inheritance we pass on to our two precious daughters. I have brothers, sisters, nieces, nephews, uncles, and cousins of every race and every hue scattered across three continents. And for as long as I live, I will never forget that in no other country on earth is my story even possible. It's a story that hasn't made me the most conventional of candidates. But it is a story that has seared into my genetic makeup the idea that this nation is more than the sum of its parts—that out of many, we are truly one.

Now throughout the first year of this campaign, against all predictions to the contrary, we saw how hungry the American people were for this message of unity. Despite the temptation to view my candidacy through a purely racial lens, we won commanding victories in states with some of the whitest populations in the country. In South Carolina, where the Confederate flag still flies, we built a powerful coalition of African Americans and white Americans. This is not to say that race has not been an issue in this campaign. At various stages in the campaign, some commentators have deemed me either "too black" or "not black enough." We saw racial tensions bubble to the surface during the week before the South Carolina primary. The press has scoured every single exit poll for the latest evidence of racial polarization, not just in terms of white and black but black and brown as well.

And yet, it's only been in the last couple of weeks that the discussion of race in this campaign has taken a particularly divisive turn. On one end of the spectrum, we've heard the implication that my candidacy is somehow an exercise in affirmative action—that it's based solely on the desire of wild and wide-eyed liberals to purchase racial reconciliation on the cheap. On the other end, we've heard my former pastor, Jeremiah Wright, use incendiary language to express views that have the potential not only to widen the racial divide but views that denigrate both the greatness and the goodness of our nation and that rightly offend white and black alike.

Now I've already condemned, in unequivocal terms, the statements of Reverend Wright that have caused such controversy and, in some cases, pain. For some, nagging questions remain: Did I know him to be an occasionally fierce critic of American domestic and foreign policy? Of course. Did I ever hear him make remarks that could be considered controversial while I sat in the church? Yes. Did I strongly disagree with many of his political views? Absolutely, just as I'm sure many of you have heard remarks from your pastors, priests, or rabbis with which you strongly disagree.

But the remarks that have caused this recent firestorm weren't simply controversial. They weren't simply a religious leader's efforts to speak out against perceived injustice. Instead, they expressed a profoundly distorted view of this country—a view that sees white racism as endemic and that elevates what is wrong with America above all that we know is right with America, a view that sees the conflicts in the Middle East as rooted primarily in the actions of stalwart allies like Israel instead of emanating from the perverse and hateful ideologies of radical Islam.

As such, Reverend Wright's comments were not only wrong but divisive, divisive at a time when we need unity—racially charged at a time when we need to come together to solve a set of monumental problems: two wars, a terrorist threat, a falling economy, a chronic health-care crisis, and potentially devastating climate change—problems that are neither black or white or Latino or Asian but rather problems that confront us all.

Given my background, my politics, and my professed values and ideals, there will no doubt be those for whom my statements of condemnation are not enough. Why associate myself with Reverend Wright in the first place?, they may ask. Why not join another church? And I confess that if all that I knew of Reverend Wright were the snippets of those sermons that have run in an endless loop on the television sets and You-Tube, if Trinity United Church of Christ conformed to the caricatures being peddled by some commentators, there is no doubt that I would react in much the same way.

But the truth is that isn't all that I know of the man. The man I met more than 20 years ago is a man who helped introduce me to my Christian faith, a man who spoke to me about our obligations to love one another, to care for the sick and lift up the poor. He is a man who served his country as a United States Marine and who has studied and lectured at some of the finest universities and seminaries in the country and who over 30 years has led a church that serves the community by doing God's work here on Earth—by housing the homeless, ministering to the needy, providing day-care services and scholarships and prison ministries, and reaching out to those suffering from HIV/AIDS.

In my first book, *Dreams from My Father*, I described the experience of my first service at Trinity, and it goes as follows:

> People began to shout, to rise from their seats and clap and cry out, a forceful wind carrying the reverend's voice up to the rafters.
>
> And in that single note—hope—I heard something else; at the foot of that cross, inside the thousands of churches across the city, I

imagined the stories of ordinary black people merging with the stories of David and Goliath, Moses and Pharaoh, the Christians in the lion's den, Ezekiel's field of dry bones.

Those stories of survival and freedom and hope became our stories, my story. The blood that spilled was our blood; the tears our tears; until this black church, on this bright day, seemed once more a vessel carrying the story of a people into future generations and into a larger world. Our trials and triumphs became at once unique and universal, black and more than black. In chronicling our journey, the stories and songs gave us a meaning to reclaim memories that we didn't need to feel shame about—memories that all people might study and cherish and with which we could start to rebuild.

That has been my experience at Trinity. Like other predominantly black churches across the country, Trinity embodies the black community in its entirety—the doctor and the welfare mom, the model student and the former gang-banger. Like other black churches, Trinity's services are full of raucous laughter and sometimes bawdy humor. They are full of dancing and clapping and screaming and shouting that may seem jarring to the untrained ear. The church contains in full the kindness and cruelty, the fierce intelligence and the shocking ignorance, the struggles and successes, the love and, yes, the bitterness and biases that make up the black experience in America.

And this helps explain, perhaps, my relationship with Reverend Wright. As imperfect as he may be, he has been like family to me. He strengthens my faith, officiated my wedding, and baptized my children. Not once in my conversations with him have I heard him talk about any ethnic group in derogatory terms or treat whites with whom he interacted with anything but courtesy and respect. He contains within him the contradictions—the good and the bad—of the community that he has served diligently for so many years.

I can no more disown him than I can disown the black community. I can no more disown him than I can disown my white grandmother, a woman who helped raise me, a woman who sacrificed again and again for me, a woman who loves me as much as she loves anything in this world but a woman who once confessed her fear of black men who passed her by on the street and who on more than one occasion has uttered racial or ethnic stereotypes that made me cringe.

These people are part of me. And they are part of America, this country that I love.

Now, some will see this as an attempt to justify or excuse comments that are simply inexcusable. I can assure you it is not. And I suppose the politically safe thing to do would be to move on from this episode and just hope that it fades into the woodwork. We can dismiss Reverend Wright as a crank or a demagogue, just as some have dismissed Geraldine Ferraro in the aftermath of her recent statements as harboring some deep-seated bias.

But race is an issue that I believe this nation cannot afford to ignore right now. We would be making the same mistake that Reverend Wright made in his offending sermons about America: to simplify and stereotype and amplify the negative to the point that it distorts reality. The fact is that the comments that have been made and the issues that have surfaced over the last few weeks reflect the complexities of race in this country that we've never really worked through, a part of our union that we have not yet made perfect. And if we walk away now, if we simply retreat into our respective corners, we will never be able to come together and solve challenges like health care or education or the need to find good jobs for every American.

Understanding this reality requires a reminder of how we arrived at this point. As William Faulkner once wrote, "The past isn't dead and buried. In fact, it isn't even past." We do not need to recite here the history of racial injustice in this country. But we do need to remind ourselves that so many of the disparities that exist between the African-American community and the larger American community today can be traced directly to inequalities passed on from an earlier generation that suffered under the brutal legacy of slavery and Jim Crow. Segregated schools were and are inferior schools. We still haven't fixed them 50 years after *Brown vs. Board of Education*. And the inferior education they provided, then and now, helps explain the pervasive achievement gap between today's black and white students.

Legalized discrimination, where blacks were prevented—often through violence—from owning property or loans were not granted to African-American business owners or black homeowners could not access FHA mortgages or blacks were excluded from unions or the police force or the fire department meant that black families could not amass any meaningful wealth to bequeath to future generations. That history helps explain the wealth and income gap between blacks and whites and the concentrated pockets of poverty that persist in so many of today's urban and rural communities. A lack of economic opportunity among black men and the shame and frustration that came from not being able to provide for one's family contributed to the erosion of black families, a problem that welfare policies for many years may have worsened. And the lack of basic services in so many urban black neighborhoods—parks for kids to play in, police walking the beat, regular garbage pick-up, building code enforcement—all helped create a cycle of violence, blight, and neglect that continues to haunt us.

This is the reality in which Reverend Wright and other African Americans of his generation grew up. They came of age in the late '50s and early '60s, a time when segregation was still the law of the land and opportunity was systematically constricted. What's remarkable is not how many failed in the face of discrimination but how many men and women overcame the odds, how many were able to make a way out of no way for those like me who would come after them.

But for all those who scratched and clawed their way to get a piece of the American Dream, there were many who didn't make it—those who were ultimately defeated, in one way or another, by discrimination. That legacy of defeat was passed on to future generations—those young men and increasingly young women whom we see standing on street corners or languishing in our prisons, without hope or prospects for the future. Even for those blacks who did make it, questions of race and racism continue to define their worldview in fundamental ways. For the men and women of Reverend Wright's generation, the memories of humiliation and doubt and fear have not gone away, nor has the anger and the bitterness of those years.

That anger may not get expressed in public, in front of white coworkers or white friends, but it does find voice in the barbershop or the beauty shop or around the kitchen table. At times, that anger is exploited by politicians to gin up votes along racial lines or to make up for a politician's own failings. And occasionally it finds voice in the church on Sunday morning, in the pulpit and in the pews. The fact that so many people are surprised to hear that anger in some of Reverend Wright's sermons simply reminds us of that old truism that the most segregated hour of American life occurs on Sunday morning.

That anger is not always productive. Indeed, all too often, it distracts attention from solving real problems. It keeps us from squarely facing our own complicity within the African-American community in our own condition. It prevents the African-American community from forging the alliances it needs to bring about real change. But the anger is real. It is powerful, and to simply wish it away—to condemn it without understanding its roots—only serves to widen the chasm of misunderstanding that exists between the races.

In fact, a similar anger exists within segments of the white community. Most working and middle-class white Americans don't feel that they've been particularly privileged by their race. Their experience is the immigrant experience. As far as they're concerned, no one handed them anything; they built it from scratch. They've worked hard all their lives, many times only to see their jobs shipped overseas or their pensions dumped after a lifetime of labor. They are anxious about their futures, and they feel their dreams slipping away. And in an era of stagnant wages and global competition, opportunity comes to be seen as a zero-sum game, in which your dreams come at my expense. So when they are told to bus their children to a school across town, when they hear that an African American is getting an advantage in landing a good job or a spot in a good college because of an injustice that they themselves never committed, when they're told that their fears about crime in urban neighborhoods are somehow prejudice, resentment builds over time.

Like the anger within the black community, these resentments aren't always expressed in polite company. But they have helped shape the political landscape for at least a generation. Anger over welfare and affirmative action helped forge the Reagan coalition. Politicians routinely exploited fears of crime for their own electoral ends. Talk show hosts and conservative commentators built entire careers unmasking bogus claims of racism while dismissing legitimate discussions of racial injustice and inequality as mere political correctness or reverse racism. And just as black anger often proved counterproductive, so have these white resentments distracted attention from the real culprits of the middle-class squeeze: a corporate culture rife with inside dealing, questionable accounting practices, and short-term greed; a Washington dominated by lobbyists and special interests; economic policies that favor the few over the many. And yet, to wish away the resentments of white Americans, to label them as *misguided* or even *racist* without recognizing they are grounded in legitimate concerns, this, too, widens the racial divide and blocks the path to understanding.

This is where we are right now.

It's a racial stalemate we've been stuck in for years. And contrary to the claims of some of my critics, black and white, I have never been so naive as to believe that we can get beyond our racial divisions in a single election cycle or with a single candidate, particularly a candidacy as imperfect as my own. But I have asserted a firm conviction, a conviction rooted in my faith in God and my faith in the American people that, working together, we can move beyond some of our old racial wounds and that, in fact, we have no choice—we have no choice if we are to continue on the path of a more perfect union.

For the African-American community, that path means embracing the burdens of our past without becoming victims of our past. It means continuing to insist on a full measure of justice in every aspect of American life. But it also means binding our particular grievances for better health care and better schools and better jobs to the larger aspirations of all Americans—the white woman struggling to break the glass ceiling, the white man who's been laid off, the immigrant trying to feed his family. And it means also taking full responsibility for our own lives—by demanding more from our fathers and spending more time with our children and reading to them and teaching them that while they may face challenges and discrimination in their own lives, they must never succumb to despair or cynicism. They must always believe that they can write their own destiny.

Ironically, this quintessentially American—and, yes, conservative—notion of self-help found frequent expression in Reverend Wright's sermons. But what my former pastor too often failed to understand is that embarking on a program of self-help also requires a belief that society can change. The profound mistake of Reverend Wright's sermons is not that he spoke about racism in our society. It's that he spoke as if our society was static, as if no progress had been made, as if this country—a country that has made it possible for one of his own members to run for the highest office in the land and build a coalition of white and black, Latino, Asian, rich, poor, young and old—is still irrevocably bound to a tragic past. What we know, what we have seen, is that America can change. That is the true genius of this nation. What we have already achieved gives us hope—the audacity to hope—for what we can and must achieve tomorrow.

Now, in the white community, the path to a more perfect union means acknowledging that what ails the African-American community does not just exist in the minds of black people—that the legacy of discrimination and current incidents of discrimination, while less overt than in the past—these things are real and must be addressed. Not just with words but with deeds—by investing in our schools and our communities, by enforcing our civil rights laws and ensuring fairness in our criminal justice system, by providing this generation with ladders of opportunity that were unavailable for previous generations. It requires all Americans to realize that your dreams do not have to come at the expense of my dreams, that investing in the health, welfare, and education of black and brown and white children will ultimately help all of America prosper.

In the end, then, what is called for is nothing more and nothing less than what all the world's great religions demand: that we do unto others as we would have them do unto us. Let us be our brother's keeper, Scripture tells us. Let us be our sister's keeper. Let us find that common stake we all have in one another, and let our politics reflect that spirit as well.

For we have a choice in this country. We can accept a politics that breeds division and conflict and cynicism. We can tackle race only as spectacle, as we did in the O.J. trial, or in the wake of tragedy, as we did in the aftermath of Katrina or as fodder for the nightly news. We can play Reverend Wright's sermons on every channel every day and talk about them from now until the election and make the only question in this campaign whether or not the American people think that I somehow believe or sympathize with his most offensive words. We can pounce on some gaffe by a Hillary supporter as evidence that she's playing the race card, or we can speculate on whether white men will all flock to John McCain in the general election regardless of his policies. We can do that. But if we do, I can tell you that, in the next election, we'll be talking about some other distraction and then another one and then another one. And nothing will change.

That is one option.

Or, at this moment, in this election, we can come together and say, "Not this time." This time, we want to talk about the crumbling schools that are stealing the future of black children and white children and Asian children and Hispanic children and Native-American children. This time, we want to reject the cynicism that tells us that these kids can't learn—that those kids who don't look like us are somebody else's problem. The children of America are not "those kids"—they are our kids, and we will not let them fall behind in a twenty-first-century economy. Not this time. This time, we want to talk about how the lines in the emergency room are filled with whites and blacks and Hispanics who do not have health care, who don't have the power on their own to overcome the special interests in Washington but who can take them on if we do it together.

This time, we want to talk about the shuttered mills that once provided a decent life for men and women of every race and the homes for sale that once belonged to Americans from every religion, every region, every walk of life. This time, we want to talk about the fact that the real problem is not that someone who doesn't look like you might take your job—it's that the corporation you work for will ship it overseas for nothing more than a profit. This time, we want to talk about the men and women of every color and creed who serve together and fight together and bleed together under the same proud flag. We want to talk about how to bring them home from a war that should've never been authorized and should've never been waged. And we want to talk about how we'll show our patriotism by caring for them and their families and giving them the benefits that they have earned.

I would not be running for president if I didn't believe with all my heart that this is what the vast majority of Americans want for this country. This union may never be perfect, but generation after generation has shown that it can always be perfected. And today, whenever I find myself feeling doubtful or cynical about this possibility, what gives me the most hope is the next generation—the young people whose attitudes and beliefs and openness to change have already made history in this election.

There's one story in particular that I'd like to leave you with today, a story I told when I had the great honor of speaking on Dr. King's birthday at his home church, Ebenezer Baptist, in Atlanta. There's a young, 23-year-old woman, a white woman named *Ashley Baia*, who organized for our campaign in Florence, South Carolina. She'd been working to organize a mostly African-American community since the beginning of this campaign, and one day, she was at a roundtable discussion where everyone went around telling their story and why they were there. And Ashley said that when she was 9 years old, her mother got cancer. And because she had to miss days of work, she was let go and lost her health care. They had to file for bankruptcy, and that's when Ashley decided that she had to do something to help her mom.

She knew that food was one of their most expensive costs, and so Ashley convinced her mother that what she really liked and really wanted to eat more than anything else was mustard and relish sandwiches because that was the cheapest way to eat. That's the mind of a nine year old. She did this for a year until her mom got better. And so Ashley told everyone at the roundtable that the reason she had joined our campaign was so that she could help the millions of other children in the country who want and need to help their parents, too.

Now, Ashley might have made a different choice. Perhaps somebody told her along the way that the source of her mother's problems were blacks who were on welfare and too lazy to work or Hispanics who were coming into the country illegally. But she didn't. She sought out allies in her fight against injustice.

Anyway, Ashley finishes her story and then goes around the room and asks everyone else why they're supporting the campaign. They all have different stories and different reasons. Many bring up a specific issue. And finally they come to this elderly black man who's been sitting there quietly the entire time. And Ashley asks him why he's there. And he doesn't bring up a specific issue. He does not say *health care* or *the economy*. He does not say *education* or *the war*. He does not say that he was there because of Barack Obama. He simply says to everyone in the room, "I am here because of Ashley." "I'm here because of Ashley."

Now, by itself, that single moment of recognition between that young white girl and that old black man is not enough. It is not enough to give health care to the sick or jobs to the jobless or education to our children. But it is where we start. It is where our union grows stronger. And as so many generations have come to realize over the course of the 221 years since a band of patriots signed that document right here in Philadelphia, that is where perfection begins.

Thank you very much, everyone. Thank you.

A Statement for Voices Unheard:
A Challenge to the National Book Awards

Adrienne Rich, Audre Lorde, and Alice Walker
Writers

At the National Book Award ceremony, Adrienne Rich read the following statement, prepared by herself, Audre Lorde, and Alice Walker—all of whom had been nominated for the poetry award. They agreed that whoever was chosen to receive the award, if any, from among the three, would read the statement.

We, Audre Lorde, Adrienne Rich, and Alice Walker, together accept this award in the name of all the women whose voices have gone and still go unheard in a patriarchal world, and in the name of those who, like us, have been tolerated as token women in this culture, often at great cost and in great pain. We believe that we can enrich ourselves more in supporting and giving to each other than by competing against each other; and that poetry—if it *is* poetry—exists in a realm beyond ranking and comparison. We symbolically join together here in refusing the terms of patriarchal competition and declaring that we will share this prize among us, to be used as best we can for women.

We appreciate the good faith of the judges for this award, but none of us could accept this money for herself, nor could she let go unquestioned the terms on which poets are given or denied honor and livelihood in this world, especially when they are women. We dedicate this occasion to the struggle for self-determination of all women, of every color, identification, or derived class: the poet, the housewife, the lesbian, the mathematician, the mother, the dishwasher, the pregnant teenager, the teacher, the grandmother, the prostitute, the philosopher, the waitress, the women who will understand what we are doing here and those who will not understand yet, the silent women whose voices have been denied us, the articulate women who have given us strength to do our work.

This presentation was given at the National Book Award ceremony, 1974. Reprinted with permission of *Ms.* Copyright © 1974.

Whose Woods These Are

Sally Miller Gearhart
Professor Emeritus, San Francisco State University

This presentation was a response to papers presented on the program, "Narrative as Communication. It was partly inspired by "It Was a Dark and Stormy Night; or, Why Are We Huddling About the Camp-fire?" by Ursula K. Le Guin.

The big stand-off was about to be over. The showdown was here. The heads of three world powers each held a thumb over a doomsday button. They had tried everything. And everything hadn't worked. Now, no one of them willing to give an inch, they prepared to send the planet into its total annihilation. The only question was, which of them would have the satisfaction of being the last to die.

Suddenly one of them, Thomas Ivanovitch Woo by name but Ivan for short, remembered a promise that in a weak moment he had made to his wife. "Wait a minute, fellows," he said. "Before we do this number we might as well give the women a chance. We got nothing to lose." The others agreed.

So Ivan called his wife and asked her how to get in touch with this Great Mother she was always talking about. His wife gave him three instructions: "Hush. Go into the woods. And listen."

So Ivan hushed, went into the only forest left on the planet and stood and listened. Pretty soon he sensed some sort of presence and he asked an old, old question: "What must we do?"

The answer was prompt and fairly direct: "Disarm."

Since that was clear enough Ivan went back to his colleagues and told them what the Great Mother had said. And they all disarmed their nations, right down to the last bullet. Ivan went back to the woods and asked the same question again. This time the answer was equally prompt: "Decentralize."

And so the world decentralized its population, its business and government. Time and again Ivan went back to the woods and time and again the Great Mother directed him in the re-making of the world. He did not even argue with some things that seemed of a strictly personal concern to her like the requirement that women be given all the say-so about sex and reproduction, and the requirement that all future planning hold the male population to twenty percent, or that the whole world acknowledge the primacy of the female of the species and embrace the values of nonviolence, nurturance, and cooperation.

This presentation was given at the Western Speech Communication Association Convention, Portland, Oregon, February 18, 1980. Used by permission of Sally Miller Gearhart.

"Yeah, yeah, yeah," said Ivan, pretty tired of it all by this time. Off he went and saw to it that all these things were accomplished.

One day when he came back to the Great Mother he was pretty smug. "Say, G.M.," he began. "It's really working. There's a pretty good world out there. Thanks a lot." And he started to go.

"Just a minute."

Ivan turned back.

"You haven't even started yet."

"Whaddya mean?"

"I've had to be pretty directive up to this point. But I won't do that much longer. It's time now for you to begin cleaning up your communication."

"My what?"

"Hush. Go deeper into the woods. Listen harder."

So Ivan went deeper into the woods and tried to listen harder. He sat for many days in the forest trying to listen. It was not at all easy. Finally a big oak tree said to him: "Hello." Ivan was so relieved that he sprang up and hugged the tree, an action pleasing to the tree since in all its experience the one thing that men do not do to trees is hug them, much less with tears running down their cheeks.

When he sat down again Ivan remembered that his mission was communication, so he tried to decide on his general purpose. Should he entertain, inform or persuade the tree? Since he had been in politics all his life he naturally decided on the persuasive mode. "Tree," he began, moving straight to his proposition, "you must help me and the rest of mankind with our communication problem. "

In response the tree cried out in pain and shrank away from him. Clearly he had done the wrong thing. "What is it, what is it? What did I do?"

"Too violent," wailed the tree. "You're trying to change me, and that hurts."

"By asking you to help me?"

"You didn't ask. You didn't even say you wanted or needed something. You told me what I must do."

"Oh," said Ivan. This was going to be difficult. He sat for a while and finally it dawned on him—if he simply opened up, said only what he wanted or needed, and was himself willing to change, then maybe he and the tree could change together. Ivan was ecstatic at this idea, and having been through EST training he was undaunted and eager to try again.

"Well, tree," he said. "I won't persuade. I'll inform you. I want to tell you something. About . . . about trees. Trees. Trees are a type of vegetation found. . . ."

Again the tree reacted, somewhat more mildly this time but enough to let him know that he was still behaving violently. "You're still trying to do something to me," said the tree. "You might just as well put a chain saw to my throat. Instead of trying to inform me you could. . . ."

"I could . . . ?" prompted Ivan.

The tree was silent.

"I could . . . ?"

"Do just what you're trying to do now?" suggested the tree.

Ivan exploded. "What I'm trying to do now? What I'm trying to do now is find out something." He stopped abruptly.

The tree seemed to smile.

And then Ivan was truly in despair. "What can I do," he said to himself. "What is there left? If I can't persuade but can only be open to change, if I can't instruct but must only discover, what can be the nature of my discourse with others?" Truly a puzzle.

He sat for many hours, thinking and listening, thinking to himself, listening to the trees, the grass, the small animals. Finally he said to the tree, "Tree, I've been sitting here for hours puzzling over this thing. First I tried reasoning it out but that didn't work. Then I tried getting in the mood of being all vulnerable and open, not trying to persuade you at all but being willing to change with you. But still nothing happened. Then I tried getting in the mood of just plain learning from you or with you but that didn't work either. Now here I sit, dog tired, and still not able to communicate with you without hurting you."

"Well, you just did it," said the tree.

"???????" said Ivan.

"You just told me a story. About what you've been going through in your head. It was in chronological order. That's the best beginning you've made."

"A story?" Then again Ivan was blessed with illumination. "Yeah! Yeah! You mean I entertained you! That's it! The only nonviolent way to communicate is to entertain! Telling stories—that's what the Toastmaster Club said all along!" He jumped up in exuberance and in sheer release of tension he began to do a buck-and-wing for the tree. "Let me entertain you," Ivan sang.

Again the tree shrank back as if offended.

Ivan stopped abruptly, mid-kick, his face a mask of astonishment. "I'm still trying to do something to you right?" he said to the tree. "*To you*, and not *for us*."

"Right."

Ivan collapsed again to his thinking/listening position. So even stories could hurt if they tried to change people or things. There must be a difference, he mused, between wanting things to change and wanting to change things. The moment he thought that, a good feeling washed over him. Then instead of entertaining the tree he could simply express himself. And then if the tree expressed itself. . . .

He tried it. "Tree, I want to tell a story." And he picked the first fairy tale that occurred to him, one that he barely remembered. But as he warmed to his task of the telling, he found that the words he was uttering themselves generated other words. Soon he began remembering easily and soon there were brand new images, new ideas and feelings that flew by so fast within him that he had trouble getting them out. He paid less and less attention to what he wanted the tree to think of him, even though he was of course still very much aware of the tree's presence, and more and more attention to the story he was telling. He began to enjoy the telling and when he had finished he was sure he heard sighs of appreciation and excitement.

To his amazement another tree in the forest spoke up. "I have a story too," it said. And when it had finished its story there was another tree and another story, another squirrel and another story. Ivan felt himself to be inside a great matrix, a womb, where he and the entire forest shared a constantly changing and intensely intimate reality.

Deep into the night trees and animals told stories of their past, of the things they had observed, of the things they had heard about. They told stories of the future, how they feared it might be, how they hoped it would be.

It was dawn when Ivan rose to his feet to start back to the world of politics. He knew now at least one way that they might begin. Good reason in controversy would have to wait a while. And so would that old taskmaster, justification. He had a story to tell. And he suspected his colleagues had some too.

When he pulled up his chair at the World Council and the whole assembly drew their attention to him, an old enemy-turned-friend said, "Well Ivan, what have you got for us this time?" The whole assembly laughed heartily. Ivan smiled.

"Hush," he said. "Let's go to the woods. And Listen."

Building Community

A Flair for Fashion:
A Welcome to New Employees

Erika Fair
Student, Ohio State University

*In this presentation, Erika Fair assumed the role of the owner of
Erika Fair's Fashion Fair International, welcoming new employees to
her company.*

Welcome to Erika Fair's Fashion Fair International. I would personally like to express my congratulations and wishes for good luck to each
of you. As you know, you were hired because of your flair for fashion and
your sense of individuality. This company is built on employees like you.

As each of you knows, my company has a very individual style. Our
clothes express the feminine side of a woman. These clothes are playful
yet sophisticated, exciting yet subtle, durable yet delicate. Our clothes
say, "I'm a professional, a mother, a wife, and even an athlete." Our
clothes are versatile. For example, with this belt and these earrings, this
outfit says, "Let's go to work, let's give a speech, or even let's have a
romantic dinner." Get rid of the belt, throw on a pair of flats, and it says,
"I'm ready for a day of shopping or just a day of relaxation."

This is where you come in. You know our reputation, you know what
our clothes say and how to wear them. All you have to do is help build
this reputation. As buyers, you are skilled enough to know what Erika
Fair says and what it doesn't. I expect each of you to assert your individuality when faced with a buying decision but at the same time to be
mindful of the company's look.

Look around you—these are your team members. You need to know
each other. You need to be able to work with each other as a family unit,
to be able to trust one another's judgments, and, at the same time, to be
able to accept one another's downfalls.

You are at the top of the line, and I already cherish each of you as a
part of the family. If you ever have a problem, feel free to contact me,
even at home, if necessary. Think of these headquarters as your home
away from home and me as your mom away from mom. I'm here not as a
disciplinarian but as an advisor, friend, and confidante.

This presentation was given at Ohio State University, Columbus, Ohio, spring 1993. Used
by permission of Erika Fair.

You were hired because you are the best at what you do, and you all are here because you know that Erika Fair Fashions is the best: The best working with and for the best—what more can we ask for?

Again, I would like to express my sincere congratulations and wishes of good luck to each of you, and I hope that your experience here at Erika Fair Fashions International is rewarding and exciting for you.

Knock, Knock

Daniel Beaty
Actor, Singer, and Writer

As a boy, I shared a game with my father.
Played it every morning 'til I was 3.
He would knock knock on my door,
and I'd pretend to be asleep
'til he got right next to the bed.
Then I would get up and jump into his arms.
"Good morning, Papa."
And my papa, he would tell me that he loved me.
We shared a game.
Knock Knock

Until that day when the knock never came,
and my momma takes me on a ride past cornfields
on this never-ending highway 'til we reach a place of high
rusty gates.
A confused little boy,
I entered the building carried in my mama's arms.
Knock Knock

We reach a room of windows and brown faces.
Behind one of the windows sits my father.
I jump out of my mama's arms
and run joyously towards my papa
only to be confronted by this window.
I knock knock, trying to break through the glass,
trying to get to my father.
I knock knock as my mama pulls me away
before my papa even says a word.

And for years, he has never said a word
And so 25 years later, I write these words
for the little boy in me who still awaits his papa's knock.

Papa, come home 'cause I miss you.
I miss you waking me up in the morning and telling me you love me.
Papa, come home 'cause there's things I don't know,
and I thought maybe you could teach me:

This presentation is from the play, Emergency, written by Daniel Beaty (2008). A video of the presentation can be viewed at http://www.liveleak.com/view?i=fc8_1247670801. Used by permission of Daniel Beaty, www.DanielBeaty.com.

How to shave;
how to dribble a ball;
how to talk to a lady;
how to walk like a man.
Papa, come home because I decided a while back
I wanted to be just like you,
but I'm forgetting who you are.

And 25 years later, a little boy cries,
and so I write these words and try to heal
and try to father myself,
and I dream up a father who says the words my father did not.

Dear Son,
I'm sorry I never came home.
For every lesson I failed to teach, hear these words:
Shave in one direction in strong deliberate strokes to avoid irritation.

Dribble the page with the brilliance of your ballpoint pen.
Walk like a god, and your goddess will come to you.
No longer will I be there to knock on your door,
So you must learn to knock for yourself.
Knock knock down doors of racism and poverty that I could not.
Knock knock down doors of opportunity
for the lost brilliance of the black men who crowd these cells.
Knock knock with diligence for the sake of your children.
Knock knock for me for, as long as you are free,
these prison gates cannot contain my spirit.
The best of me still lives in you.
Knock knock with the knowledge that you are my son, but you are not
my choices.
Yes, we are our fathers' sons and daughters,
But we are not their choices.
For despite their absences, we are still here.
Still alive, still breathing
With the power to change this world,
One little boy and girl at a time.
Knock knock
Who's there?
We are.

Poverty, Money—and Love

Jessica Jackley
Co-Founder and Former Chief Marketing Officer of Kiva Microfunds;
Founder and Chief Executive Officer of ProFounder

The stories we tell about each other matter very much. The stories we tell ourselves about our own lives matter. And, most of all, I think the way that we participate in each other's stories is of deep importance.

I was six years old when I first heard stories about the poor. Now, I didn't hear those stories from the poor themselves, I heard them from my Sunday school teacher and Jesus, via my Sunday school teacher. I remember learning that people who were poor needed something material—food, clothing, shelter—that they didn't have. And I also was taught, coupled with that, that it was my job—this classroom full of five- and six-year-old children—it was our job, apparently, to help. This is what Jesus asked of us. And then he said, "What you do for the least of these, you do for me." Now, I was pretty psyched. I was very eager to be useful in the world. I think we all have that feeling. Also, it was interesting that God needed help. That was news to me, and it felt like it was a very important thing to get to participate in.

But I also learned very soon thereafter that Jesus also said, and I'm paraphrasing, "the poor would always be with us." This frustrated and confused me. I felt like I had been just given a homework assignment that I had to do—and I was excited to do—but no matter what I would do, I would fail. So I felt confused, a little bit frustrated, and angry, like maybe I'd misunderstood something here. And I felt overwhelmed. For the first time, I began to fear this group of people and to feel negative emotion towards a whole group of people. I imagined in my head a long line of individuals who were never going away—that would always be with us. They were always going to ask me to help them and give them things, which I was excited to do, but I didn't know how it was going to work. And I didn't know what would happen when I ran out of things to give, especially if the problem was never going away.

In the years following, the other stories I heard about the poor growing up were no more positive. For example, I saw pictures and images frequently of sadness and suffering. I heard about things that were going wrong in the lives of the poor. I heard about disease. I heard about war. They always seemed to be kind of related. And in general, I got this idea that the poor in the world lived lives that were wrought with suffering and sadness, devastation, hopelessness.

This presentation was filmed at TEDGlobal July 2010, and posted October 2010. A video of the presentation can be viewed at http://www.ted.com/talks/jessica jackley_poverty_money_and_love.html. Used with permission of Jessica Jackley.

After a while, I developed what I think many of us do, this predictable response, where I started to feel bad every time I heard about them. I started to feel guilty for my own relative wealth because I wasn't doing more, apparently, to make things better. And I even felt a sense of shame because of that. So, naturally, I started to distance myself. I stopped listening to their stories quite as closely as I had before, and I stopped expecting things to really change.

Now, I still gave. On the outside, it looked like I was still quite involved. I gave of my time and my money. I gave when solutions were on sale. The cost of a cup of coffee can save a child's life, right? I mean who can argue with that? I gave when I was cornered; when it was difficult to avoid; and I gave, in general, when the negative emotions built up enough that I gave to relieve my own suffering, not someone else's. The truth be told, I was giving out of that place, not out of a genuine place of hope and excitement to help and of generosity. It became a transaction for me; it became sort of a trade. I was purchasing something. I was buying my right to go on with my day and not necessarily be bothered by this bad news. And I think the way that we go through that sometimes can, first of all, disembody a group of people, individuals out there in the world. And it can also turn them into a commodity, which is a very scary thing. So as I did this, and as I think many of us do this, we buy our distance, we buy our right to go on with our day. I think that exchange can actually get in the way of the very thing that we want most. It can get in the way of our desire to really be meaningful and useful in another person's life and, in short, to love.

Thankfully, a few years ago, things shifted for me because I heard this gentleman speak, Dr. Muhammad Yunus. I know many in the room probably know exactly who he is, but to give the shorthand version for any who have not heard him speak, Dr. Yunus won the Nobel Peace Prize a few years ago for his work pioneering modern microfinance. When I heard him speak, it was three years before that. But basically, microfinance—if this is new to you as well—think of it as financial services for the poor. Think of all the things you get at your bank and imagine those products and services tailored to the needs of someone living on a few dollars a day. Dr. Yunus shared his story, explaining what that was, and what he had done with his Grameen Bank. He also talked about, in particular, microlending, which is a tiny loan that could help someone start or grow a business.

Now, when I heard him speak, it was exciting for a number of reasons. First and foremost, I learned about this new method of change in the world that, for once, showed me, maybe, a way to interact with someone and to give, to share of a resource in a way that wasn't weird and didn't make me feel bad. That was exciting. But more importantly, he told stories about the poor that were different than any stories I had heard before. The fact that the individuals he talked about were poor was sort of a side note. He was talking about strong, smart, hardworking entrepreneurs who woke up every day and were doing things to make their lives and their families' lives better. All they needed to do that more quickly and to do it better was a little bit of capital. It was an amazing sort of insight for me.

I, in fact, was so deeply moved by this—it's hard to express now how much that affected me—but I was so moved that I actually quit my job a few weeks later, and I moved to East Africa to try to see for myself what this was about. For the first time in a long time, I wanted to meet those individuals. I wanted to meet these entrepreneurs and see for myself what their lives were actually about. So I spent three months in Kenya, Uganda, and Tanzania interviewing entrepreneurs who had received 100 dollars to start or grow a business.

In fact, through those interactions, for the first time, I was starting to get to be friends with some of those people in that big amorphous group out there that was supposed to be far away. I was starting to be friends and to get to know their personal stories. And over and over again, as I interviewed them and spent my days with them, I did hear stories of life change and amazing little details of change. So I would hear from goat herders who had used that money that they had received to buy a few more goats. Their business trajectory would change. They would make a little bit more money. Their standard of living would shift and would get better. And they would make really interesting little adjustments in their lives, like they would start to send their children to school. They might be able to buy mosquito nets. Maybe they could afford a lock for the door and feel secure. Maybe it was just that they could put sugar in their tea and offer that to me when I came as their guest, and that made them feel proud. But there were these beautiful details, even if I talked to 20 goat herders in a row, and some days that's what happened—these beautiful details of life change that were meaningful to them.

That was another thing that really touched me. It was really humbling to see for the first time—to really understand—that even if I could have taken a magic wand and fixed everything, I probably would have gotten a lot wrong. Because the best way for people to change their lives is for them to have control and to do that in a way that they believe is best for them. So I saw that, and it was very humbling.

Anyway, another interesting thing happened while I was there. I never once was asked for a donation, which had kind of been my mode, right? There's poverty, you give money to help. No one asked me for a donation. In fact, no one wanted me to feel bad for them at all. If anything, they just wanted to be able to do more of what they were doing already and to build on their own capabilities. So what I did there, once in a while, was to give people a loan—I thought that sounded very reasonable and really exciting.

And, by the way, I was a philosophy and poetry major in school, so I didn't know the difference between profit and revenue when I went to East Africa. I just got this impression that the money would work. My introduction to business was in these $100 little infuses of capital. I learned about profit and revenue, about leverage, about all sorts of things from farmers, from seamstresses, from goat herders. So this idea that these new stories of business and hope might be shared with my friends and family and, through that, maybe we could get some of the money that they needed to be able to continue their businesses as loans, that's this little idea that turned into Kiva.

A few months later, I went back to Uganda with a digital camera and a basic website that my partner, Matthew, and I had built and took pictures of seven of my new friends; posted their stories—these stories of entrepreneurship—up on the website; spammed friends and family; and said, "We think this is legal. Haven't heard back yet from SEC on all the details, but do you want to help participate in this and provide the money that they need?" The money came in basically overnight. We sent it over to Uganda. Over the next six months, a beautiful thing happened. The entrepreneurs received the money; they were paid; and their businesses, in fact, grew, and they were able to support themselves and change the trajectory of their lives.

In October of '05, after those first seven loans were paid, Matt and I took the word *beta* off of the site. We said, "Our little experiment has been a success. Let's start for real." That was our official launch. And then that first year, October '05 through '06, Kiva facilitated $500,000 in loans. The second year, it was a total of 15 million. The third year, the total was up to around 40. The fourth year, we were just short of 100. And today, less than five years in, Kiva's facilitated more than 150 million dollars, in little 25-dollar bits, from lenders and entrepreneurs—more than a million of those, collectively, in 200 countries.

So that's where Kiva is today, just to bring you right up to the present. And while those numbers and those statistics are really fun to talk about, and they're interesting, to me, Kiva's really about stories. It's about retelling the story of the poor, and it's about giving ourselves an opportunity to engage that validates their dignity, validates a partnership relationship, not a relationship that's based on the traditional sort of donor-beneficiary weirdness that can happen. Instead, it's a relationship that can promote respect and hope and this optimism that, together, we can move forward. So what I hope is that not only can the money keep flowing forth through Kiva—that's a very positive and meaningful thing—but I hope Kiva can blur those lines, like I said, between the traditional rich and poor categories that we're taught to see in the world, this false dichotomy of us and them, have and have not. I hope that Kiva can blur those lines. Because as that happens, I think we can feel free to interact in a way that's more open, more just, and more creative—to engage with each other and to help each other.

Imagine how you feel when you see somebody on the street who is begging, and you're about to approach them. Imagine how you feel. And then imagine the difference when you might see somebody who has a story of entrepreneurship and hard work who wants to tell you about their business. Maybe they're smiling, and they want to talk to you about what they've done. Imagine if you're speaking with somebody who's growing things and making them flourish; somebody who's using their talents to do something productive; somebody who's built their own business from scratch; someone who is surrounded by abundance, not scarcity, who's in fact creating abundance; somebody with full hands with something to offer, not empty hands asking for you to give them something. Imagine if you could hear a story you didn't expect of somebody who wakes up every day and works very, very hard to make their life better. These stories can really change the way that we think about each other. And if we can catalyze a supportive community to come around these individuals and to participate in their story by lending a little bit of money, I think that can change the way we believe in each other and each other's potential.

Now for me, Kiva is just the beginning. As I look forward to what is next, it's been helpful to reflect on the things I've learned so far. The first one is, as I mentioned, entrepreneurship was a new idea to me. Kiva borrowers, as I interviewed them and got to know them over the last few years, have taught me what entrepreneurship is. And I think, at its core, it's deciding that you want your life to be better. You see an opportunity, and you decide what you're going to do to try to seize that. In short, it's deciding that tomorrow can be better than today and going after that. The second thing that I've learned is that loans are a very interesting tool for connectivity. They're not a donation. Yes, maybe it doesn't sound that much different. But, in fact, when you give something to someone and they say, "Thanks," and let you know how things go, that's one thing. When you lend them money and they slowly pay you back over time, you have this excuse to have an ongoing dialogue. This continued attention—this ongoing attention—is a really big deal to build different kinds of relationships among us. And then third, from what I've heard from the entrepreneurs I've gotten to know, when all else is equal, given the option to have just money to do what you need to do or money plus the support and encouragement of a global community, people choose the community plus the money. That's a much more meaningful combination, a more powerful combination.

So with that in mind, this particular incident has led to the things that I'm working on now. I see entrepreneurs everywhere now—now that I'm tuned into this. And one thing that I've seen is there are a lot of supportive communities that already exist in the world. With social networks, it's an amazing way to grow the number of people that we all have around us in our own supportive communities, rapidly. And so, as I have been thinking about this, I've been wondering: How can we engage these supportive communities to catalyze even more entrepreneurial ideas and to catalyze all of us to make tomorrow better than today? As I've researched what's going on in the United States, a few interesting little insights have come up. One is that, of course, as we all might expect, many small businesses in the US and all over the world still need money to grow and to do more of what they want to do, or they might need money during a hard month. But there's always a need for resources close by. Another thing is, it turns out, those resources don't usually come from the places you might expect—banks, venture capitalists, other organizations and support structures. They come from friends and family. Some statistics say 85 percent or more of funding for small businesses comes from friends and family. That's around 130 billion dollars a year. It's a lot. And third, as people are doing this friends-and-family-fundraising process, it's very awkward. People don't know exactly what to ask for, how to ask, and what to promise in return, even though they have the best of intentions and want to thank those people who are supporting them.

So to harness the power of these supportive communities in a new way and to allow entrepreneurs to decide for themselves exactly what that financial exchange should look like, exactly what fits them and the people around them, this week, we're quietly doing a launch of Profounder, which is a crowd-funding platform for small businesses to raise what they need through investments from their friends and family. And it's investments—not donations, not loans—but investments that have a dynamic return. The mapping of participating in the story actually flows with the up and down. In short, it's a do-it-yourself tool for small businesses to raise these funds. And what you can do is go onto the site, create a profile, and create investment terms in a really easy way. We make it really, really simple for me as well as anyone else who wants to use the site. And we allow entrepreneurs to share a percentage of their revenues. They can raise up to a million dollars from an unlimited number of unaccredited, unsophisticated investors—everyday people, heaven forbid—and they can share those returns over time, again, using whatever terms they set. As investors choose to become involved based on those terms, they can either take their rewards back as cash, or they can decide in advance to give those returns away to a nonprofit. So they can be a cash or a cause investor. It's my hope that this kind of tool can show anybody who has an idea a path to go do what they want to do in the world and to gather the people around them that they already have—the people who know them best and who love them and want to support them—to gather them to make this happen.

So that's what I'm working on now. And to close, I just want to say, look, these are tools. Right now, Profounder's right at the very beginning, and it's very palpable—it's very clear to me—that it's just a vessel, it's just a tool. What we need are for people to care, to actually go use it, just like they've cared enough to use Kiva to make those connections. But the good news is I don't think I need to stand here and convince you to care. I'm not even going to try. I don't think, even though we often hear the ethical and moral reasons, the religious reasons, "Here's why caring and giving will make you happier." I don't think we need to be convinced of that. I think we know. In fact, I think we know so much and it's such a reality that we care so deeply that, in fact, what usually stops us is that we're afraid to try and to mess up because we care so very much about helping each other and being meaningful in each other's lives.

I've given you my story today, which is the best I can do. And I think I can remind us that we do care. I think we all already know that. And I think we know that love is resilient enough for us to get out there and try. For me, the best way to be inspired to try is to stop and to listen to someone else's story. I'm grateful that I've gotten to do that here at TED. I'm grateful that, whenever I do that, guaranteed, I am inspired, I am inspired by the person I am listening to. And I believe more and more every time I listen in that person's potential to do great things in the world and in my own potential to maybe help. Forget the tools, forget the moving around of resources—that stuff's easy. Believing in each other—really being sure when push comes to shove that each one of us can do amazing things in the world—that is what can make our stories into love stories and our collective story into one that continually perpetuates hope and good things for all of us. This belief in each other—knowing that without a doubt and practicing that every day in whatever you do—that's what I believe will change the world and make tomorrow better than today.

Inch by Inch

Al Pacino, Actor
Playing Coach Tony D'Amato in *Any Given Sunday*

I don't know what to say, really. Three minutes 'til the biggest battle of our professional lives all comes down to today. Now either we heal as a team or we're gonna crumble, inch by inch, play by play, 'til we're finished.

We're in hell right now, gentlemen, believe me. And, we can stay here—get the shit kicked out of us—or we can fight our way back into the light. We can climb outta hell one inch at a time.

Now, I can't do it for you. I'm too old. I look around. I see these young faces, and I think—I mean—I made every wrong choice a middle-aged man can make. I pissed away all my money, believe it or not. I chased off anyone who's ever loved me. And lately, I can't even stand the face I see in the mirror.

You know, when you get old in life, things get taken from you. I mean that's part of life. But, you only learn that when you start losing stuff. You find out life's this game of inches. So is football. Because in either game, life or football, the margin for error is so small—I mean one-half a step too late or too early and you don't quite make it. One-half second too slow, too fast, you don't quite catch it.

The inches we need are everywhere around us.

They're in every break of the game, every minute, every second.

On this team, we fight for that inch. On this team, we tear ourselves and everyone else around us to pieces for that inch. We claw with our fingernails for that inch because we know when we add up all those inches, that's gonna make the fuckin' difference between winning and losing! Between livin' and dyin'!

I'll tell you this: In any fight, it's the guy who's willing to die who's gonna win that inch. And I know if I'm gonna have any life anymore, it's because I'm still willin' to fight and die for that inch. Because that's what livin' is! The six inches in front of your face!!

Now I can't make you do it. You got to look at the guy next to you. Look into his eyes! Now I think you're gonna see a guy who will go that inch with you. You're gonna see a guy who will sacrifice himself for this team because he knows, when it comes down to it, you're gonna do the same for him!

That's a team, gentleman!

And, either we heal, now, as a team, or we will die as individuals.

That's football, guys.

That's all it is.

Now, what are you gonna do?

Any Given Sunday was produced by Oliver Stone, 1999. A video of the presentation can be viewed at www.americanrhetoric.com/.../moviespeechonanygivensunday.html

⟍

Seeking Adherence

Who Is a True Friend?

Christa C. Porter
Student, Ohio State University

*In this presentation, Christa C. Porter assumed the role of a teacher of
a high-school Sunday school class.*

Good morning, y'all.
Class members: Good morning.
Today, we're going to talk about something you all know a lot about;
I hope we'll get some new ideas on the subject that will stay in your
heads when you leave and get on the church bus. We're going to talk
about friendship. Anybody here have friends?
Class members: Yes.
What is your definition of a true friend? Someone give me a defini-
tion of a true friend.
Class member: Somebody who's loyal and who can be trusted.
OK! Somebody else?
Class member: Somebody you can talk with.
All right. Anyone else?
Class member: Someone to do things with and have fun with.
OK. Everyone has their own definition of a friend. I'd like to add mine
to the list. One of my definitions is that a friend is someone who will
respect what I say. Even if my opinions are different from theirs, they'll
still respect me and won't call me stupid. A friend is also someone I can
call at 3:00 in the morning and say, "I need somebody to talk to," and
she'll talk to me. That's what I consider a friend. Even if she has to wake
up at 3:00 in the morning, she's willing to talk to me when I need help.

The Bible has some things to say about friends. Proverbs 18:24 says a
friend is closer than any brother. Proverbs 27:10: Far better is the neigh-
bor that is nearer than a brother that is far off. And greater love hath no
man than this that a man lay down his life for his friend.

OK, you've given me your definitions of a friend, I've given you my
definition, and I've given you some of what the Bible says about friends.
We've been looking at friendship from our perspective here—of what
friends do for us. How about looking at friendship from the other side?
How can we be a good friend? Would I wake up at 3:00 in the morning

This presentation was given at Ohio State University, Columbus, Ohio, spring 1993. Used
by permission of Christa C. Porter.

for my friend—to listen to her? If your friend were stranded 20 miles away, would you go pick her up? So, a lot of times, we think about what we want our friends to do, but we never think about what we would do for our friends.

One of the ways in which we can be good friends to others is by being trustworthy, which Regina mentioned in her definition of a friend. Can I keep a secret? Can I be trusted? Trust. That's a common word that is used in the definition of a friend. You've probably all had the experience of having friends talk about you behind your back, they say bad things about you, they tell your business to everyone. The Bible recognizes this potential problem. Proverbs 18:24 says that he that maketh many friends doeth it to his own destruction. A prime example: If you tell your friend something, your friend could have a friend who has a friend who has a friend. And the next thing you know, your business is around the whole school.

Help me out here—you stand up. Now pick out somebody real quick who's your friend. OK, now you pick out somebody who's your friend, and you stand up. One more time—you pick out someone who is your friend. Now, I could tell her about my conversation with a guy from school, she could tell her something, and she could tell him something, and he then tells it to his friend, over here. And by the time it gets back to me, according to the story, I've had a date with this guy, we've had sex, I got pregnant, and I had an abortion—all that from just telling one person one thing. That's what happens when you have a lot of friends, especially the kind who aren't trustworthy.

The whole point of this is the person you can really have trust in is God. You don't have to worry about Him coming down and saying, "Guess what she did last night?" He's going to be there for you regardless, he's going to listen to you, and he's going to give you the best advice. Our friends can be wonderful, but God is the best friend of all.

Everest Swim

Lewis Pugh
Swimmer and Environmentalist

Last year, when I was here, I was speaking to you about a swim which I did across the North Pole. And while that swim took place three years ago, I can remember it as if it was yesterday. I remember standing on the edge of the ice, about to dive into the water, and thinking to myself, I have never ever seen any place on this earth which is just so frightening. The water is completely black. The water is minus 1.7 degrees centigrade, or 29 degrees Fahrenheit. It's flipping freezing in that water. And then a thought came across my mind: If things go pear-shaped on this swim, how long will it take for my frozen body to sink the four-and-a-half kilometers to the bottom of the ocean? And then I said to myself, I've just got to get this thought out of my mind as quickly as possible. And the only way I can dive into that freezing cold water and swim a kilometer is by listening to my iPod and really revving myself up, listening to everything from beautiful opera all the way across to Puff Daddy and then committing myself a hundred percent—there is nothing more powerful than the made-up mind—and then walking up to the edge of the ice and just diving into the water.

And that swim took me 18 minutes and 50 seconds, and it felt like 18 days. And I remember getting out of the water and my hands feeling so painful and looking down at my fingers, and my fingers were literally the size of sausages. You know, we're made partially of water; when water freezes it expands, and so the cells in my fingers had frozen and expanded and burst. And the most immediate thought when I came out of that water was the following: I'm never ever going to do another cold-water swim in my life again.

Anyway, last year, I heard about the Himalayas and the melting of the glaciers because of climate change. I heard about this lake, Lake Imia. This lake has been formed in the last couple of years because of the melting of the glacier. The glacier's gone all the way up the mountain and left in its place this big lake. And I firmly believe that what we're seeing in the Himalayas is the next great, big battleground on this earth. Nearly two billion people—so one in three people on this earth—rely on the water from the Himalayas. And with a population increasing as quickly as it is and with the water supply from these glaciers—because of climate change—decreasing so much, I think we have a real risk of instability. North, you've got China; south, you've India, Pakistan, Bangladesh, all these countries.

This presentation was filmed at TEDGlobal July 2010 and posted October 2010. A video of the presentation can be viewed at http://www.ted.comitalks/lewispugh_s_mind_shifting_mt_everest_swim.html. Used with permission of Lewis Pugh.

And so I decided to walk up to Mt. Everest, the highest mountain on this earth, and go and do a symbolic swim underneath the summit of Mt. Everest. Now, I don't know if any of you have had the opportunity to go to Mt. Everest, but it's quite an ordeal getting up there. Twenty-eight great, big, powerful yaks carrying all the equipment up onto this mountain—I don't just have my Speedo. But there's a big film crew who then sends all the images around the world. The other thing which was so challenging about this swim is not just the altitude. I wanted to do the swim at 5,300 meters above sea level, so it's right up in the heavens. It's very, very difficult to breathe. You get altitude sickness. It feels like you've got a man standing behind you with a hammer just hitting your head all the time.

That's not the worst part of it. The worst part was that this year was the year where they decided to do a big cleanup operation on Mt. Everest. Many, many people have died on Mt. Everest, and this was the year they decided to go and recover all the bodies of the mountaineers and then bring them down the mountain. And when you're walking up the mountain to attempt to do something which no human has ever done before, and, in fact, no fish—there are no fish up there swimming at 5,300 meters—when you're trying to do that and then the bodies are coming past you, it humbles you, and you also realize very, very clearly that nature is so much more powerful than we are.

And we walked up this pathway, all the way up. And to the right-hand side of us was this great Khumbu Glacier. And all the way along the glacier, we saw these big pools of melting ice. And then we got up to this small lake underneath the summit of Mt. Everest, and I prepared myself the same way as I've always prepared myself for this swim, which was going to be so very difficult. I put on my iPod, I listened to some music, I got myself as aggressive as possible—but controlled aggression—and then I hurled myself into that water.

I swam as quickly as I could for the first hundred meters, and then I realized very, very quickly I had a huge problem on my hands. I could barely breathe. I was gasping for air. I then began to choke, and then it quickly led to me vomiting in the water. And it all happened so quickly—I don't know how it happened, but I went underwater. And, luckily, the water was quite shallow, and I was able to push myself off the bottom of the lake and get up and then take another gasp of air. And then I said, "Carry on. Carry on. Carry on." I carried on for another five or six strokes, and then I had nothing in my body, and I went down to the bottom of the lake. And I don't know where I got it from, but I was able to somehow pull myself up and as quickly as possible get to the side of the lake. I've heard it said that drowning is the most peaceful death that you can have. I have never ever heard such utter bollocks. It is the most frightening and panicky feeling that you can have.

I got myself to the side of the lake. My crew grabbed me, and then we walked as quickly as we could down—over the rubble—down to our camp. And there, we sat down, and we did a debrief about what had gone wrong there on Mt. Everest. And my team just gave it to me straight. They said, "Lewis, you need to have a radical tactical shift if you want to do this swim. Every single thing which you have learned in the past 23 years of swimming, you must forget. Every single thing which you learned when you were serving in the British army about speed and aggression, you put that to one side. We want you to walk up the hill in another two day's time. Take some time to rest and think about things. We want you to walk up the mountain in two day's time and, instead of swimming fast, swim as slowly as possible. Instead of swimming crawl, swim breaststroke. And remember, never ever swim with aggression. This is the time to swim with real humility."

And so we walked back up to the mountain two days later. And I stood there on the edge of the lake, and I looked up at Mt. Everest—and she is one of the most beautiful mountains on the earth—and I said to myself, "Just do this slowly." And I swam across the lake. And I can't begin to tell you how good I felt when I came to the other side.

But I learned two very, very important lessons there on Mt. Everest. And I thank my team of Sherpas who taught me this. The first one is that just because something has worked in the past so well doesn't mean it's going to work in the future. And similarly, now, before I do anything, I ask myself what type of mindset do I require to successfully complete a task. And taking that into the world of climate change, which is, frankly, the Mt. Everest of all problems, just because we've lived the way we have lived for so long, just because we have consumed the way we have for so long and populated the earth the way we have for so long doesn't mean that we can carry on the way we are carrying on. The warning signs are all there. When I was born, the world's population was 3.5 billion people. We're now 6.8 billion people, and we're expected to be 9 billion people by 2050.

And then the second lesson, the radical, tactical shift. And I've come here to ask you today: What radical tactical shift can you take in your relationship to the environment which will ensure that our children and our grandchildren live in a safe world and a secure world and, most importantly, in a sustainable world? And I ask you, please, to go away from here and think about that one radical tactical shift which you could make, which will make that big difference, and then commit a hundred percent to doing it. Blog about it, tweet about it, talk about it, and commit a hundred percent. Because very, very few things are impossible to achieve if we really put our whole minds to it.

Winning the Cultural War

Charlton Heston
Actor and President of the National Rifle Association of America

I remember my son when he was five, explaining to his kindergarten class what his father did for a living. "My Daddy," he said, "pretends to be people."

There have been quite a few of them. Prophets from the Old and New Testaments, a couple of Christian saints, generals of various nationalities and different centuries, several kings, three American presidents, a French cardinal and two geniuses, including Michelangelo. If you want the ceiling re-painted I'll do my best. There always seem to be a lot of different fellows up here. I'm never sure which one of them gets to talk. Right now, I guess I'm the guy.

As I pondered our visit tonight it struck me: If my Creator gave me the gift to connect you with the hearts and minds of those great men, then I want to use that same gift now to re-connect you with your own sense of liberty... your own freedom of thought... your own compass for what is right.

Dedicating the memorial at Gettysburg, Abraham Lincoln said of America, "We are now engaged in a great Civil War, testing whether this nation or any nation so conceived and so dedicated can long endure."

Those words are true again. I believe that we are again engaged in a great civil war, a cultural war that's about to hijack your birthright to think and say what resides in your heart. I fear you no longer trust the pulsing lifeblood of liberty inside you... the stuff that made this country rise from wilderness into the miracle that it is.

Let me back up. About a year ago I became president of the National Rifle Association, which protects the right to keep and bear arms. I ran for office, I was elected, and now I serve... I serve as a moving target for the media who've called me everything from "ridiculous" and "duped" to a "brain-injured, senile, crazy old man." I know... I'm pretty old but I sure Lord ain't senile.

As I have stood in the crosshairs of those who target Second Amendment freedoms, I've realized that firearms are not the only issue. No, it's much, much bigger than that.

I've come to understand that a cultural war is raging across our land, in which, with Orwellian fervor, certain acceptable thoughts and speech are mandated.

For example, I marched for civil rights with Dr. King in 1963—long before Hollywood found it fashionable. But when I told an audience last

This presentation was given at the Harvard Law School Forum, Boston, Massachusetts, February 16, 1999. Used with permission.

year that white pride is just as valid as black pride or red pride or anyone else's pride, they called me a racist.

I've worked with brilliantly talented homosexuals all my life. But when I told an audience that gay rights should extend no further than your rights or my rights, I was called a homophobe.

I served in World War II against the Axis powers. But during a speech, when I drew an analogy between singling out innocent Jews and singling out innocent gun owners, I was called an anti-Semite.

Everyone I know knows I would never raise a closed fist against my country. But when I asked an audience to oppose this cultural persecution, I was compared to Timothy McVeigh.

From *Time* magazine to friends and colleagues, they're essentially saying, "Chuck, how dare you speak your mind. You are using language not authorized for public consumption!"

But I am not afraid. If Americans believed in political correctness, we'd still be King George's boys—subjects bound to the British crown.

In his book, *The End of Sanity,* Martin Gross writes that "blatantly irrational behavior is rapidly being established as the norm in almost every area of human endeavor. There seem to be new customs, new rules, new anti-intellectual theories regularly foisted on us from every direction. Underneath, the nation is roiling. Americans know something without a name is undermining the nation, turning the mind mushy when it comes to separating truth from falsehood and right from wrong. And they don't like it."

Let me read a few examples. At Antioch College in Ohio, young men seeking intimacy with a coed must get verbal permission at each step of the process from kissing to petting to final copulation . . . all clearly spelled out in a printed college directive.

In New Jersey, despite the death of several patients nationwide who had been infected by dentists who had concealed their AIDS—the state commissioner announced that health providers who are HIV-positive need not . . . need not . . . tell their patients that they are infected.

At William and Mary, students tried to change the name of the school team "The Tribe" because it was supposedly insulting to local Indians, only to learn that authentic Virginia chiefs truly like the name.

In San Francisco, city fathers passed an ordinance protecting the rights of transvestites to cross-dress on the job, and for transsexuals to have separate toilet facilities while undergoing sex change surgery.

In New York City, kids who don't speak a word of Spanish have been placed in bilingual classes to learn their three R's in Spanish solely because their last names sound Hispanic.

At the University of Pennsylvania, in a state where thousands died at Gettysburg opposing slavery, the president of that college officially set up segregated dormitory space for black students.

Yeah, I know . . . that's out of bounds now. Dr. King said "Negroes." Jimmy Baldwin and most of us on the March said "black." But it's a no-no now. For me, hyphenated identities are awkward . . . particularly "Native-American." I'm a Native American, for God's sake. I also happen to be a blood-initiated brother of the Miniconjou Sioux. On my wife's side, my grandson is a thirteenth generation native American . . . with a capital letter on "American."

Finally, just last month . . . David Howard, head of the Washington D.C. Office of Public Advocate, used the word "niggardly" while talking to colleagues about budgetary matters. Of course, "niggardly" means stingy or scanty. But within days Howard was forced to publicly apologize and resign.

As columnist Tony Snow wrote: "David Howard got fired because some people in public employ were morons who (a) didn't know the meaning of 'niggardly,' (b) didn't know how to use a dictionary to discover the meaning, and (c) actually demanded that he apologize for their ignorance."

What does all of this mean? It means that telling us what to think has evolved into telling us what to say, so telling us what to do can't be far behind.

Before you claim to be a champion of free thought, tell me: Why did political correctness originate on America's campuses? And why do you continue to tolerate it? Why do you, who're supposed to debate ideas, surrender to their suppression?

Let's be honest. Who here thinks your professors can say what they really believe? It scares me to death, and should scare you too, that the superstition of political correctness rules the halls of reason.

You are the best and the brightest. You, here in the fertile cradle of American academia, here in the castle of learning on the Charles River, you are the cream. But I submit that you, and your counterparts across the land, are the most socially conformed and politically silenced generation since Concord Bridge.

And as long as you validate that . . . and abide it . . . you are—by your grandfathers' standards—cowards.

Here's another example. Right now at more than one major university, Second Amendment scholars and researchers are being told to shut up about their findings or they'll lose their jobs. Why? Because their research findings would undermine big-city mayors' pending lawsuits that seek to extort hundreds of millions of dollars from firearm manufacturers.

I don't care what you think about guns. But if you are not shocked at that, I am shocked at you. Who will guard the raw material of unfettered ideas, if not you? Who will defend the core value of academia, if you supposed soldiers of free thought and expression lay down your arms and plead, "Don't shoot me."

If you talk about race, it does not make you a racist. If you see distinctions between the genders, it does not make you a sexist. If you think critically about a denomination, it does not make you anti-religion. If you accept but don't celebrate homosexuality, it does not make you a homophobe.

Don't let America's universities continue to serve as incubators for this rampant epidemic of new McCarthyism.

But what can you do? How can anyone prevail against such pervasive social subjugation?

The answer's been here all along. I learned it 36 years ago, on the steps of the Lincoln Memorial in Washington, D.C., standing with Dr. Martin Luther King and two hundred thousand people.

You simply . . . disobey. Peaceably, yes. Respectfully, of course. Nonviolently, absolutely. But when told how to think or what to say or how to behave, we don't. We disobey social protocol that stifles and stigmatizes personal freedom.

I learned the awesome power of disobedience from Dr. King . . . who learned it from Gandhi, and Thoreau, and Jesus, and every other great man who led those in the right against those with the might.

Disobedience is in our DNA. We feel innate kinship with that disobedient spirit that tossed tea into Boston Harbor, that sent Thoreau to jail, that refused to sit in the back of the bus, that protested a war in Viet Nam.

In that same spirit, I am asking you to disavow cultural correctness with massive disobedience of rogue authority, social directives and onerous law that weaken personal freedom.

But be careful . . . it hurts. Disobedience demands that you put yourself at risk. Dr. King stood on lots of balconies.

You must be willing to be humiliated . . . to endure the modern-day equivalent of the police dogs at Montgomery and the water cannons at Selma.

You must be willing to experience discomfort. I'm not complaining, but my own decades of social activism have taken their toll on me. Let me tell you a story.

A few years back I heard about a rapper named Ice-T who was selling a song called "Cop Killer" celebrating ambushing and murdering police officers. It was being marketed by none other than Time/Warner, the biggest entertainment conglomerate in the world.

Police across the country were outraged. Rightfully so—at least one had been murdered. But Time/Warner was stonewalling because the CD was a cash cow for them, and the media were tiptoeing around it because the rapper was black. I heard Time/Warner had a stockholders meeting scheduled in Beverly Hills. I owned some shares at the time, so I decided to attend.

What I did there was against the advice of my family and colleagues. I asked for the floor. To a hushed room of a thousand average American stockholders, I simply read the full lyrics of "Cop Killer"—every vicious, vulgar, instructional word.

"I GOT MY 12 GAUGE SAWED OFF,
I GOT MY HEADLIGHTS TURNED OFF,

I'M ABOUT TO BUST SOME SHOTS OFF,
I'M ABOUT TO DUST SOME COPS OFF . . ."

It got worse, a lot worse. I won't read the rest of it to you. But trust me, the room was a sea of shocked, frozen, blanched faces. The Time/Warner executives squirmed in their chairs and stared at their shoes. They hated me for that.

Then I delivered another volley of sick lyrics brimming with racist filth, where Ice-T fantasizes about sodomizing two 12-year old nieces of Al and Tipper Gore.

"SHE PUSHED HER BUTT AGAINST MY . . ."

Well, I won't do to you here what I did to them. Let's just say I left the room in echoing silence. When I read the lyrics to the waiting press corps, one of them said "We can't print that." "I know," I replied, "but Time/Warner's selling it."

Two months later, Time/Warner terminated Ice-T's contract. I'll never be offered another film by Warners, or get a good review from *Time* magazine. But disobedience means you must be willing to act, not just talk.

When a mugger sues his elderly victim for defending herself . . . jam the switchboard of the district attorney's office.

When your university is pressured to lower standards until 80% of the students graduate with honors . . . choke the halls of the board of regents.

When an 8-year-old boy pecks a girl's cheek on the playground and gets hauled into court for sexual harassment . . . march on that school and block its doorways.

When someone you elected is seduced by political power and betrays you . . . petition them, oust them, banish them.

When *Time* magazine's cover portrays millennium nuts as deranged, crazy Christians holding a cross as it did last month . . . boycott their magazine and the products it advertises.

So that this nation may long endure, I urge you to follow in the hallowed footsteps of the great disobediences of history that freed exiles, founded religions, defeated tyrants, and yes, in the hands of an aroused rabble in arms and a few great men, by God's grace, built this country.

If Dr. King were here, I think he would agree.

Thank you.

—

Discovering Knowledge and Belief

Focus-Group Discussion of *The Lantern*

Randi Lewis
Student, Ohio State University

In this presentation, Randi Lewis uses a focus group to generate feed-back for the staff of the student newspaper at Ohio State University, The Lantern. *Her words are included below, although the answers her audience gave are not.*

In public relations, we do a lot of focus groups to find out who our audience is, what they think about a product, or what they like about a product or service. As students at OSU, I'm assuming most of you read *The Lantern*, so that will be the focus of this discussion today. I'd like to begin by welcoming you all to this focus group. Thank you for taking time out of your busy schedules to participate in this session. I will be asking several open-ended questions about *The Lantern* and would like you to be honest in answering them.

There are several goals we are trying to accomplish by conducting this focus group. First, we'd like to find out the aspects you like and dis-like about our student newspaper. Second, we want to hear what you think about the stories we've been running the past three quarters. Last, we want to get some suggestions from you—the students who read our paper—on how we can serve you better. The paper is here for you, and we want to do the best job that we can in meeting your needs.

Before we begin the discussion, I would like to give you a little bit of background about *The Lantern*. It is a student-run newspaper that is writ-ten and put together entirely by journalism students in the news and public relations tracks. The paper is published every day, Monday through Friday, during autumn, winter, and spring quarters and bi-weekly during the summer quarter. It is funded and supported totally by advertising dollars.

With this background in mind, let's get started with the focus-group questions. You can raise your hand or jump right in, whatever you're most comfortable doing. I'm going to be taking notes while you're talk-ing in order to get your suggestions down.

- How many of you read *The Lantern* on a regular basis?
- How many of you read it more than 3 times a week?

This presentation was given at Ohio State University, Columbus, Ohio, spring 1993. Used by permission of Randi Lewis.

- How many of you read *The Lantern* as a primary source for your news?
- What are the sections you flip to first or the ones you read most often?
- What about sports? Do you feel we should be including more articles about sports—not just those at OSU but nationally?
- What about the editorial page/letters to the editor? Do you all read that section? What do you think about that section?
- What are some of the stories that stood out for you in *The Lantern* over the past three quarters? Why do you remember those stories in particular?
- What are some of the things you like about *The Lantern*?
- What are some of the things you dislike about *The Lantern*?
- You've given me several valuable suggestions for *The Lantern*. There is one specific question I'd like to ask you. Do you feel we should print Associated Press (or AP) articles in *The Lantern*? There are two schools of thought in journalism. Some think that we should have totally student-written articles—no AP articles whatsoever. Others argue that, for many students, this is their only source of news, so we need to include a balance between AP and student-written articles about campus. What's your feeling on that?

This has been a very productive discussion, but unfortunately, I need to wrap up here. Let me summarize the main ideas you've given me: We need more accurate reporting, more careful attention to grammar and spelling, a more professional look generally, and more in-depth coverage of OSU sports. In terms of AP articles, you believe they are appropriate to include not as major sources of news but to acknowledge certain world events—such as when a prominent person dies. All of these suggestions are extremely valuable.

I want to thank you all for participating in this focus-group discussion. As I said before, you, the students, are the primary audience that we're trying to serve, so your input is greatly appreciated. I want you to know all of your suggestions will be carefully considered by *The Lantern* staff. Thank you all again.

Selecting a Conference Site for ZAPPlication.org®

Anthony J. Radich
Executive Director, Western States Arts Federation (WESTAF)

This presentation was held to select a city in which to hold the annual conference of artists and arts administrators affiliated with ZAPPlication.org® (ZAPP®). ZAPP® is an online software system designed to help artists enter art fairs and to make the administrative management of art fairs more efficient. Participants in the discussion were: Leah Charney, manager, ZAPPlication.org® project; Christina Villa, program assistant, ZAPPlication.org® project; and Adrianne Devereux, finance officer, ZAPPlication.org® project.

Anthony: Thank you for taking the time to meet. Our goal at this meeting is to decide where we will hold our ZAPP® conference in 2011. I am going to turn to Leah and ask her to define the problem.

Leah: Okay, we just completed our second annual ZAPP® conference. This is, as you know, a professional development conference for artists and administrators of art fairs. The first conference was in August 2009, and the conference was held in Denver. The second year, it was held in September in St. Louis, so now we are looking to plan our third annual conference. We're searching for another location outside of Denver—a location on the East Coast or in the Southeast—and we want to hold it again in the fall, so August, September, or perhaps October are the months we are looking at.

Anthony: And why are you thinking the East Coast or the Southeast for this conference?

Leah: Sure. We selected Denver for the first year of the conference. Denver is our home city—and when you're launching something, that makes sense. Keep it close to home. Then we moved it to the Midwest for a more central location. So now we're thinking that either the East Coast or the Southeast region makes sense demographically. Moving it there will allow us to attract different folks who may not have been able to join us in the conference's first two years.

Anthony: That makes sense. Thank you. And now shall we turn to brainstorming possible locations for the conference that are in the Southeast or on the East Coast? These also need to be places where we could hold a conference in the fall.

Leah: How about Atlanta or Florida?

Adrianne: Or maybe Pennsylvania?

This presentation was delivered at Denver, Colorado, on November 5, 2010. Used by permission of Anthony J. Radich.

Christina: I'd like to suggest Virginia.

Anthony: Terry Adams mentioned Kentucky as a possible site when I had lunch with him yesterday. He's the director of the Cherry Creek Arts Festival. Kentucky isn't very far east, but it's east of Denver. Any other suggestions? So far, we have Atlanta, Florida, Pennsylvania, Virginia, and Kentucky on our list.

Christina: I can't think of any others I would propose.

Leah: Me, neither.

Anthony: OK, then, let's turn to evaluating these locations. What criteria do you think we need to use to select a city for the conference?

Leah: We need a city that has either a large artist community or a reputable art fair or arts event. If we held our conference before or after an art fair or other such event, there might be a lot of artists or show administrators who would be interested in coming to that city and staying for the conference. They may even be willing to arrive early for the conference and stay for the art fair. I think we would want to hold the conference before such an event because holding it after a large arts fair probably wouldn't attract the artist population we want.

Anthony: Okay, and why would that be?

Christina: The artists are tired after doing a huge art fair. They would be tired and not inclined to attend a conference right after spending several days at a fair.

Anthony: This is good to know. Anything else for criteria?

Leah: We also would like it to be somewhere that is accessible for many people, so either near a major airport or a major highway.

Anthony: That makes sense. I'm going to now turn to Adrianne. From your work in preparing meetings, are there other criteria you would suggest?

Adrianne: We need to consider whether the location is going to be in a hotel or whether we're going to find a space sponsored by an art fair. In some of the cities on our list, it would be easier to find a space in connection with an art fair, and that could save us some money.

Anthony: Okay.

Adrianne: We also should consider the cost of flying to places. We want something where we can get a good deal even if we're not paying for it. I'm sure more people will come if air fares are not high.

Leah: Not everyone is going to fly to the conference, so we want a site accessible to large numbers of artists traveling by car. We did very well last year attracting local artists—artists in a 300- or 400-mile region—who were willing to drive to the conference.

Anthony: That's an excellent consideration. I want to go back to what Adrianne said and underscore the sponsored space. We had a reception at the St. Louis Artists' Guild that I thought was really lovely and fit us size wise, and I think people really liked it. We can't always come up with something like that for our conference, but I think getting people out in the community beyond the hotel is good. So I would like one of our criteria to be whether we might be able to get a space like this. Christina, are there other criteria you want to add?

Christina: I can't think of any.

Adrianne: Neither can I.

Leah: I think we have the main ones we need to take into account.

Anthony: Our criteria, then, seem to be: The city has an art fair or event that is held in the fall and with which we could coordinate, it is easily accessible by plane or car, it is a city that is cheap to fly to, and it might have a space we could use that is linked to the art event or an arts organization in the city. So now let's go through each site suggested and evaluate it against our criteria.

Leah: I'd like to start with Florida. In talking to the Artists Advisory Committee, it seems like the trend was that the market was really good in Florida, so everyone flocked there, and now artists are trying to stay away from there. So cities in Florida might not meet our criterion of accessibility to artists—at least not to good artists.

Anthony: Okay.

Adrianne: On the other hand, there are definitely more shows in Florida than anywhere else.

Anthony: Really?

Adrianne: Yes, so Florida might give us more opportunities for partnering. We might even be able to sandwich between two prominent events if there is one happening one weekend and another happening the following weekend. If our conference were in the middle, we might attract a different audience. So Florida might meet our criterion of a city where we could link up with arts festivals or events.

Christina: Florida is relatively easy to get to from the Midwest and the East.

Anthony: If we were to hold it in Florida, where in Florida would we do it?

Leah: Miami.

Anthony: Okay.

Leah: Or West Palm Beach, Boca, or Bonita Springs.

Anthony: Okay.

Adrianne: We have some art shows in the Orlando area, but I would say a lot of our shows are in Palm Beach County.

Anthony: So the southern area of Florida.

Adrianne: Yes.

Leah: Yes, Coconut Grove and West Palm Beach.

Anthony: Okay. And how does a site in Florida fit our other criteria? I guess flying there is average in terms of price.

Christina: Getting into Miami is pretty easy, I would say, but accessibility might be an issue if a hurricane comes up. The fall is hurricane season.

Anthony: Yes, between Ft. Lauderdale and Miami, it's pretty inexpensive to get in most of the time, but possible hurricanes could be an issue.

Leah: Yes. Flights are probably cheap, but, yes, we could run into weather issues.

Christina: I like the idea of Coconut Grove or Boca Raton, but many of the significant shows in this area are in the spring, so they don't fit our criterion of being connected to a major art show.

Anthony: Okay.

Adrianne: Like SunFest is in Palm Beach County, but it's in April. Coconut Grove is also in April or May. They do a lot of off-season shows because people go down there in the winter time.

Anthony: Florida, then, seems to meet some criteria, but we're not so sure that it would meet the criterion of being accessible to artists simply because of the unique situation there in terms of perception. Access also might be an issue if there's a hurricane. Does anyone know about spaces in any cities in Florida where we might hold the conference other than a hotel?

Adrianne: No, I don't. I've never been to Florida.

Anthony: How about you, Leah and Christina? Any idea about whether some kind of interesting space might be available to us because of the presence of an arts festival or an arts organization?

Leah: No. This is something we'd have to look into.

Anthony: Yes. Should we move on to another site on our list?

Christina: What about Virginia?

Adrianne: I know there are two major arts festivals in the Virginia Beach and Norfolk area—the Boardwalk Arts Show and the Neptune Festival. The Boardwalk attracts somewhere in the range of 500 to 800 applicants. It's in the summer, though, so we couldn't connect up with that, and it's certainly the major one. Neptune isn't as prominent a show.

Anthony: Okay, so Virginia perhaps doesn't meet our criterion of connecting to a major arts festival because we want our conference to be in the fall.

Christina: It is an accessible location, though—it's sort of in the middle of the area we're trying to reach. People could even fly into Baltimore, which Southwest Airlines serves, and drive down to Virginia Beach. That is about a four-hour drive, though.

Anthony: That's true, so Virginia is somewhat accessible and relatively cheap to reach. I'm familiar with that area, and I think finding an interesting art space in which to hold our conference would be possible. There's a contemporary art center in Virginia

Beach, for example. Virginia seems a possible location, then, in that it meets many of our criteria. If we held it in Virginia Beach, though, the art fair available to us in the fall isn't very large or very renowned, so that might be a problem. Let's turn to Kentucky. I'm the one who mentioned Kentucky. I was thinking of Louisville simply because St. James is a partner, which means we could connect with a large art show and might be able to find a good space in which to hold the conference as a result.

Leah: Yes, and St. James is the main show, but then there are also three other events that happen simultaneously within a mile the first weekend of October. So it might be a great way to capture a lot of artists just because there are four arts events happening simultaneously.

Adrianne: Yes. There are 400 to 600 artists right there.

Christina: Kentucky isn't quite as accessible by plane and car as some other locations, but the fact that there will be so many artists already there helps.

Anthony: Good summary. Shall we take a look at Atlanta?

Leah: Well, I think one thing to note about Atlanta is that you have an easy airport. Many airlines have hubs there, and it's easy to get in and out of the city. It's also often cheap to fly into Atlanta.

Anthony: Okay, so Atlanta meets our criteria of accessibility and cheapness. Atlanta doesn't have hurricanes that might cause problems for accessibility. That's a plus.

Adrianne: They do have a lot of shows in the fall.

Anthony: Okay. Anyone familiar with spaces where we could hold a conference in Atlanta other than in a hotel?

Christina: I'm not that familiar with Atlanta.

Leah: I'm not, either.

Adrianne: It's probably time to turn to Pennsylvania. I suggested it, and I like the idea of Pennsylvania, but I'm thinking now that it probably doesn't meet many of our criteria. There's a great art show affiliated with ZAPP®, but it's out there in central Penn in the middle of nowhere.

Anthony: And I don't think Philly or Pittsburgh would be especially attractive for our target audience.

Leah: Pennsylvania is also pretty far from many areas of the country with large art shows. I'm thinking we should eliminate Pennsylvania from consideration.

Anthony: Okay with everyone?

Adrianne,
Leah, and
Christina: Yes.

Anthony: So let's see where we are. Florida is still in the running, but I think it is lower on our list because, although it's cheap to get to, accessibility might be compromised by the fact that some artists don't want to go there now, and the weather might keep people away. Also, many of the good shows that we'd want to connect with are not in the fall. We don't know enough about possible spaces in the various cities in Florida to tell yet whether we could find someplace to hold the conference that's interesting.

Virginia is still on the list. We could say Virginia Beach is accessible because it's only four hours from D.C. or Baltimore, but it's also not accessible for that reason—some people might balk at that drive. We know there are good spaces there to which we'd have access, but the art show that is held in the fall in Virginia Beach isn't one of the major fairs. So that's a mark against it as a site for the conference.

In Kentucky, we have several arts events held in the same weekend, so we'd already have a lot of potential audience members there, even though accessibility usually wouldn't be quite as easy for many people. Because of the art events going on, we probably could find a good place to hold the conference. Atlanta is a good contender in that it is accessible by plane or car, is cheap to get to, and we know there are art shows there in the fall. We don't know much about potential spaces there, though. And we decided to delete Pennsylvania from consideration simply because the major show there is in a remote location and doesn't meet the criterion of accessibility.

Have I accurately summarized your perceptions of where we are in assessing the sites?

Leah: Yes.

Christina: Yes.

Anthony: How about this? We might be able to select from these four options more easily if we had a bit more information.

For our next meeting, Leah, would you come with the names and dates and number of participants in the art shows held in the fall in these four locations?

Christina, would you bring a list of the ZAPP® partners who are located in these cities?

Adrianne, would you do a quick check via Orbitz or Expedia to see how much it tends to cost to fly into these cities? Maybe take two cities in the East or South—places that have a lot of artists—and see how much it would cost to fly into these cities?

We still don't know all that much about interesting spaces in which to hold our conference in these cities, but I'm thinking that's something we can investigate once a site is chosen, especially if we have a partner in the area.

Once we have the information on art shows, partners, and cost of flights, I think we'll be able to select a city pretty easily that we are confident meets our criteria. How does that sound?

Leah: Sounds good.

Adrianne: Yes, I'll bring that information to our next meeting.

Anthony: Shall we plan to meet next Tuesday at this same time?

Christina: That works for me.

Leah: Me, too.

Adrianne: Yes, I'll be here.

Anthony: Great! Thank you for your input and time. I think we'll be able to make our decision at the next meeting.

Endnotes

➤ CHAPTER 1

[1] Thomas L. Friedman, *The World is Flat: A Brief History of the Twenty-first Century* (New York: Farrar, Straus and Giroux, 2005), 49.

[2] Sam Howe Verhovek, *Jet Age: The Comet, the 707, and the Race to Shrink the World* (New York: Avery/Penguin, 2010), 205.

[3] Friedman, *The World is Flat*, 7.

[4] Friedman, *The World is Flat*, 8.

[5] Friedman, *The World is Flat*, 8.

[6] Friedman, *The World is Flat*, 9.

[7] Friedman, *The World is Flat*, 9.

[8] Friedman, *The World is Flat*, 9 [Italics added].

[9] Friedman, *The World is Flat*, 9.

[10] Friedman, *The World is Flat*, 10.

[11] Friedman, *The World is Flat*, 10 [Italics added].

[12] Friedman, *The World is Flat*, 9.

[13] Friedman, *The World is Flat*, 10.

[14] Friedman, *The World is Flat*, 10.

[15] Friedman, *The World is Flat*, 10.

[16] Friedman, *The World is Flat*, 11.

[17] Jamake Highwater, *The Primal Mind: Vision and Reality in Indian America* (New York: Meridian, 1981), 65.

[18] The terms *conquest* and *conversion* to describe modes of rhetoric were developed by Sally Miller Gearhart in "The Womanization of Rhetoric," *Women's Studies International Quarterly* 2 (1979): 196. The terms *advisory* and *invitational rhetoric* and the general schema for the modes of rhetoric were developed by Sonja K. Foss and Cindy L. Griffin in an early draft of "Beyond Persuasion: A Proposal for an Invitational Rhetoric," *Communication Monographs* 62 (1995): 2–18. The term *benevolent rhetoric* was developed by Barbara J. Walkosz in a conversation with Sonja K. Foss, 1999.

[19] Suzette Haden Elgin, *How to Disagree Without Being Disagreeable: Getting Your Point Across with the Gentle Art of Verbal Self-Defense* (New York: John Wiley, 1997), 80.

[20] Margaret J. Wheatley, *Leadership and the New Science: Discovering Order in a Chaotic World*, 2nd ed. (San Francisco: Berrett-Koehler, 1999), 147.

[21] Wheatley, *Leadership and the New Science*, 65.

[22] Wheatley, *Leadership and the New Science*, 67.

[23] Annette Simmons, *A Safe Place for Dangerous Truths: Using Dialogue to Overcome Fear & Distrust at Work* (New York: American Management Association, 1999), 20.

[24] Jon Kabat-Zinn, *Full Catastrophe Living*, 15th ed. (New York: Delta/Bantam Dell/Random House, 2009), 9.

[25] Dalai Lama and Howard C. Cutler, *The Art of Happiness: A Handbook for Living* (New York: Riverhead, 1998), 173–74.

[26] Kabat-Zinn, *Full Catastrophe Living*, 154.

[27] Gord Cunningham and Alison Mathie, "Asset-Based Community Development: An Overview." Presented at the meeting of Synergos, Bangkok, Thailand, February 21, 2002, http://www.Synergos.org/knowledge/02/abcdoverview.htm.

[28] Ali Bulent Cambel, *Applied Chaos Theory: A Paradigm for Complexity* (New York: Academic/Harcourt Brace, 1993), 1.

[29] Edward N. Lorenz, *The Essence of Chaos* (Seattle: University of Washington Press, 1993), 69, 102.

[30] Stephen H. Kellert, *In the Wake of Chaos: Unpredictable Order in Dynamical Systems* (Chicago: University of Chicago Press, 1993), 12.

[31] Stephen Hawking, *Black Holes and Baby Universes* (New York: Bantam, 1993), 150.

[32] Malcolm Gladwell, *The Tipping Point: How Little Things Can Make a Big Difference* (New York: Little, Brown, 2000), 8, 9.

[33] Much of this description of invitational rhetoric is from Foss and Griffin, "Beyond Persuasion," 2–18.

[34] Foss and Griffin, "Beyond Persuasion," p. 5.

[35] James S. Baumlin and Tita French Baumlin, "Rogerian and Platonic Dialogue in—and Beyond—the Writing Classroom," in *Rogerian Perspectives: Collaborative Rhetoric for Oral and Written Communication*, ed. Nathaniel Teich (Norwood, NJ: Ablex, 1992), 128.

[36] Carl R. Rogers, *A Way of Being* (Boston: Houghton Mifflin, 1980), 143.

[37] Simmons, *A Safe Place for Dangerous Truths*, 99.

[38] Sara Lawrence-Lightfoot, *Respect: An Exploration* (Reading, MA: Perseus, 1999), 9, 10.

[39] Martha C. Nussbaum, *Cultivating Humanity: A Classical Defense of Reform in Liberal Education* (Cambridge: Harvard University Press, 1997), 10–11.

[40] The term *trial empathy* is suggested by Heinz Kohut, *The Restoration of the Self* (New York: International Universities Press, 1977), 168; *trial identification* comes from Stanley L. Olinick, "A Critique of Empathy and Sympathy," in *Empathy I*, ed. Joseph Lichtenberg, Melvin Bornstein, and Donald Silver (Hillsdale, NJ: Lawrence Erlbaum, 1984), 137–66; and *transient identification* is a label proposed by James H. Spencer Jr., "Discussion," in *Empathy I*, ed. Joseph Lichtenberg, Melvin Bornstein, and Donald Silver (Hillsdale, NJ: Lawrence Erlbaum, 1984), 37–42.

[41] Anatol Rapoport, quoted by Daniel C. Cennett in his book review of *The God Delusion* by Richard Dawkins, *Free Inquiry* 27 (December 2006/January2007): 66.

[42] Lisbeth Lipari, "Listening, Thinking, Being," *Communication Theory* 20 (2010): 350.

[43] Krista Ratcliffe, "Rhetorical Listening: A Trope for Interpretive Invention and a 'Code of Cross-Cultural Conduct,'" *College Composition and Communication* 51 (1999): 205, 207.

[44] Michael P. Nichols, *The Lost Art of Listening* (New York: Guilford, 1995), 250.

[45] Lipari, "Listening, Thinking, Being," 355.

[46] Abraham Kaplan, "The Life of Dialogue," in *The Reach of Dialogue: Confirmation, Voice, and Community*, ed. Rob Anderson, Kenneth N. Cissna, and Ronald C. Arnett (Cresskill, NJ: Hampton, 1994), 40.

[47] Lipari, "Listening, Thinking, Being," 355.

[48] Lipari, "Listening, Thinking, Being," 350–51.

[49] "Improving Listening Skills," www.livestrong.com/article/14657-improving-listening-skills/.

[50] Gearhart, "The Womanization of Rhetoric," 195.

[51] Ursula K. Le Guin, "Bryn Mawr Commencement Address (1986)," *Dancing at the Edge of the World: Thoughts on Words, Women, Places* (New York: Grove, 1989), 150–51.

[52] Sonia Johnson, *The Ship that Sailed into the Living Room: Sex and Intimacy Reconsidered* (Estancia, NM: Wildfire, 1991), 162.

[53] Charles Hauss, *Beyond Confrontation: Transforming the New World Order* (Westport, CT: Praeger, 1996), 101.

[54] Hauss, *Beyond Confrontation*, 101.

[55] Starhawk, *Truth or Dare: Encounters with Power, Authority, and Mystery* (San Francisco: Harper & Row, 1987), 9–10.

[56] Starhawk, *Truth or Dare*, 11.

[57] Myles Horton with Judith Kohl and Herbert Kohl, *The Long Haul: An Autobiography* (New York: Doubleday, 1990), 16.

[58] Gearhart, "The Womanization of Rhetoric," 198.

[59] Dennis A. Lynch, Diana George, and Marilyn M. Cooper, "Moments of Argument: Agonistic Inquiry and Confrontational Cooperation," *College Composition and Communication* 48 (1997): 80.

[60] Carl R. Rogers, *On Becoming a Person: A Therapist's View of Psychotherapy* (Boston: Houghton Mifflin, 1961), 333.

[61] Simmons, *A Safe Place for Dangerous Truths*, 57.

[62] Simmons, *A Safe Place for Dangerous Truths*, 45.

[63] Martin Buber, *Between Man and Man*, trans. Ronald Gregor Smith (New York: Macmillan, 1965), xiv.

[64] Sally Miller Gearhart, quoted in Eric Mills, "Enriching and Expanding the Animal Movement: Dr. Sally Gearhart Talks about Sexism, Racism and Coalition-Building," *Agenda* 111 (1983): 5.

[65] Deborah Tannen, *The Argument Culture: Stopping America's War of Words* (New York: Ballantine, 1998), 14.

[66] Tannen, *The Argument Culture*, 3.

[67] Suzette Haden Elgin, "Peacetalk 101," 2000, preface, www.forloving-kindness.org/peacetalk2.html.

[68] Charles Simic, quoted in Tannen, *The Argument Culture*, 7–8.

[69] Janice Moulton, "A Paradigm of Philosophy: The Adversary Method," in *Discovering Reality: Feminist Perspectives on Epistemology, Metaphysics, Methodology, and Philosophy of Science*, ed. Sandra Harding and Merrill B. Hintikka (Boston: D. Reidel, 1983), 151.

➤ CHAPTER 2

[1] Lloyd F. Bitzer, "The Rhetorical Situation," *Philosophy and Rhetoric* 1 (1968): 1–14.

[2] Bitzer, "The Rhetorical Situation," 6.

[3] Kenneth Burke, *The Philosophy of Literary Form: Studies in Symbolic Action* (Berkeley: University of California Press, 1973), 1.

[4] Thomas J. Gallagher, "Native Participation in Land Management Planning in Alaska," *Arctic* 41 (1988): 96.

[5] Kate Lorenz, "Warning: Social Networking Can be Hazardous to Your Job Search," October 11, 2009, http://www.careerbuilder.com/Article/CB-533-Job-Search-Warning-Social-Networking-Can-Be-Hazardous-to-Your-Job-Search.

[6] Richard M. Weaver, *Language is Sermonic: Richard M. Weaver on the Nature of Rhetoric*, ed. Richard L. Johannesen, Rennard Strickland, and Ralph T. Eubanks (Baton Rouge: Louisiana State University Press, 1970), 222.

[7] Weaver, *Language is Sermonic*, 224.

[8] Kenneth Burke, *A Rhetoric of Motives* (New York: Prentice-Hall, 1950), 55.

[9] Burke, *The Philosophy of Literary Form*, 146.

[10] Nelle Morton, *The Journey is Home* (Boston: Beacon, 1985), 202–07.

➤ CHAPTER 3

[1] These conditions are derived, in part, from Sonja K. Foss and Cindy L. Griffin, "Beyond Persuasion: A Proposal for an Invitational Rhetoric," *Communication Monographs* 62 (1995): 2–18.

[2] Nancy Signorielli, "Television's Mean and Dangerous World: A Continuation of Cultural Indicators Perspective," in *Cultivation Analysis: New Directions in Media Effects Research*, ed. Nancy Signorielli and Michael Morgan (Newbury Park, CA: Sage, 1990), 85–106.

[3] For an overview of physical and intellectual safety as conceptualized and practiced in contemporary schools, see "Safety in the Schools," special issue, *Educational Horizons* 83 (2004): 17–76.

[4] Annette Simmons, *A Safe Place for Dangerous Truths: Using Dialogue to Overcome Fear & Distrust at Work* (New York: American Management Association, 1999), 82.

[5] Simmons, *A Safe Place*, 80–81.

[6] For a discussion of how talk affects participation in civic life, see Robert O. Wyatt, Joohan Kim, and Elihu Katz, "How Feeling Free to Talk Affects Ordinary Political Conversation, Purposeful Argumentation, and Civic Participation," *Journalism and Mass Communication Quarterly* 77 (2000): 99–114.

[7] Mary Alice Speke Ferdig, "Exploring the Social Construction of Complex Self-Organizing Change: A Study of Emerging Change in the Regulation of Nuclear Power" (Ph.D. diss., Benedictine University, 2001), 187.

[8] Sally Miller Gearhart, "Womanpower: Energy Re-Sourcement," in *The Politics of Women's Spirituality: Essays on the Rise of Spiritual Power within the Feminist Movement*, ed. Charlene Spretnak (Garden City, NY: Doubleday, 1982), 95.

[9] Bill Amend, "FoxTrot," *The Albuquerque Journal*, January 12, 2002, F3.

[10] Starhawk, *Truth or Dare: Encounters with Power, Authority, and Mystery* (San Francisco: Harper & Row, 1987), 5.

[11] Suzette Haden Elgin, *How to Disagree Without Being Disagreeable: Getting Your Point Across with the Gentle Art of Verbal Self-Defense* (New York: John Wiley, 1997), 145–46.

[12] Adrienne Rich, Audre Lorde, and Alice Walker, "A Statement for Voices Unheard: A Challenge to the National Book Awards," *Ms.*, September 1974, 38.

➤ CHAPTER 4

[1] Elizabeth Kirk, quoted in Andrew Harnack and Eugene Kleppinger, *Online! A Reference Guide to Using Internet Sources* (New York: Bedford/St. Martin's, 2000), 51-64.

➤ CHAPTER 5

[1] Christine Todd Whitman, "Statement of Governor Christine Todd Whitman, Administrator, US Environmental Protection Agency, Before the Subcommittee on VA, HUD, and Independent Agencies of the Committee on Appropriations," November 28, 2001, http://yosemite1.epa.gov/opa/admpress.nsf/12a744ff56dbff8585257590004750b6/98cdc2362a6eb7aa8525701a0052e42f!OpenDocument.

[2] David Boaz, "The Public School Monopoly: America's Berlin Wall," *Vital Speeches of the Day* 58 (June 1, 1992): 507–11.

[3] Hans Rosling, "Asia's Rise—How and When," TEDIndia, November 2009, http://www.ted.com/talks/hans_rosling_asia_s_rise_how_and_when.html.

[4] Richard R. Kelley, "Prospering in '92: How to Avoid a Cold When the World is Sneezing," *Vital Speeches of the Day* 58 (June 1, 1992): 333–36.

[5] The motivated sequence was developed by Alan Monroe. See Bruce E. Gronbeck, Raymie E. McKerrow, Douglas Ehninger, and Alan H. Monroe, *Principles and Types of Speech Communication*, 12th ed. (New York: HarperCollins College, 1994), 193–223.

[6] Joe Jackson and Bill Hutchinson, "Plan for Mosque Near World Trade Center Site Moves Ahead," October 7, 2010, nydailynews.com/ny_local/2010/05/06/2010-05-06_plan_for_mosque_near_world_trade_center_site_moves_ahead.html; "If That 'Mosque' ISN'T Built, This Is No Longer America . . . a Letter from Michael Moore,"

http://www.michaelmoore.com/words/mike-friends-blog/if-mosque-isnt-built-no-longer-america; Lauren Russell, "Church Plans Quran-Burning Event," July 30, 2010, http://articles.cnn.com/2010-07-29/us/florida.burn.quran.day_1_american-muslims-religion-cair-spokesman-ibrahim-hooper?_s=PM:US; "Fla. Pastor Will 'Not Today, Not Ever' Burn Quran," September 11, 2010, news.yahoo.com/s/ap/quran_burning.

[7] Ursula K. Le Guin, "The Princess," *Dancing at the Edge of the World: Thoughts on Words, Women, Places* (New York: Harper & Row, 1989), 75.

[8] Steve Jobs, "How to Live Before You Die," Commencement Address, Stanford University, Palo Alto, CA, June 10, 2005, http://www.youtube.com/watch?v=UF8uR6Z6KLc.

[9] Ben Bernanke, "On the Outlook for the Economy and Policy," Economic Club of New York, October 15, 2008, New York City, http://www.americanrhetoric.com/speeches/benbernankenewyorkeconomicclub.htm.

➤ CHAPTER 6

[1] L. Paul Bremer III, "Keynote Address to the TD Waterhouse Investment Conference," February 4, 2005, San Diego, CA, www.americanrhetoric.com.

[2] Harvey Milk, "Milk Forum: My Concept of a Legislator," *Bay Area Reporter*, May 27, 1976, n.p.

[3] Ursula K. Le Guin, "A Left-Handed Commencement Address," *Dancing at the Edge of the World: Thoughts on Words, Women, Places* (New York: Harper & Row, 1989), 116.

[4] Bill Gates, "Remarks by Bill Gates, 2002 International Consumer Electronics Show, January 7, 2002, Las Vegas, NV, http://www.microsoft.com/presspass/exec/billg/speeches/2002/01-07ces.aspx.

[5] Alan Chapman, "Clichés and Expressions Origins," http://www.businessballs.com/clichesorigins.htm.

[6] Christopher Reeve, "Democratic National Convention Address," August 26, 1996, Chicago, IL, http://www.americanrhetoric.com/speeches/christopherreeve1996dnc.htm.

[7] Martin Luther King Jr., "I Have a Dream," August 28, 1963, Washington, DC, http://www.americanrhetoric.com/speeches/mlkihaveadream.htm.

[8] Cal Ripken Jr., "Farewell to Baseball Address," September 9, 2001, Baltimore, MD, http://www.americanrhetoric.com/speeches/calripkenjr.htm.

[9] Gwen Moffat, quoted in Nina Winter, *Interview with the Muse: Remarkable Women Speak on Creativity and Power* (Berkeley, CA: Moon, 1978), 123.

[10] Charlton Heston, "Winning the Cultural War," February 16, 1999, Boston, MA, http://www.theblessingsofliberty.com/articles/article9.html.

[11] Tiger Woods, "Apology," February 19, 2010, Ponte Vedra Beach, FL, http://articles.cnn.com/2010-02-19/us/tiger.woods.transcript_1_elin-behavior-core-values?_s=PM:US.

[12] Jessica Lynch, "Opening Statement Before House Oversight and Government Reform Committee," US Congress, April 24, 2007, Washington, DC, http://www.americanrhetoric.com/speeches/jessicalynchopeningstatement.htm.

[13] William Jefferson Clinton, "Democratic Presidential Nomination Acceptance Address," July 16, 1992, New York City, http://www.americanrhetoric.com/speeches/wjclinton1992dnc.htm.

[14] Hillary Clinton, "Democratic National Convention Keynote Address," August 26, 2008, Denver, CO, http://www.americanrhetoric.com/speeches/convention2008/hillaryclinton2008dnc.htm.

[15] George W. Bush, "9/11 Address to the Nation," September 11, 2001, Washington, DC, http://www.americanrhetoric.com/speeches/gwbush911addresstothenation.htm.

[16] Sarah Palin, "Resignation Announcement," July 3, 2009, Wasilla, AK, http://www.huffingtonpost.com/2009/07/03/sarah-palin-resignation-s_n_225557.html.

[17] Walt Bresette, "We Are All Mohawks," *Green Letter* [Winter 1990]: 50.

[18] Annie Dillard, *The Writing Life* (New York: HarperCollins, 1989), 16.

[19] Andrei Codrescu, "What Central-European Artists and Writers Can Do for Us, with Remarks on Missouri," *Artlogue* [Missouri Arts Council] 12 (1991): 7.

[20] Conan O'Brien, Harvard (Class Day) Commencement Speech, June 7, 2000, Cambridge, MA, http://www.scribd.com/doc/1312/Harvard-Graduation-Speech-by-Conan-OBrien.

[21] Chief Weninock, quoted in T. C. McLuhan, ed., *Touch the Earth: A Self-Portrait of Indian Existence* (New York: Touchstone, 1971), 10.

[22] Patti P. Gillespie, "1987 Presidential Address: Campus Stories, or The Cat Beyond the Canvas," *Spectra* [Speech Communication Association] (January 1988): 3.

[23] William Shakespeare, *As You Like It*, II, vi, 139.

[24] Tim Tebow, "Remarks at Presidential Prayer Breakfast," February 4, 2010, Washington, DC, http://www.freerepublic.com/focus/f-news/2446851/posts.

[25] Barbara Brown Zikmund, "What is Our Place?," in *And Blessed Is She: Sermons by Women*, ed. David Albert Farmer and Edwina Hunter (San Francisco: Harper & Row, 1990), 233.

[26] Janet Hughes, "Exhibiting with Pride," statement presented at the opening of the Missouri Visual Artists' Biennial, March 5, 1993, University of Missouri, Columbia, MO.

[27] Bill Cosby, "Address at the 50th Anniversary of *Brown v. Board of Education*," May 17, 2004, Washington, DC, http://www.americanrhetoric.com/speeches/billcosbypoundcakespeech.htm.

[28] Alice Walker, "Sent by Earth: A Message from the Grandmother Spirit," *We are the Ones We Have Been Waiting For: Inner Light in a Time of Darkness* (New York: New, 2006), 208.

[29] Maya Angelou, "Remarks at the Funeral Service for Coretta Scott King," February 7, 2008, Lithonia, GA, http://www.americanrhetoric.com/speeches/mayaangeloueulogyforcorettaking.htm.

[30] Barack Obama, "A More Perfect Union," March 18, 2008, Philadelphia, PA, http://www.americanrhetoric.com/speeches/barackobamaperfectunion.htm.

[31] Theodor Seuss Geisel, "My Uncle Terwilliger on the Art of Eating Popovers," Lake Forest College, June 4, 1977, Lake Forest, IL, http://humanity.org/voices/commencements/speeches/index.php?page=seuss_commencement_poem.

[32] Diane Stein, *Casting the Circle: A Woman's Book of Ritual* (Freedom, CA: Crossing, 1990), 178.

[33] Barbara Kingsolver, *The Bean Trees* (New York: Harper Perennial, 1988), 163.

[34] David E. Thigpen, "A New Kind of Homeless," *Time*, December 31, 2001/January 7, 2002, 30.

[35] J. D. Salinger, *The Catcher in the Rye* (New York: Bantam, 1951), 58.

[36] Michelle Obama, "Democratic National Convention Keynote Address," August 25, 2008, Denver, CO, http://www.americanrhetoric.com/speeches/convention2008/michelleobama2008dnc.htm.

[37] Mary Catherine Batson, *Composing a Life* (New York: Penguin, 1989), 240.

⟡ CHAPTER 7

[1] Sonia Sotomayor, "Opening Statement to the Senate Judiciary Committee," July 13, 2009, Washington, DC, http://www.americanrhetoric.com/speeches/soniasotomayoropeningstmt.htm.

[2] Billy Collins, "Introduction to Poetry," *The Apple that Astonished Paris* (Fayetteville: University of Arkansas Press, 1998), 58.

[3] Jessica Jackley, "Poverty, Money—and Love," TEDGlobal, July 2010, http://www.ted.com/talks/jessica_jackley_poverty_money_and_love.html.

[4] Terry Russell and Renny Russell, *On the Loose* (San Francisco: Sierra Club, 1967), 45.

[5] Nancy Pelosi, "Helen Keller's Statue," October 7, 2009, Washington, DC, http://www.speaker.gov/newsroom/speeches?id=0221.

[6] Dan Rather, "CBS Evening News Signoff," March 9, 2005, New York, NY, http://www.americanrhetoric.com/speeches/danrathersignoff.htm.

[7] Al Sharpton, "Eulogy for Michael Jackson," July 7, 2009, Los Angeles, CA, http://www.americanrhetoric.com/speeches/alsharptoneulogyformichaeljackson.htm.

[8] Tom Delay, "Farewell Address to the House of Representatives," June 8, 2006, Washington, DC, http://www.americanrhetoric.com/speeches/alsharptoneulogyformichaeljackson.htm.

[9] Karen A. Carlton, "Our Lives, One Life," commencement speech, College of Arts and Humanities, Humboldt State University, May 22, 1993, Arcata, CA.

[10] General Norty Schwartz, "Medal of Honor Ceremony for Richard Etchberger," September 22, 2010, Washington, DC, http://www.af.mil/shared/media/document/AFD-100922-038.pdf. Etchberger received the Medal of Honor for his heroic actions in combat in Laos on March 11, 1968. After deliberately exposing himself to enemy fire in order to place three surviving wounded comrades in rescue slings, permitting them to be airlifted to safety, he himself was fatally wounded. See http://en.wikipedia.org/wiki/Richard_Etchberger.

[11] Billy Joel, Commencement Address, Berklee College of Music, May 11, 1993, Boston, MA, http://www.berklee.edu/commencement/past/bjoel.html.

[12] Pete Geren, Secretary of the Army, "Salute to the Military," December 5, 2007, Corpus Christi, TX, http://www.army.mil/-speeches/2007/12/05/6973-secretary-of-the-army-salute-to-the-military-speech-corpus-christi-chamber-of-commerce/.

[13] Dan George, quoted in T. C. McLuhan, ed., *Touch the Earth: A Self-Portrait of Indian Existence* (New York: Touchstone, 1971), 162.

[14] Madeleine Albright, "White House Address Commemorating International Women's Day," March 8, 2010, Washington, DC, http://www.americanrhetoric.com/speeches/madeleinealbrightinternationalwomensdayspeech.htm. The poem "The Low Road" can be found in Marge Piercy, *The Moon Is Always Female* (New York: Alfred A. Knopf, 1980), 44–45.

[15] Lewis Pugh, "Everest Swim," TEDGlobal, July 2010, http://www.ted.com/talks/lewis_pugh_s_mind_shifting_mt_everest_swim.html.

[16] Oprah Winfrey, "Commencement Address at Stanford University," June 15, 2008, Palo Alto, CA, http://www.americanrhetoric.com/speeches/oprahwinfreystanfordcommencement.htm.

[17] Christine D. Keen, "May You Live in Interesting Times: The Workplace in the '90s," *Vital Speeches of the Day* 58 (November 15, 1991): 83–86.

[18] Steve Spurrier, "Resignation Statement," January 4, 2002, Gainesville, FL, http://www.americanrhetoric.com/speeches/stevespurrierfloridaresignation.htm.

[19] Pete Sampras, "International Tennis Hall of Fame Induction Address," July 14, 2007, Newport, RI, http://www.americanrhetoric.com/speeches/petesamprastennishofinductionspeech.htm.

[20] George W. Bush, "Hurricane Relief Address to the Nation," September 15, 2005, New Orleans, LA, http://www.americanrhetoric.com/speeches/gwbushhurricanekatrinarelief.htm.

[21] Barack Obama, "Father's Day Address," June 21, 2010, Washington, DC, http://www.americanrhetoric.com/speeches/barackobama/barackobamafathersday2010.htm.

[22] Reese Witherspoon, "I'm Just Trying to Matter," March 5, 2006, Los Angeles, CA, http://www.americanrhetoric.com/speeches/reesewitherspoonoscaraward.htm.

[23] Julius Genachowski, "On a National Mobile Broadband Plan," February 24, 2010, Washington, DC, http://www.americanrhetoric.com/speeches/juliusgenachowskimobilebroadbandspeech.htm.

⏤ CHAPTER 8

[1] Umberto Eco, *The Open Work*, trans. Anna Cancogni (Cambridge: Harvard University Press, 1989), 166.

[2] Bill Gates, "Remarks at the 2002 International Consumer Electronics Show," January 7, 2002, Las Vegas, NV, http://www.microsoft.com/billgates/speeches/2002/01-07ces.asp.

[3] Barack Obama, "Remarks by the President on Comprehensive Immigration Reform," July 1, 2010, School of International Service, American University, Washington, DC,

http://www.whitehouse.gov/the-press-office/remarks-president-comprehensive-immigration-reform.

4 Gates, "Remarks at the 2002 International Consumer Electronics Show."

5 Michele Kurtz, "Sentence for Junta May Hinge on Past," *Boston Globe*, January 25, 2002, B1.

➤ CHAPTER 9

1 Garr Reynolds, *Presentation Zen: Simple Ideas on Presentation Design and Delivery* (Berkeley, CA: New Riders, 2008), 10.

2 Elisabeth Bumiller, "We Have Met the Enemy and He Is PowerPoint," *New York Times*, April 27, 2010, www.nytimes.com.

3 Seth Godin, quoted in Reynolds, *Presentation Zen*, 10.

4 David Byrne, *Envisioning Emotional Epistemological Information* (n.p.: Todomundo, 2003), "Exegesis," 1.

5 Byrne, *Envisioning Emotional Epistemological Information*, "Exegesis," 1–2.

6 Jens E. Kjeldsen, "The Rhetoric of PowerPoint," Seminar.net 2 (2006): 2.

7 Edward R. Tufte, *The Cognitive Style of PowerPoint: Pitching Out Corrupts Within* (Cheshire, CT: Graphics, 2006), 4.

8 Kjeldsen, "The Rhetoric of PowerPoint," 4.

9 Tufte, *The Cognitive Style of PowerPoint*, 12.

10 Tufte, *The Cognitive Style of PowerPoint*, especially 12, 15, 16, and 24; and Gordon Shaw, Robert Brown, and Philip Bromiley, "Strategic Stories: How 3M is Rewriting Business Planning," *Harvard Business Review* 76 (1998): 44.

11 Bumiller, "We Have Met the Enemy."

12 Robin Williams, *The Non-Designer's Presentation Book: Principles for Effective Presentation Design* (Berkeley, CA: Peachpit, 2010), 17.

13 Duarte, quoted in Reynolds, *Presentation Zen*, 90.

14 Kjeldsen, "The Rhetoric of PowerPoint," 12.

15 Reynolds, *Presentation Zen*, 122.

16 Reynolds, *Presentation Zen*, 145.

17 Kjeldsen, "The Rhetoric of PowerPoint," 13.

18 Andy Goodman, *Why Bad Presentations Happen to Good Causes and How to Ensure They Won't Happen to Yours* ([Los Angeles, CA]: Cause Communications, 2006), 66.

19 Williams, *The Non-Designer's Presentation Book*, 127.

20 Goodman, *Why Bad Presentations Happen*, 67.

21 Williams, *The Non-Designer's Presentation Book*, 126.

22 Tufte, *The Cognitive Style of PowerPoint*, 30.

23 Suzette Haden Elgin, *The Last Word on the Gentle Art of Verbal Self-Defense* (New York: Prentice Hall, 1987), 143.

24 Elgin, *The Last Word*, 142.

25 Albert Ellis and Robert A. Harper, *A New Guide to Rational Living* (North Hollywood, CA: Melvin Powers, 1975), 146.

26 This discussion of irrational anxiety is adapted from Ellis and Harper, *A New Guide to Rational Living*, 145–57.

27 Adapted from Elgin, *The Last Word*, 166.

28 For an account of the history of women speakers in the United States, see Karlyn Kohrs Campbell, *Man Cannot Speak for Her: A Critical Study of Early Feminist Rhetoric*, vol. 1 (New York: Greenwood, 1989).

Index